The Way Forward?

Christian Voices on Homosexuality and the Church

Edited by Timothy Bradshaw

Second Edition

scm press

British Library Cataloguing in Publication data

A catalogue record for this book is available
from the British Library

0 334 02934 1

First published in Great Britain 1997
by Hodder and Stoughton Ltd

Second edition published 2003
by SCM Press
9–17 St Albans Place, London N1 0NX

www.scm-canterburypress.co.uk

SCM Press is a division of
SCM-Canterbury Press Ltd

Printed and bound in Great Britain by
Bookmarque, Croydon, Surrey

Contents

Contributors 2003

The Right Reverend Professor Stephen W. Sykes is Principal of St John's College, and Professor of Theology, in the University of Durham.

Professor Gerald Bray is Anglican Professor of Divinity at Beeson Divinity School, Samford University, Birmingham, Alabama. Formerly tutor in Christian Doctrine at Oak Hill College, London. Recent Publications include *The Doctrine of God* and *Biblical Interpretation* (both IVP); he has edited three volumes in the Ancient Christian Commentary series, as well as the historic canons of the Church of England. He is presently working on an edition of the convocation records of the English and Irish churches.

Dr Tom Brown is Consultant Psychiatrist, West Lothian Healthcare NHS Trust.

Dr John Colwell is tutor in Christian Doctrine and Ethics at Spurgeon's College. He is author of *Actuality and Provisionality: A Study in the Theology of Karl Barth* (Rutherford House) and *Living the Christian Story: The Distinctiveness of Christian Ethics* (T. & T. Clark).

Martin Hallett is Director for the True Freedom Trust, a Christian organisation helping those with homosexual feelings, their relatives and their friends. He is author of *I am Learning to Love* (Marshall Pickering), *Out of the Blue* (Hodder) and *Sexual Identity and Freedom in Discipleship* (Grove Books).

Dr Jeffrey John taught New Testament Theology in the University of Oxford for ten years before becoming Vicar of Holy Trinity, Eltham. He is Canon Theologian of Southwark Cathedral. He has written *Permanent, Faithful, Stable: A Study of Same-Sex Relationships* (DLT).

Dr Dave Leal is Lecturer in Philosophy at Brasenose College, Oxford, and teaches philosophy and theology in the University of Oxford. He is author of *On Marriage as Vocation* and *Debating Homosexuality* (Grove Books).

Professor Oliver O'Donovan is Regius Professor of Moral and Pastoral Theology in the University of Oxford and Canon of Christ Church. Among his publications are *Resurrection and Moral Order: An Outline for Evangelical Ethics* (IVP) and *The Desire of the Nations: Rediscovering the Roots of Political Theology* (CUP).

Professor Elizabeth Stuart is Professor of Christian Theology at King Alfred's College, Winchester. She has written extensively on theology and sexuality. Her latest book *Gay and Lesbian Theologies: Repetitions with Critical Difference* is published by Ashgate.

Professor Anthony Thiselton is Professor of Christian Theology and Head of the Department of Theology at the University of Nottingham. He is Canon Theologian of Leicester Cathedral. His publications include *The Two Horizons, New Horizons in Hermeneutics: The Theory and Practice of Transforming Bible Reading* (Paternoster), and his recent commentary, *The First Epistle to the Corinthians: A Commentary on the Greek Text* (Eerdmans/Paternoster).

Dr Simon Vibert is Vicar of St Luke's Wimbledon Park and Chairman of Fellowship of Word and Spirit. He has authored a number of their Orthos publications including *Conduct Which Honours God? The Question of Homosexuality*. His Doctor of Ministry thesis was on the subject of the ultimate purpose of marriage.

Michael Vasey taught worship at Cranmer Hall, St John's College, Durham. He was a member of the Liturgical Commission of the Church of England. He wrote *Strangers and Friends: A New Exploration of Homosexuality and the Bible* (Hodder). Michael died tragically and prematurely several months after publishing his essay in this collection.

The Most Reverend Rowan Williams is Archbishop of Canterbury. He has written several books and articles on subjects ranging from the history of Christian spirituality to issues on literature, ethics and social philosophy.

Dr Timothy Bradshaw is currently Acting Principal and Senior Tutor of Regent's Park College in the University of Oxford, where he teaches systematic and historical theology. He serves on the Faith and Order Advisory Group of General Synod, and the Anglican–Orthodox Theological Commission. He has written on Barth, Pannenberg and ecclesiology.

Foreword

The second edition of *The Way Forward?* reminds us that discussion of homosexuality is an ecclesial-political as well as a theological matter. The reality of this is effectively illustrated by the participation in the book of two theologians, Rowan Williams and Jeffrey John, whose lives and opinions now have an inescapably political dimension. The writings and actions of both men are subject to scrutiny by people who are not interested in theological discussion because they have already made up their minds; their concern is rather with the implication of what has been written for processes of decision-making in the Church – thus for politics.

Such is the reputation of the political that it would not be difficult to portray this movement into politics as a kind of decline. Theological discussion occupies the pure world of ideas in which intelligent people freely respond to serious argument – so the assumption goes; politics is contaminated by passion and power. But the mere naming of this dichotomy reveals its inadequacy. Ideas are propounded by people. People have a variety of motives, concerns and intentions which are embodied in the language they use. When this language bears upon or is connected to the making of decisions, it inescapably carries political connotations. It is never the vehicle of 'pure ideas'. And why should it be assumed that the exercise of power is *ipso facto* an abuse of power or a morally undesirable event? Is the mere fact of a theologian taking on the responsibilities and influence of a leader in the Church a giving way to temptation?

The examples are to hand. Rowan Williams' accession as Archbishop of Canterbury means, inevitably, that he is not free to articulate his convictions without consideration of the consequences for the Anglican Communion. Cardinal Ratzinger, who regularly had his opinions as a theologian quoted against his decisions as a Curial official, used to say that he could not have anticipated the significance of his later role. Not that a theologian should be thought of as devoid of responsibility for the life of the Church. But the fact is – and I can confirm it from my own experience – the conversations and reading matter of a church leader are simply different from those of a theologian. As a consequence a church leader's mind is formed by a different range of influences, broader in social range and experience perhaps, and narrower in analytical capacity. A theologian, of course, should be a worshipper and ought to have a care for the communion of saints. But a theologian's encounter with sanctity may well be more limited than that of a church leader (it is refreshing indeed when it is not!) and thus the imaginative vision may be slighter.

The ecclesial-political dimension of a Christian life can thus present itself as having a positive dimension, an expansion of a person's range of interests, concerns and sympathies. But there can be a downside. Rowan Williams, on becoming Archbishop of Canterbury, stated that he would not use his position as a platform from which to propagate his views on homosexuality. In other words he was conscious of a temptation to abuse his power on a matter on which a decision in favour of his view had not been reached. That declaration was a complex recognition of the possibility of distinguishing public responsibilities and less public (hardly private!) convictions. It tacitly recognised the proper domain of the ecclesial-political and the desirability of the Church making an authentic, unpressured decision. It openly acknowledged that, as a church leader, he would be self-critical in his attitude towards the power of his office.

It is not necessary to defend the view that all language is political for it to be true that the language in which argument about homosexuality is conducted is, at the present time, inescapably political. The reason for this is that for a Christian of gay or lesbian desire the Church has a decision or decisions to make which would reverse its traditional teaching. All argument, therefore, has the capacity to be deployed as advocacy in favour of, or contrary to, those decisions. Several of the authors in this collection will be familiar with the process by which carefully formulated argument is summarised, abbreviated, truncated or quoted in part, or their scholarly reputations harnessed to political bandwagons not of their creation.

Dismaying though this may be it is inevitable, and in part desirable. Decision-making in most non-Roman Catholic churches involves a synodical element. Even in the Catholic Church the faithful are supposed to be consulted. The Orthodox theory of the episcopate is that they should be inseparable from their people. Exquisite ambiguity and irresolution is the privilege of the few. Scholars are not infrequently to blame for not making their meaning clear, or even for deliberately cultivating obscurity as if it were a guarantee of intellectual quality. But the process of arriving at a decision, or non-decision, is a complex one involving many people for whom the dispassionate weighing of argument is an unfamiliar exercise. It is often said that the simplest form of human judgment is by character. If a person is thought to be good, kindly and reliable, then the opinions they espouse will be seen in a positive light. Similarly if they are shifty, angry and unpredictable, their views will not commend themselves. One of the explicit aims of the St Andrew's Day Statement and this collection of essays is precisely to 'have done with all spite and bad temper, with rage, insults and slander, with evil of any kind' (Eph. 4:31, REB). It is an invitation to all participants, of whatever convictions, to put themselves (and thus their arguments) at best advantage in an avowedly political context.

But there is a difficulty here which needs to be faced on both sides of the debate. According to traditional teaching the genital sexual expression of homosexual feeling is incompatible with a life of Christian holiness. That is, so the tradition goes, to be taught in the Church, not obsessively indeed as though the Church thought that failure in this matter would be the sin of all sins, but simply as an integral matter of living the Christian life (much as one might teach about fornication or adultery). Inevitably this is connected to the Christian theme of judgment, the discriminating of right from wrong and the baptismal rejection of all that is evil. Of course such a 'judgment' offends against the modern ban on judgmentalism. (One has lost count of the times that the modern media insist that to make *this* judgment is to be judgmental; or, indeed, to be unhealthily obsessed with homosexuality.) But for the argument to continue as argument there must surely be a way in which orthodox Christian believers can assert definitely, but without stridency, that such behaviour has the nature of sin.

Can such an utterance be made without the Christian who is in a loving, permanent, sexually active, gay or lesbian relationship reacting as to a personal insult or attack? The evidence, of course, is that such a view is felt to be quite unacceptable. The consequences are, inevitably, verbal reprisal and the avoidance of the company of people or groups unable to make that judgment. An anonymous priest in a gay partnership, writing in the *Guardian*, makes clear his bile by speaking of 'Carey' and the 'decade of evangelism' with undisguised contempt. One can only presume that he is not in any state of reconciliation with his local evangelical clergy. That is the human reality and it is understandable. It is also the political seed from which schism grows, the 'party-spirit' which was undermining the life of the Christian community in Corinth. But is it inevitable?

A first answer to that question bears upon the tone in which such a judgment is made. Here the phenomenon of disgust has to be confronted. For reasons which are possibly biological, though social conditioning also plays a role, it is not difficult for heterosexual people of traditional views to draw upon a reservoir of strongly felt rejection in relation to the expression of same-sex affectivity. Is it reasonable to ask Christians who hold such expression of love to be sinful, even in the context of a permanent faithful partnership, not to tinge that judgment with the overtones of disgust? That is a matter of self-control, and self-control is a justifiable demand of the godliness of a Christian. For a person in a gay partnership not to feel the pressure of disgust from a fellow Christian would be a modest, but real step towards an improvement of relationship.

The second answer takes us further, but inevitably places a severe additional burden upon persons in gay partnerships. That is the suggestion that they should not regard disapproval of such behaviour as a pretext for social withdrawal or other retaliatory action. Is that even remotely conceivable? A somewhat similar situation already exists in those churches, notably the Church of England, which have ended the rule restricting ordination to men, but have allowed men (and lay women) to continue to oppose women's ordinations from an honoured position inside the Church. Ordained women are thus confronted – and not infrequently affronted – by those who say, with impunity, that they are not truly ordained. The analogy is not precise, however, because (so far as I know) no one has suggested that ordained women are in a state of sin as a result of claiming to be ordained. Moreover, they enjoy the support of the majority of members of the institution. Christians in lesbian or gay partnerships are a minority. There is a public history of the persecution of this minority. It is wholly understandable when proponents of the case for lesbian and gay partnerships say that the case for which they are arguing is not met so long as what they see as an excluding judgment is not withdrawn.

But what, politically, is foreseeable? On current evidence one can only suppose that there will continue to be those who believe that what they regard as the scripturally endorsed states of life, chastity and life-long marriage, are part of Christian holiness. It is not foreseeable that such convictions will simply disappear. One question which faces those who urge an abandonment of that rule is what place they accord those professing conservative views. Are they to be labelled unchristian and homophobic? If so, we are certainly heading in all our churches for a *de facto* or *de iure* schism. A *de facto* schism would exist when different dioceses, parishes or congregations announced the sort of policy they pursued and became what the American sociologist Robert Bellah called 'life-style enclaves'. *De iure* schism would follow when proponents or opponents of a certain policy attempted to embody it in legislation. All denominations except the most resolutely conservative would become, at best, federations embodying contradictory solutions.

I have been asking whether such a development is inevitable, and the answer seems to me that, humanly speaking, it is very probable. But by implication it is not strictly inevitable if my two conditions can be met, that is, if those urging the continuation of the tradition on this matter renounce the temptation to mobilise the negativities which so easily fuel the use of language, and if those urging the abandonment of the tradition do not react to the conservative use of the language of sin. That the greater burden is placed on the latter is apparent, much as a greater burden weighs upon ordained women in the Church than upon men. A rather different analogy is the current situation of Roman Catholics who remarry during the lifetime of a divorced partner. Their second marriage means that they are automatically excommunicated – but in best Catholic pastoral practice it does not mean that they are shunned or vilified. They are, objectively, said to be living in sin, but not for that reason thought of as beyond God's grace. This comparison is not meant to imply that the practice is satisfactory; but it illustrates the pastoral possibility of not invoking the sanction of separation and the withdrawal of kindness.

One last consideration relates to the complexities of communication across cultures. It is a feature of the modern world that the news desks of Western studios of newspapers have the telephone numbers of bishops in other countries, where the phenomena of homosexuality are not openly spoken of. It is not difficult to elicit the kind of comment which plays to the dramatising instincts of a modern journalist. The predictable condemnation is swiftly followed by a call to the headquarters of the church involved. A first-rate row is on the cards; rows create readers and readers sell advertising space. The linkages of sex, power and money are an irresistible combination but it is the financial interest which is usually concealed. In this context Christian leaders certainly need the virtue of wisdom, if what they say is not simply to be highjacked for a business which does not have their concerns at heart. It is in part tragic when the main impression of what Christian leaders have to say on this matter is received from a medium whose implicit intention is to maximise the degree of conflict within its own context, and whose only concern with the situation elsewhere is its potential to increase the pressure locally.

Stephen W. Sykes
Principal of St John's College
and Professor of Theology
University of Durham
July 2003

Preface to the Second Edition

This symposium originated from the desire to seek common ground on which a proper theological discussion might take place, in an appropriate spirit of Christian courtesy. The need for this has hardly diminished since 1997. The Lambeth Conference of 1998 saw a great struggle over the question of homosexuality in the Church, leading to encouragement and vindication for those supporting the traditional view but a grave disappointment for those proposing change. The Lambeth Conference texts on this topic in places patch in elements of the St Andrew's Day Statement, the initial theological text to which the essays in this symposium respond.

Although passed by a large majority of the Anglican bishops worldwide, the Lambeth Conference Resolution on this topic was ignored by the movement and campaign for change, notably in North America. In the Diocese of New Westminster, Canada, Bishop Ingham in 2003 introduced the practice of blessing homosexual partnerships, attracting immense criticism from African and Asian Anglicans especially, but also from traditionalists in Britain and North America. In the same year the American Diocese of New Hampshire elected Gene Robinson as its new Bishop, a self-declared practising homosexual who had formerly had a wife and family. Loud protests and declarations of impaired communion resulted. Secular Western culture has seen the campaign for gay rights succeeding dramatically, to the extent of quasi-marital status being legally recognised in law for homosexual couples. This secular ethos surrounds the Church's debate in the West, whereas in Africa and Asia the context, often of a resurgent and proselytising Islam, is very different.

Bishop Stephen Sykes in his Foreword to this second edition discusses the intense controversy caused by the selection of Jeffrey John, a contributor to the symposium, as Bishop of Reading designate, a position he relinquished in order to preserve the peace of the Church. This withdrawal was deeply ironic in that Canon John had formally declared himself now abstinent and willing to uphold the Church's teaching: it has never been part of the traditional Christian ethic to ban those with homosexual feelings, or 'orientation', who are content to uphold celibacy in their friendships. The controversy arose because of his dissent from the traditional teaching, as exemplified by his essay herein, advocating the legitimacy of a homosexual element to a 'covenanted' partnership.

This takes us to the core of the debate, probed by the St Andrew's Day Statement, which asks some questions yet to be even considered by our secular press in its voracious and simplistic coverage of this issue. The Christian ethical tradition encourages friendship of a deep kind between friends male and female. The disagreement arises over how such friendship is to be conducted when sexual desire maps onto it: is this to be regarded as a problem to be coped with pastorally to prevent a sinful pattern of life, or something to be celebrated and implemented as a good? Connected with this are the questions of ontology and identity raised by the St Andrew's Day Statement, and the suggestion that we all have multifaceted sexual potentialities, capable of being shaped in particular directions in particular contexts. How should we conduct ourselves so as to live out the creative intention of God for the common good of humanity?

The re-publication of this symposium has been requested to help the Church consider these deeply fraught and painful questions. One of its contributors, Michael Vasey, tragically died prematurely shortly after his contribution was published. Another is now Archbishop of Canterbury. The authors continue in their different ministries to engage with the issue in Christian seriousness and care. Bishop Stephen Sykes, Professor of Theology in Durham, has kindly provided a Foreword to this edition. Otherwise the essays remain unchanged apart from minor corrections. An index, list of Scripture references, and bibliography for further reading across the range of opinion, have been added.

Timothy Bradshaw
Acting Principal and Senior Tutor
Regent's Park College, University of Oxford
July 2003

Introduction

THE ST ANDREW'S DAY Statement was produced by a group of theologians concerned at the fevered conflict over homosexuality gripping the Church. There seemed a need for some careful theological consideration of the question, and in particular of the claims that quasi-marital relationships between people of the same sex be given legitimacy and that practising homosexuals should be allowed to proceed to ordination. The list of those who produced the Statement is rather longer than the official list of signatories, including some, with personal experience of homosexuality, who wanted to remain anonymous.

The style of the Statement was deliberately detached and low-key, adopting a tone which did not collude with the dramatics of campaigners. It was no surprise, therefore, that the media showed little interest in the document. Whereas fierce dialectic and polarised rhetoric are 'news', attempts to find common ground tend to spoil the media fun.[1] The document did, however, attract the attention, as was hoped, of readers across the range of opinion. The authors of the Statement wished to listen to the responses of such people in the Church, to seek to clarify points of common understanding and to identify the key points of genuine disagreement, in an atmosphere free of the hostility and abuse of much of the conflict.

We are very grateful to all those who took the time and trouble to respond carefully and honestly to the Statement. Some came in person to talk to us in Oxford, as well as providing a written contribution, which often was revised after our personal conversation. We were genuinely keen to hear what they had to say to us, and regard this set of essays as an exercise in courteous listening to many voices, an exercise in respect as well as honesty. The much-abused 'ivory tower' can be of use to the Church in its concern for detachment as a context for discussion, and perhaps this has been so. The discussions, however, have been far from abstract and have insisted on concrete experience being a vital focus.

No fruitful dialogue can be without a context, without parameters: open-ended anarchy can be the only result of an undefined project. This discussion has been set in the Church's context, that is in the setting of the orthodox faith in the revealed action of the triune God, hence the credal principles set out early in the Statement. They are principles to which all participants in the discussion are committed and to which they may appeal. It is noteworthy that all the contributors expressed satisfaction with them.

Politically such a collection of essays from the full spectrum of opinion is bound to be delicate. We have sincerely tried to elicit responses from all viewpoints, inviting honest criticism and counter-argument. This means that the symposium, focused on the initial Statement, will contain some essays with which every reader will disagree. It may be the first exposure some readers will have had to views expressed here, with which they may well continue to disagree, but the very process will be educative. It will be evident that the essays do not fall neatly into two camps. Authors from the more revisionist wing, for example, will be found to argue some conflicting emphases, one obvious example being between those advocating marriage as a model for same-sex relationships, others advocating friendship as this model. More interestingly still, readers will be able to detect similar points being made by authors writing from 'opposite camps', for example on the linking of celibacy to homosexual inclination. Themes criss-cross tantalisingly through the essays, and the Statement receives robust criticism and questioning from opposing quarters.

The contributors represent different subject areas and realms of experience, giving another spectrum of variation, probing the themes of human desire and imagination in relation to contemporary social patterns and to moral order rooted in the risen Christ. The 'hermeneutical gap' between 'then' and 'now' can be absolutised by some and relativised by others; some judging the views of Paul of Tarsus irrelevant in some respects for today, others judging these views to be decisive in shaping contemporary patterns of behaviour. How can deep commitments held by authors be detached from their arguments, and indeed should they be? History, psychology, socio-cultural analysis, biblical scholarship, hermeneutics, pastoral experience, theology: so many disciplines are needed to explore this question, indeed even to frame the right questions. The mix of essays will at least show this complexity.

Two longer papers have been included among the essays. First Professor Oliver O'Donovan offered the publication of his lecture delivered in Berlin, an offer too good to miss, in which he advances some speculative constructs which he floats as possibilities for making a kind of pontoon bridge between opposite banks of the divide. Both Professor O'Donovan and the other authors of the Statement underline the fact that these constructs emanate from his theological imagination alone. Shortly thereafter Professor Anthony Thiselton offered his long essay on the hermeneutical state of play regarding the debate, which again seemed a resource too valuable to omit from a collection aiming to help the Church at a pressing time. Bishop John Austin Baker's lecture,[2] another initiative to take the debate further in the Church of England, was delivered as the final essay was being written, and so note has been taken of that lecture in the interests of his desire for real theological engagement. The authors of the Statement asked their chairman to write a concluding essay in the light of the contributions, and this comes with their commendation.

We are keenly aware of the pressure on all the contributors, and so are sincerely thankful to all of them for managing to produce their responses, in which they have succeeded in raising key questions, offering telling criticisms, making imaginative suggestions and counter-proposals to those of the Statement, and doing so with passion and sincerity. The reader will have to form a view whether the considerable burden of proof to support a major change in the Church's teaching and practice has been met. The authors of the St Andrew's Day Statement, for their part, do not think that it has.

Our prayer is that this focused set of essays will contribute not only to the peace of the Church, but to clarity of apostolic modes of life and faithfulness to our baptismal covenant of dying into Christ and rising with him. The dialogue presented by these essays, ecumenical in scope, is offered to the Church as a resource for the debate called for by General Synod.

Notes

1. Rowan Williams, drawing on Walter Benjamin, speaks of 'the succession of "shocks", apparently self-contained instants of presentation assaulting your awareness. It is an accurate forecast of what is normally thought of as "news" today.' *The Truce of God* (Fount, 1983), p. 99.
2. *Homosexuality and Christian Ethics: A New Way Forward Together*, April 1997 (delivered at, and available from, St-Martin-in-the-Fields church, London WC2N 4JJ).

St Andrew's Day Statement

An Examination of the Theological Principles Affecting the Homosexuality Debate

Introduction

Faced with practical questions which arouse strong and conflicting passions, the church has only one recourse: to find in the Gospel a starting-point of common faith from which those who differ can agree to proceed in their discussions. Such a question now before the Church of England is how we should respond to those, including clergy, seeking to live in quasi-marital relations with a partner of the same sex. The purpose of the following statement is to provide some definition of the theological ground upon which the issue should be addressed and from which any fruitful discussion between those who disagree may proceed.

By defining its fundamental agreements more clearly, the church may lighten the weight which is at present laid upon a practical question not without importance in its own right but in danger of being over-freighted with symbolic resonances. This in turn may create a context for principled pastoral care which is more responsive to particular individual circumstances and less to political meanings that can be read into them. That the issue should have become so highly dramatised calls for repentance on the part of all members of the church. It suggests that the Gospel has not been directing the acts, words and thoughts of Christians on this subject.

To emphasise its purpose the statement is in two parts, the first an affirmation of credal principles, the second an application of these principles to the question of homosexuality as it presents itself to the church today. It is not intended to cover every issue that must be considered in this context, and nothing should be inferred from what the statement does not say. If its assertions prove susceptible of being accommodated within more than one interpretation of present disputes, that will be an advantage, since it hopes to include all who do not intend a decisive break with orthodox Christianity. Of those who, nevertheless, find that they cannot agree, it is asked only that they should be precise about their disagreements, so that the extent of common ground available to the church may become clear.

Principles

I

Jesus Christ is the one Word of God. He came in human flesh, died for our sins and was raised for our justification. In the flesh he lived for us a life of obedience to the will of God; on the cross he bore God's judgement on our sin; and in his resurrection our human nature was made new. In him we know both God and human nature as they truly are. In his life, death and resurrection we are adopted as children of God and called to follow in the way of the cross. His promise and his call are for every human being: that we should trust in him, abandon every self-justification, and rejoice in the good news of our redemption.

II

The Spirit of Jesus Christ bears witness to the Gospel in Holy Scripture and in the ministry of the people of God. He directs us in the task of understanding all human life and experience through the Scriptures. And so, guided by the Spirit of God to interpret the times, the church proclaims the Word of God to the needs of each new age, and declares Christ's redeeming power and forgiveness in mutual encouragement and exhortation to holiness.

III

The Father of Jesus Christ restores broken creation in him. For he himself is its fulfilment: in him the church learns by its life and witness to attest to the goodness and hope of creation. The Spirit gives us strength and confidence to live as men and women within the created order, finding peace and reconciliation and awaiting the final revelation of the children of God.

Application

I

'In him' – and in him alone – 'we know both God and human nature as they truly are'; and so in him alone we know ourselves as we truly are. There can be no description of human reality, in general or in particular, outside the reality in Christ. We must be on guard, therefore, against constructing any other ground for our identities than the redeemed humanity given us in him. Those who understand themselves as homosexuals, no more and no less than those who do not, are liable to false understandings based on personal or family histories, emotional dispositions, social settings, and solidarities formed by common experiences or ambitions. Our sexual affections can no more define who we are than can our class, race or nationality. At the deepest ontological level, therefore, there is no such thing as 'a' homosexual or 'a' heterosexual; there are human beings, male and female, called to redeemed humanity in Christ, endowed with a complex variety of emotional potentialities and threatened by a complex variety of forms of alienation.

'Adopted as children of God and called to follow in the way of the cross', we all are summoned to various forms of self-denial. The struggle against disordered desires, or the misdirection of innocent desires, is part of every Christian's life, consciously undertaken in baptism. In any individual case, the form which this struggle takes may be determined by circumstances (wealth or poverty, illness or health, educational success or failure). Often these are not open to choice, but are given to us as a situation in which we are to live faithfully. We are not promised that the struggle will be quickly and triumphantly resolved, nor even that it will be successful at every point along the way; only that it will be crowned at last by a character formed through patience to be like Christ's.

II

The interpretation of homosexual emotion and behaviour is a Christian 'task', still inadequately addressed. 'Guided by God's Spirit', the church must be open to empirical observation and governed by the authority of the apostolic testimony. According to this testimony the rebellion of humankind against God darkens our mind and subverts our understanding of God and creation (Acts 26:18; Rom. 1:19–32; Eph. 4:17–19). For the biblical writers the phenomena of homosexual behaviour are not addressed solely as wilfully perverse acts but in generalised terms, and are located within the broader context of human idolatry (Rom. 1:26–7 with 1:19–32; 1 Cor. 6:9–10 with 6:12–20).

Many competing interpretations of the phenomena can be found in contemporary discussion, none of them with an unchallengeable basis in scientific data. The church has no need to espouse any one theory, but may learn from many. To every theory, however, it must put the question whether it is adequate to the understanding of human nature and its redemption that the Gospel proclaims. Theories which fail this test can only imprison the imagination by foreclosing the recognition of emotional variety and development. To 'interpret the times' in the midst of this theoretical confusion, the church must avoid being lulled by the vague idea that there is a transparent and necessary progress of thought working itself out in history, with which it has only somehow to keep abreast. It must search for conceptual and theological clarification. Without this there are dangers in a wide-ranging programme of discussions which, with insufficient support from the church's teaching, may serve merely to amplify the Babel of confused tongues.

The primary pastoral task of the church in relation to all its members, whatever their self-understanding and mode of life, is to re-affirm the good news of salvation in Christ, forgiveness of sins, transformation of life and incorporation into the holy fellowship of the church. In addressing those who understand themselves as homosexual, the church does not cease to speak as the bearer of this good news. It assists all its members to a life of faithful witness in chastity and holiness, recognising two forms or vocations in which that life can be lived: marriage and singleness (Gen. 2:24; Matt. 19:4–6; 1 Cor. 7 *passim*). There is no place for the church to confer legitimacy upon alternatives to these. Pastoral care, however, needs a certain flexibility, taking note of the circumstances which make each individual case different from every other, and discerning ways in which the Gospel touches people in different situations. The church, then, will give constant encouragement in following Christ not only to those who conform to one of these two vocations, but to all who seriously intend discipleship in fellowship with the body of the church. It is in this sense that the Bishops' Statement (*Issues in Human Sexuality*, 1991) is to be understood when it speaks of 'respecting the integrity' (cf. 5:21) of those who conscientiously dissent from the biblical teaching as the church understands it. While this teaching applies to all – for the priesthood of believers consecrates all Christians to a life of holiness – the Bishops have Scripture on their side in arguing that special considerations affect the behaviour of the clergy, who have a particular commission to expound and exemplify the teachings of the church (cf. 1 Tim. 3:1–13; 4:12–13; 5:19–20; Tit. 1:5–9; Jas. 3:1; 2 Pet. 2:2).

III

The 'fulfilment' of all creation is found in Christ (Eph. 1:23; Col. 1:15–19). Our own fulfilment, therefore, is not merely a private one but a communal, even a cosmic one. Both marriage and singleness in their different ways point forward to this fulfilment in the fellowship of God with his redeemed creation. In neither vocation, then, does fulfilment require or allow the exercise of every power or the satisfaction of every desire that any individual may reasonably have: a life may be fulfilled without occasion to employ the power of sexual expression, just as it may without occasion to exploit the potential for education, parenthood or mobility.

Both vocations in their different ways give equal expression to the blessing of human friendship, which is sanctified by Christ who calls us his friends (John 15:13–15; cf. Isa. 41:8) and elevated in him to become the 'fellowship of the Holy Spirit' (2 Cor. 13:14). Every aspect of our common life in Christ, friendship included, has a properly exploratory character: understanding our humanity in him, we are freed from human constructs to search out and discover the richness of creation that is opened to us by God's redeeming work. This search finds its fulfilment as it is directed by the hope for the final appearing of Jesus, the Son obedient to the Father who will put all things in subjection to him.

For the grace of God has appeared, bringing salvation to all, training us to renounce impiety and worldly passions, and in the present age to live lives that are self-controlled, upright, and godly, while we wait for the blessed hope and the manifestation of the glory of our great God and Saviour, Jesus Christ. He it is who gave himself for us that he might redeem us from all iniquity and purify for himself a people of his own who are zealous for good deeds. Declare these things; exhort and reprove with all authority. Let no one look down on you. (Titus 2:11–15)

St Andrew's Day 1995

Michael Banner
F. D. Maurice Professor of Moral and Social Theology, King's College, London

Markus Bockmuehl
University Lecturer in Divinity and Fellow of Fitzwilliam College, Cambridge

Timothy Bradshaw (chairman)
Dean of Regent's Park College, Oxford

Oliver O'Donovan
Regius Professor of Moral and Pastoral Theology, Oxford

Ann Holt
Director of Care for Education

William Persson
Formerly Bishop of Doncaster

David Wright
Senior Lecturer in Ecclesiastical History, University of Edinburgh

Knowing myself in Christ

Rowan Williams

THE MOST WELCOME contribution made by the Statement is at the level of method. Ours is a time in which it is depressingly easy to make this or that issue a test of Christian orthodoxy in such a way as to make wholly suspect the theology of anyone disagreeing on the issue in question; in other words, the possibility is neglected that Christians beginning from the same premises and convictions may yet come to different conclusions about particular matters without thereby completely voiding the commonness of their starting-point. It is really a matter of having a language *in which* to disagree rather than speaking two incompatible or mutually exclusive tongues. Of late, attitudes to sexuality have come to be seen as a clear marker of orthodoxy or unorthodoxy in many circles; and it is true that there are plenty of people for whom the casting off of 'traditional' or even scriptural norms to do with certain kinds of sexual behaviour is part of a general programme of emancipation from the constraints of what they conceive to be orthodoxy, part of a package that might include a wide-ranging relativism, pluralism in respect of other faiths, agnosticism about various aspects of doctrine or biblical narrative, and so on. However, it seems to me that the Statement, beginning as it does with proposed principles for theological discussion, recognises that the *assumption* that revisionism on one question entails wholesale doctrinal or ethical relativism is dangerous for the future of reasoned Christian disagreement of a properly theological character. What follows is based upon an unqualified agreement with the principles enunciated; which is to say that the qualifications and questions I want to enter are matters which I should see as rooted in the same fundamental concerns. I now turn to the Application.

I

'Our sexual affections can no more define who we are than can our class, race or nationality.' No more, but perhaps also no less: to acknowledge a human identity centred in, determined by, Christ is not the same as saying that such an identity is, apart from Christ, abstract and unhistorical, shaped only by maleness and femaleness 'called to redeemed humanity in Christ'. This first section of Application raises two questions in my mind. Does it presuppose that 'sexual affections' (which is a phrase I assume refers obliquely to sexual 'orientation') are a datum of historical humanity on much the same level as race or class? If so, the analogies would be interesting to pursue – and quite complex in character. 'Race' is a non-negotiable aspect of where I stand as an historical human subject; in some environments, it forecloses certain options for me (because of the way my society as a whole organises itself), and in any case it will always as a matter of bare fact be something true of me. Christians generally and black Christians in this century particularly have wanted to add that racial identity can be touched and redeemed by Christ in the sense that the particular ways of living associated with this racial and cultural history may by the grace of Christ be shown as transparent to Christ, ways of expressing and witnessing to the richness that is in him. And at the same time, there may be aspects of that culture opaque to Christ – a history of idolatry, aggression, servility, internalised assumptions of inferiority and so on, depending on whether the cultural history is or is not one of triumphant negotiation or domination of others. There is a long job of cultural discernment ahead; but we can at least say that it won't do either to say that a particular racial identity is incapable of carrying the meanings of Christ or that such an identity is epiphenomenal, a matter pretty well irrelevant to the concrete working out of what it is to be alive in Christ. Class, on the other hand, is not so straightforward. My class origins are, like my racial identity, simply a matter of bare fact. But, unlike my racial identity, my actual class position may change. It depends upon the vagaries of corporate and personal history: on how power is distributed and redistributed. Christians have got into trouble in the past for apparently encouraging people to assume that their position in the distribution of power and wealth was an absolute given, like race or gender. We couldn't say quite so easily that any class identity was in a merely static way capable of being transparent to Christ; what is significant here is how I come to terms with the power I have, with the limits of my possibilities, with the morality of effecting change for myself or others. I suspect that one of the areas of disagreement between those who do and those who don't wish to reaffirm the Church's historical position on homosexuality could be characterised according to whether sexual orientation was seen as more like race than class or vice versa.

But the second paragraph of section I of the Application seems to tilt the analogy a little more towards class. Hence my second question: is the mere fact of homosexual desire something against which struggle is imperative? Is it always and necessarily a desire comparable to the desire for many sexual partners or for sexual gratification at someone else's expense – comparable, more broadly, to the desire for revenge or the desire to avoid speaking an unwelcome or disadvantageous truth? I think the paragraph assumes that it is, and that it is therefore one of those 'given' constraints on proper moral freedom that in fact surround the moral life as lived in an historical environment where ideal conditions of freedom are not to be found. Now certainly this grants that human agents as we know them do not simply exist at that 'deepest ontological level' where there is no problem of sexual orientation. At such a level, there is no wealth or poverty or education or lack of it; but it is not at that level that we have to make specific moral options. The first section of Application thus nudges us towards a picture of homosexual desire as in some sense given, in the way a racial identity is given, but at the same time necessarily a kind of obstacle, not capable of quite the same sort of positive transfiguration as racial identity.

II

Both these questions on the first section obviously raise the further question of how it is that sexual desire directed towards the same sex comes to be construed in this prima facie rather problematical way; and the second section offers an answer. 'The phenomena of homosexual behaviour' are seen in a particular light in Scripture – not as a uniquely awful perversion, but as an instance of the effect upon the human mind of rebellion against God, a symptom of that confusion that comes from failing to identify correctly and worship unreservedly the one true God. While this takes the focus helpfully away from individual culpability and refuses to muddy the waters by simply stirring up disgust, it makes it plain that homosexual desire is of its nature a pointer to something in need of healing and correction. Thus the homosexually inclined person does not truly know himself or herself. This in turn makes it plain that in an important respect sexual orientation is *not* like racial identity, perhaps not even like class; it is never simply a matter of bare fact, at least at the deepest level of the self (where, in any case, as we have been told, the categories of 'heterosexual' and 'homosexual' are inappropriate). This must mean that any sense on the part of the homosexually inclined person that significant elements of their human identity in the broader sense are shaped by their sexual orientation must in some way be rooted in error. I would want only to note that this could pose some fairly serious difficulties as a basis for Christian nurture, since one of the recurring problems the Christian pastor has to face in counselling the homosexually inclined person is dealing with inner alienation and self-hatred. That is not quite the point I want to draw out here. This reading of the scriptural evidence takes it for granted (and this is a little in tension with the second paragraph of Application II) that, whatever the aetiology of homosexual desire, it cannot represent a 'neutral' given in anyone's situation.

In reflecting about this, I ask if there is not an unclarity over the basic categories. Mention is made of 'the phenomena of homosexual behaviour' as understood in Scripture. But in spite of the range of New Testament allusion, direct reference is really restricted to Romans 1. What makes this text less than completely decisive for some contemporary Christian interpreters is that the 'phenomena' in view here are described in terms of considerable imaginative 'violence' – the blind abandonment of what is natural and at some level known to be so, and the deliberate turning in rapacity to others. To see this as an account of 'the phenomena of homosexual behaviour' is to beg the question somewhat, when it is cast as a self-conscious flouting of a truth already made known. It would have to be said, if this passage is indeed to be read as about the phenomena of homosexual behaviour in general, that homosexual desire is not only intrinsically disordered but intrinsically rapacious in a way that other kinds of desire are not. The writers of the Statement are – creditably – reluctant to draw such a consequence of their reading. Yet the passage from reference to 'phenomena of behaviour' in the first paragraph, with Romans 1 adduced as a point of reference, to 'phenomena' in general – evidently, from the context, the wider phenomena of *desire* itself – in the second might leave some readers uneasy, however willing they might be to agree the folly of approaching this question with a bland assumption that we are so much better than our forebears at making sense of these things. It is quite possible, without subscribing to any such flannel, to ask whether and how we can be sure that the 'phenomena' under review are the same. Christians have applied this technique with notable success and sophistication to the matter of lending money for interest or deliberately slaughtering the innocent. Is it not a fair question to ask whether conscious rebellion and indiscriminate rapacity could be presented as a plausible account of the essence of 'homosexual behaviour', let alone homosexual desire, as it may be observed around us now? It may even be that such an argument simply mirrors the excesses of some sorts of gay militants in supposing there to be an essence of 'homosexual identity' after all.

However, if the basic point that homosexual desire is always the symptom of a fundamental spiritual confusion or error is accepted, what follows makes good sense. The Church proclaims good news to 'those who understand themselves as homosexual' by accepting them into the Church's fellowship and offering the possibility of change – which in practice (if I read the document rightly) means the possibility of controlling homosexual desire rather than any speculation about a supposed change of orientation, a complex and dangerous area in which there is plenty of evidence of well-meaning damage done. The Church cannot publicly endorse any form of life other than singleness or monogamous heterosexual marriage as a legitimate expression of response to God's call. To the Christian homosexual who does not see his or her desire as essentially disordered, the Church allows a conscientious discretion, so it seems, discerning according to individual circumstances – though this is admitted to apply somewhat more narrowly to ordained ministers.

A difficulty remains. In what sense does the Church actually proclaim good news to the homosexually inclined person who does not see their condition as a mark of rebellion or confusion? They are told that they are tolerated, even respected; but their own account of themselves before God is not to be recognised. I am not talking here, I should add, about what any self-described homosexual *does*, only about their understanding of their own condition. And the question is about the basis on which a description of 'homosexual behaviour' and desire centred around Romans 1 can be given a privileged position over, let us say, a conscientious self-description by a homosexual person in terms of his or her longing to live a life in which their sexual desire, like other aspects of their identity, can come to image the love and the justice of Christ. It is not simply and not always a matter of an individual setting up a self-justifying account of their desires or acts over against the Word of God; there are plenty of Christians of homosexual inclination who would say something like this:

I want to live in obedience to God; I truly, prayerfully and conscientiously do not recognise Romans 1 as describing what I am or what I want. I am not rejecting something I know in the depths of my being. I struggle against the many inducements to live in promiscuous rapacity – not without cost. I do not believe my identity as a desiring being is a complicated and embarrassing extra in my humanity as created by God. And it is hard to hear good news from the Church if it insists that my condition is in itself spiritually compromised.

If the Church is to 'give constant encouragement in following Christ' even to those who do not settle for either celibacy or marriage because of their orientation, can it really and honestly do so without at least admitting that an account of homosexual identity dominated by Romans 1 cannot be the whole story? Even the homosexually inclined person living faithfully in a celibate state might well ask whether their prayerful self-understanding was properly respected by the model that I think the document as a whole assumes.

III

The kind of person I am imagining (not without a good many actual prototypes in mind) would also have something to say about the monitions in the third section. Vocation is never simply 'fulfilment'; 'indeed', the imagined interlocutor might say,

> I am not asking just for fulfilment. I want to know how my human and historical being, enacting itself through the negotiation of all sorts of varied desires and projects, may become transparent to Jesus, a sign of the kingdom. I do not seek to avoid cost. But for the married, that cost is worked out in the daily discipline of a shared life, which, by the mutual commitment it embodies, becomes a means of grace and strength for the bearing of the cost.

Of course lives may be and some lives apparently must be lived without sexual expression in the usual sense of the term. But if you do not accept that homosexual desire is itself a mark of disorder, can you confidently say that the presence of this desire must always be a sign that sexual expression is ruled out?

How does the homosexually inclined person show Christ to the world? That must be the fundamental question, and theological and pastoral discussion of this theme ought to begin from there rather than from rights on the one hand or law on the other. There is a now fairly familiar suggestion that, if what is symbolically central in the scriptural view of marriage, in Old and New Testaments, is not an arrangement for procreation but a condition of living 'under promise', living in commitment *usque ad mortem . . . crucis*, then the partnership of two persons of the same sex is in some way 'showing' what marriage shows of the God who promises and who remains faithful. This is arguably very different from a claim to some right to fulfilment or self-expression; it is only a claim in the sense that a Christian may claim the freedom to be a bearer of the crucifying fidelity of God in the structures and shapes of his or her daily life. I think that this is an area in which further theological debate should develop. It does not, of course, settle the matter: many would respond immediately by saying that the covenantal imagery of Scripture always presupposes the order of creation as between man and woman. But this in turn would need further glossing and grounding. My hope is that the method set out in the document under review would allow a constructive exploration of these matters to go forward. And a major goal in what I have written here is to enter a plea for some recognition of the fact that those who want to argue what I have called a revisionist position on the possible legitimacy of 'sexual expression' for the person of homosexual inclination may, like their opponents, be trying to find a way of being faithful and obedient to the givens of revelation. As with other issues, most of them related to gender and sexuality for some reason, the assumption is very readily made that an impassable gulf divides people called 'liberals' from people called 'traditionalists'. This Statement is careful to avoid such glib sloganeering. 'In him we know both God and human nature as they truly are': that is a good place to begin, and to end. What we disagree about is, I hope, not that principle but how that knowledge-in-Christ is mediated and made actual in the Church's life.

2

Homosexuality in the Church: Can there be a fruitful theological debate?

Oliver O'Donovan

THE TITLE SHOULD be understood literally. It is not my intention to explain my opinions about homosexuality, but simply to ask how a fruitful debate can proceed in the Church. Putting the question that way, of course, implies that a fruitful debate is not now taking place. Certainly there is a debate – as the bibliographies attest – and not only about homosexuality as such but about the particular questions that trouble the Church. But one must say, it is a debate 'about', not a debate 'with'. For a truly theological debate to occur, the Church must be able to speak 'with' its homosexual members who have something they wish to say to it. There must be a 'conciliar process', as Bernd Wannenwetsch has finely described it.[1] Yet at this point we encounter much dispute, no debate.

A debate occurs when people take up the arguments that others have raised against them, and try to give serious answers. To do that they must think their opponents mistaken, certainly, but not wholly foolish or malicious. They must suppose that some misconception, or some partial truth not fully integrated into other truths, has limited their vision. They must accept the burden of showing how the partial truth fits in with other truths, or of identifying and resolving the misconception. This cannot happen while there is still a struggle for rhetorical dominance; that is to say, while each side hopes to win a monopoly for the categories in which they themselves frame the question. For while that goal is in view, it is a matter of strategy to ignore the alternative categories in which the opponent is thinking. One may not grant the opponent the courtesy of direct quotation, but can only attribute to him or her positions framed in one's own categories, which, predictably, will look ridiculous. This describes, not too unjustly I hope, the style of the disagreement heard in the British churches, and even more in the North American; and I need hardly comment on the tendency of media involvement to reinforce their stubborn and bitter character. Sorry as this situation is, we need not suppose that it arises simply from malice or ill-will. It has an epistemological source. When people find themselves moved by convictions which for them have immediate certainty, not subject to dialectical questioning, they will find it imaginatively impossible to accept that there are other certainties, other ways of construing the situation, which may be held without disingenuousness. In this position the only way forward is through debate — real debate, that is, and not mere regulation, by some means or other, of the dispute. I say a 'theological' debate, though that term should be otiose if one takes with due seriousness the fact that this debate must occur within the Church. I do not mean a debate confined to theologians, but a debate which has a theological purpose, to comprehend the truth of the homosexual phenomenon, whatever it may be, in the light of the Christian Gospel.

That this debate has not yet begun, does not mean that new pastoral initiatives, such as that taken recently by the Evangelische Kirche in Germany to authorise non-liturgical blessings for certain homosexual couples, are premature. The logical order may be to achieve a common clarity first, and only then implement it in pastoral action. But this is never actually the order of events. Our search for clarity makes its way forward through thought and action simultaneously. What it does mean, however, is that pastoral decisions made in this context can have only a provisional and experimental character. They cannot provide firm ground upon which we can build, for they do not rest upon the catholic conviction of the Church. *Lex orandi lex credendi* is, in my view, a perilous dictum; and most of all when it suggests that one may dictate *lex credendi* by the shrewd measure of gaining or retaining control over *lex orandi*. This caution applies not only to innovatory practices, such as that recently adopted by the EKD, but conservative practices too. In 1991 the Bishops of the Church of England avowed a policy of not ordaining candidates for ministry who were in homosexual partnerships. This was only a continuation of what had been undeclared practice from time immemorial; but, as those who attacked it quickly appreciated, because of the current confusion in the Church it could have only a hypothetical status. Confusion is precisely the state in which tradition is impotent to exercise its authority over us. Tradition depends for its authority on the general perception that it faithfully mediates the faith and practice of the Gospel.

Here, then, is a task for the Church, and one in which the theologians, though having no monopoly, will have their work cut out. For a long time, I must admit, I held back from engagement with this question, partly out of distaste at the sheer bad temper that it generated, partly because, although I had my own opinions – which of us does not? – I had no clear view of the contribution that a moral theologian ought to make. For the task of the theologian is not simply to engage in the debate on the side that appears to have the greater right; it is to safeguard the Gospel integrity of the debate, by clarifying what the questions are that must be at issue. This point should not be misunderstood. It does not mean that there are no right and wrong decisions, whether at the level of definite action or at the level of rules and principles. Not everything is shrouded in moral ambiguity! Nor does it mean that the theologian must assume a specious irresolution when the argument points irresistibly in one direction. (Karl Rahner's remarks on the false consciousness of moral theologians in the Vietnam War must not be forgotten at this point!) It means simply that, like Ezekiel's watchman on the walls, the theologian has a specific responsibility, which is to make things clear. Whatever decisions are taken in the city, whether in faith or in wilful disobedience, the watchman must ensure they are taken in full consciousness of what is at stake.

In 1995, as the dispute blazed hotter and more virulently within our Church, a small group of theological colleagues and I produced the short position-paper which was called, from the date of its publication, the St Andrew's Day Statement. It was not an 'agreed statement' in the ecumenical mould, composed by representatives of opposed groups. It was the work of an *ad hoc* group that shared a common mind. But its mind was not about the rights and wrongs of homosexuality as such, but about certain key theological principles that it saw implicit in the discussion and believed should be brought to the fore. It was an attempt, in other words, to describe the parameters of a debate which was lacking in the Church, by inviting protagonists to turn back from their immediate certainties and counter-certainties to the ultimate certainties which they would share with other Christian believers. Since the publication of this statement the process has entered a second stage: a series of meetings between its authors and individuals who can be identified as theological voices on either side of the dispute, to explore with them how far the parameters described in the Statement allow them room to formulate positions they wished to put before the Church. Its theological strategy, then, was, after all, ecumenical: it aimed to provide a catholic agreement in faith within which disagreements could be located and pursued constructively.

The St Andrew's Day Statement suggests an answer to one objection that I can envisage being raised against that search. 'What we need', someone might say, 'is not a debate, but a Confession. It is built into the process of debate that the outcome will be some kind of compromise. If we believe that the tradition as we have received it is good and lifegiving, then we ought simply to declare it. Anything else is a fine cloak for retreat and withdrawal.' I take this objection seriously, despite its intransigent sound, because there is plenty of evidence that what it fears will happen, does happen. Light and lazy talk about 'development' and 'new insights' may often do no more than announce a change of fashion. What intellectual historian can deny that great intellectual changes may be brought about by quite unintellectual causes, such as shifts in economic power, collapsing educational institutions and so on? We are right to fear that kind of change in the Church. For we are right to fear unfaithfulness.

We should want not to lose our institutional memories, forsake our loyalties and succumb to the forces of irrational change that dictate intellectual currents without intellectual accountability. These are all forms of godlessness, of bondage to arbitrary powers.

In answer to this not negligible anxiety, however, I make two points. First, to describe the parameters of a true Church-debate is already to make a Confession. The St Andrew's Day Statement is a form of Confession as well as a proposal for debate, in that it attempts to declare no more and no less than what the Church must be able to say together if it is to debate fruitfully. Secondly, no Confession, if it is undertaken as a venture in the witness of the Spirit, could be a static affair. It must lead the Church forward. The St Andrew's Day Statement describes the enterprise as follows: 'The Spirit of Jesus Christ . . . directs us in the task of understanding all human life and experience through the Scriptures. And so, guided by the Spirit of God to interpret the times, the church proclaims the Word of God to the needs of each new age' (p. 6). If we put ourselves in the way of that ministry to us, and under that authority, then we are in the way of a true development of Christian understanding as well as being protected against pseudo-developments. It implies learning things we did not know, not randomly substituting new and untried for old and tried wisdom, but by an ordered and coherent growth of Christian testimony, as the Gospel sheds illumination on the needs of a new period of history. Our first and last duty in this sphere is to discern the light the Gospel sheds on the gay movement of our time. The Church must learn to attest its faith in the Gospel before this cultural phenomenon. The gay Christian must learn to attest the truth of the gay self-consciousness in the light of the Gospel. What we commit ourselves to, when we commit ourselves to true debate, is no more and no less than this learning. But let nobody presume to announce in advance what we are going to learn before we come to learn it! That, indeed, is the mark of a false prophet!

In asking how a debate may proceed fruitfully, I consider first how it identifies its object, then the canons of theological understanding that it brings to bear upon it.

Such a debate will not assume that we know precisely what homosexuality is. It will operate in an open theoretical field. If there is anything more disconcerting than the hesitation and uncertainty with which theologians propose their answers on this subject, it is the dogmatic certainty with which they frame their questions. Here, it seems, science and statistics allow us a security that neither faith nor pastoral experience can sustain! Yet while the theologians embrace empirically based accounts, these are more and more repudiated by the intellectuals of the gay movement itself. Inspired in part by Foucault's historical sociology of knowledge, the critique of the 'medicalisation' of homosexuality has become vigorous. The debates pursued within the gay intelligentsia – and especially the debate between the 'essentialist' and 'constructionist' accounts of homosexuality – are important for the Church to overhear, if it is to encompass the full width of the theoretical possibilities, free of pseudo-certainties which are invoked simply to settle questions quickly. Of course, some theories are better supported than others – there is no need for infinite patience with the fantastic. Some theories are more capable of bearing weight – and why should not medical ones be among those that are more worthy of confidence? The point is not to banish all theories but to keep them in play, open to supplement and qualification, to doubt and to testing against experience. 'The true homosexual has no freedom of choice in the matter'; 'the incidence of homosexuality is uniform in all societies, only the recognition of it is variable'; 'homosexuality is the expression of a deeper personality disorder'; 'homosexuality is the product of rapid social change'; 'one is born with a sexual orientation that does not change, only manifests itself'; these are all examples of claims which are often made far too strong. They belong in our discussion only when deployed hypothetically, in a self-conscious strategy of exploration.

And we must bear in mind the fact – here, surely, the word 'fact' is in place – that the homosexual phenomenon is changing before our eyes. Whatever the truth about homosexuality was, we must now reckon also with a cultural movement that has acquired its own social reality. When a group of people with a common cause gains a sense of its own solidity, it develops as a cultural force, defining its aesthetic preferences, its critique of the hegemonic culture, its practices of association and communication, and, of course, its recruiting mechanisms. These, indeed, have given rise to some of the sharpest pastoral, indeed political difficulties, when they have been directed, as they naturally are, at the young. For this cultural movement I use the term 'gay' – its own self-chosen style in the English-speaking lands – while 'homosexual' refers simply to the psychosexual patterns of emotion. To be 'gay' one must have a prevailing interest in homosexuality, an identification with homosexual people, and an assertive programme which may often present itself as a series of demands for accommodation though in some forms of assertiveness, especially those of an artistic order, demand is much less significant than display. Within this description many theoretical and practical differences are accommodated. The gay consciousness is loosely knit theoretically; it has no orthodoxy; which is why a certain *orthopraxis* of aggressive protest and loyal mutual defence is important to its sense of identity. But it is equally clear that not all who think of themselves as homosexual, especially within the Church, want any part of the gay movement. Some of the hostility in the debate arises from the resentment this causes; just as some of the hostility of feminists has been directed not against men but against conservative women.

A good debate will need to be open not only to many theories but to many experiences. In the first place there is the major difference to be noticed between women's and men's experience. A special importance attaches to the female gay culture as it forms a channel by which serious philosophical reflection, largely derived from the French feminists, has influenced the movement. Then we must attend to the experience of those who have been in the gay culture and left it, while still thinking of themselves as homosexual; of those who have been homosexual and have ceased to be; of those who have married and become homosexual subsequently, sometimes in middle life; those who identify with the gay culture aesthetically and morally, though only doubtfully homosexual; literary and cultural gays; educationally low-achieving gays of deprived backgrounds, and so on. All of them demand distinct pastoral, as well as theoretical, recognition. And here I must interject a word about another category, that of the so-called 'bisexual'. The early medical theorists attempted to describe what they called 'true' homosexuality, distinguishing it from various shadow manifestations such as that which occurs in adolescence or in intense single-sex communities. This created a still-current style of psychotherapy which proposed to assist the patient by making an authoritative resolution of ambiguities, pronouncing decisively on whether he or she was a 'true' homosexual. Considering the criticism addressed to other psychotherapeutic techniques in this field, one can only be surprised at the complaisance with which this technique has been accepted. But if statistics do anything useful, they warn us of the dangers of this either–or categorisation. A larger proportion of the human race, apparently, has the capacity to respond to sexual stimuli of both same-sex and other-sex types than responds only to same-sex types. What is needed is not to sweep this considerable number of moderately sensitive human beings into one or the other of two abstract categories, but to develop a less rigid view of how sexual stimulation affects the whole personality. Here, too, the problem is that we are theory-bound.

Beside listening to theories and experiences, a debate will attend to proposals from the gay culture, and will take them the more seriously the more they rise above the level of demand and recrimination and begin to articulate what the movement stands for, its vision and its critique of society. Some gay thinkers have located themselves within the various strands of modernity-criticism; that alone must give what they say a particular interest. I mention, as an engaging example, the Canadian writer Scott Symons, who in 1965 left his marriage and his career, choosing (as he insists!) to adopt a gay lifestyle in protest against the dominance of the Liberal Party in Canadian politics, the stranglehold of Presbyterian and Methodist traditions in Ontario (he himself being an occasional Anglican worshipper), and the syllabus for teaching English literature at the University of Toronto. He said: 'there was a sense of vocation, and a sense of civic action . . . I knew that this was where one had to move, to open the doors to male sentience'.[2] What would this programme mean? How does the 'erotisation of society', to use a phrase which has gained some currency, offer liberation from sin and oppression to all of us? Could it even be a serious alternative to the *sexualisation* of society, which we experience at present without any of the beauty or the joy in creation that eros may be thought to connote? Could it mean a liberation, that is, from the legacy of Sigmund Freud? Of course, I do not know the answers to these questions; but they are questions which would certainly be asked in the course of a good debate.

Addressing now the theological content of the debate, we begin with a brief prolegomenon. The theological weight cannot rest wholly upon biblical exegesis. In theological circles where the need for debate has been felt, this, understandably, has been the first route taken, and much thought has been given to the brief and uncompromisingly negative references to homosexuality in Scripture, either explaining their tone as responses to special cultural features which were an aspect of that practice in biblical times, or insisting on the essential identity of the phenomenon despite variations. (A third type of proposal has been to dismiss the whole attempt to get insight from exegesis, a move which in my view lacks theological responsibility.) In finding the exegetical discussion inconclusive, I do not think it can be dispensed with – wearisome as some aspects of it have been. Faced with yet another attempt to get at the meaning of *arsenokoites* by philology, I cry: Enough! You have satisfied the curiosity of a generation!

It is a principle in the hermeneutics of biblical ethics, that scriptural precepts bear upon us as they are mediated through evangelical doctrine. The difficulty with the biblical references to homosexuality is that they are so incidental that they give us little help in situating them doctrinally. The famous discussion in Romans 1, however, is an exception, articulating a connection between homosexuality and idolatry, which are treated as two aspects of a cultural development. (A mirror-image, one might think of the view of Scott Symons, for whom marriage had become the emblem of the idolatrous ex-Puritanism that had dominated Canadian society.) If we could explore the relation between worship and patterns of sexual behaviour to which St Paul points us, we could, I think, achieve a more effective grip on the problems before us. We need, however, a broader doctrinal base than those texts on their own afford, yet not forgetting that they, too, demand an account.

Let us begin, then, from a systematic question, the question of *identity*. What can be meant by this term, and can there be such a thing as a homosexual identity? 'I have become a great question to myself' (Augustine, *Conf.* IV. 4. 9). We ask ourselves 'Who am I', 'What am I?', and the term 'identity' serves to sum up the answers we reach. But Christians believe there is a definite order to be observed in finding those answers. We may not simply consult the most immediate data of our self-consciousness; the risk of self-misunderstanding is never absent from those data and is always perilous. Our identities, the Gospel tells us, are given us in Christ risen from the dead; they are to be found within that lordly humanity which stands before God in the 'last Adam'. Other identities, whether national, class, family or whatever, are relative and secondary. But there can be no fundamental divisions within that restored human nature. Even the division between male and female is, from the point of view of Galatians 3:28, eschatologically suspended, though it is given back to us as an element of restored creation, to be reclaimed and reinterpreted. What status, then, has the identity–claim 'I am a homosexual'? In the minds of those who make this claim, is there a division between homosexual and heterosexual, fundamental to the human race, like that described, for example, in Aristophanes' speech in Plato's *Symposium*? Such a conception could have no theological standing. Even the male–female division itself is acknowledged only to the extent that it serves as an integrating factor in the redeemed human race: 'The woman is not without the man nor the man without the woman in the Lord' (1 Cor. 11:11), a remark which reaches beyond sexual attraction to encompass all the varied ways in which our awareness of our own humanity is given to us through the mediation of the opposite sex. The formal distinction between this division and a supposed hetero-/homosexual division is plain: heterosexuals are not drawn to homosexuals nor homosexuals to heterosexuals, as men are drawn to women and women to men. Where the division between the sexes functions as a polar structure that ensures relationship, the division between the sexual orientations would be a structure of apartness. The authors of the St Andrew's Day Statement, then, concluded that they must make a definite denial: 'At the deepest ontological level . . . there can be no such thing as "a" homosexual or "a" heterosexual; there are human beings, male and female, called to redeemed humanity in Christ.' I am bound to say that I think this denial essential: it marks a limit upon what the Church can, with any integrity, contemplate. If it is asked to adopt some alternative myth of creation-order to replace that in which Adam acclaims Eve as 'bone of my bone and flesh of my flesh', it can only refuse.

But short of this confessional point there may be ways in which a homosexual identity can be contemplated, just as forms of national and class-identity can be contemplated, within the Christ-given human identity that admits of no division. Not every form of apartness is a denial of that fundamental togetherness. We have been used in this century to confronting potentially or actually idolatrous forms of national apartness; perhaps this has made us too slow to recognise non-idolatrous forms, which offer service to the unity and co-ordination of the whole. Lest I be suspected here of advocating the characteristic British view of national identities, let me mention a very different example. I have a special concern for small and threatened linguistic communities, which preserve in their separate speech a special poetry and a special insight without which the world would be poorer. At Pentecost all heard the Gospel in their own language; none had to abandon their linguistic identity to hear it. But a small language needs a certain cultural apartness; it can be too easily destroyed by the erosion of a powerful lingua franca. To assist such a community to find the shelter that it needs could be a service offered in good conscience to God, and also to the wider human community which needs pluriformity of language and culture to fulfil its calling. In that case an 'identity' assumed within this community would not be a stubborn element of alien loyalty which resisted Christ's identity, but a 'vocation' to serve in a certain distinct context and manner. Could we find an analogy here? Could a homosexual 'identity' become a vocation?

The concept of vocation is a differentiated one. It arises in the first place from the passage of 1 Corinthians 7 where St Paul advises newly converted Christians to remain in the state 'in which' they were called. A vocation is here the objective social condition within which one finds oneself, so that one's first duty, though not necessarily one's last, is to occupy it as a Christian witness. But the use of the term extends further, especially in Reformed thought, to include what St Paul calls a *charisma*, something one is given in particular by God. And this again has two senses. Elsewhere in the same chapter Paul refers to the alternative states of marriage and singleness as 'gifts': 'each has his own gift from God, one this way, one that' (7:7). This is a personal fitness for one of these two forms of social existence. But in 1 Corinthians 12 the term recurs in a yet more individualised sense, as an endowment of the Holy Spirit to enable the individual to exercise a special function within the body which will complement the functions of others. This gives us three senses, then, of ascending force, in which we might ask whether there could be such a thing as a vocation to be a homosexual Christian: an objective condition 'within which' one must learn to serve Christ; a fitness for either marriage or singleness; and an equipment for a special service one may render the whole body.

But together with the notion of vocation we must explore the notion of *sin*. That these two conceptions of the gay Christian's position, apparently opposed, must be considered together, should not surprise us, if we are alert to the dynamics of the concept of vocation in Paul's thought: his example of a condition within which one is called is slavery – which he views as prima facie contrary to the liberty of a Christian ('I do not want you to be slaves of men'), and his argument for marriage as a state for which some are fitted turns upon the problem of *porneia*. The difficulty we feel in bringing together the notions of vocation and sin arises from the shrinking of our conception of sin to a voluntarist idea of particular transgression, torn out of the wider context of need and despair which are so important if we are to grapple with the relation of sin to the emotions. I take it that the Vatican was seen to be adopting this shrunken and legalistic idea when it spoke (in the SCDF's *Personae Humanae* of 1975) of 'homosexual acts' as 'intrinsically disordered and . . . never to be approved'; and that this is one reason why those words won so few friends even in churches inclined to a conservative view.

This perception may have some justice. Still, there is another reason why one might reasonably confine one's negative judgment to homosexual *acts*, and that is to leave questions about emotion, patterns of affection and, most strikingly, domestic provision, questions which the moral tradition as a whole has never been under pressure to resolve decisively, wide open. It is also to distance this judgment from judgments about the attribution of personal fault, of which it is said twice in the same paragraph that there is no straightforward correlation between the one judgment and the other. Of course, in noticing this point one should not credit the Vatican with the view – indefensible in itself as well as alien to Roman Catholic teaching – that the objective assessment of an act and the subjective obligation of an agent are quite separable and unrelated matters. It is simply that the correlation of objective and subjective is complex. And if we assume charitably that the complexity was mentioned at that point in the document not as a way of cutting the discussion short but of opening it up, then we have here, too, an encouragement to undertake the kind of debate we envisage: one which is open at once both to the question of a homosexual vocation and to the judgment, so strongly supported by Scripture, that in the sexual act performed between persons of the same sex we confront a manifestation of the fallen and sinful character of our humanity. The essential element, as I suppose, in this latter judgment is that human powers of *physical sexual* expression are tied decisively to the polar opposition of the two sexes and so to their mutual attraction. The ground for taking up the question of vocation, on the other hand, is that the *emotional and affective* expressiveness of human beings, closely intertwined with the sexual powers from a psychological point of view, are not simply bi-polar but multifaceted. To give the physical polarity its due, and at the same time to give the affective variety its due, is the demanding task which confronts any responsible description; and for this we need to deploy both the category of sin and the category of vocation.

One could imagine a minimal claim for a homosexual 'vocation' in the weakest sense of that word: someone already living in a partnership becomes a Christian, and conceives him- or herself to have a primary duty of fidelity to the partner – not excluding the duty to maintain a sexual relationship on which the other is dependent. This claim could be made by someone who accepted *au pied de la lettre* the traditional assessment of homosexual acts, since it requires only a generous concept of pastoral expediency. It would be analogous to policies now not infrequently admitted by churches in polygamous cultures, of permitting a new male convert to preserve a polygamous household.

A second, stronger claim could arise from the idea of vocation as a fitness for marriage. If this fitness is discerned in terms of a lack of fitness for the celibate life, then it would seem that some people are fitted for intimate partnership but not with the opposite sex. The same emotional need, the same threatening possibility of *porneia* and the disintegration that it brings in its train, require us to acknowledge para-marital states in which the couple assist each other in their discipleship by mutual affection and faithfulness. This claim does not require the additional insistence, which on our grounds would make it inherently unacceptable, that homosexual and heterosexual marriage have equal ontological status. It is perfectly compatible with the belief that heterosexual marriage is the norm, homosexual 'marriage' the adaptation. To that extent it can retain the judgment that homosexual acts are 'intrinsically disordered'; but it cannot retain the corollary, 'never to be approved'. For the sake of remedy for sin, the argument goes, this accommodation should be approved, since it is what these disciples are fitted for and to that extent called to. The nearest analogy for such a para-marital condition, besides the polygamous one already suggested, lies in the way those who think marriage intrinsically indissoluble view the second marriages – for them, 'marriages' – of divorced people: not marriages in the full sense, but an approximation to marriage which may be the best course morally available for those involved. (This analogy, of course, carries less weight in a mainstream Protestant tradition where such marriages are viewed as ontologically real marriages, though they may be regrettable ones.)

It has been widely assumed in the Church that some form of claim for homosexual marriage is *the* challenge that the gay movement presents. This, however, has been put in question recently by two gay Christian writers, Elizabeth Stuart and Michael Vasey (who contribute to this volume), who have argued independently that marriage is not the right paradigm for homosexual relations, but that 'affective friendship' is what the homosexual is fitted for. For Vasey an important reference point within the tradition is the role of single-sex monastic communities which illustrate how structures may be devised for unmarried Christians to find scope for committed relationships within the context of shared domestic life.[3] (This is the correct use to be made of Aelred of Rievaulx's *On Spiritual Friendship*, a work from which much more tendentious conclusions have sometimes been drawn.) On this account the sexual element in a homosexual friendship is neither so important to the relation itself nor so important a problem to be got over in defending it. If the marriage-model builds on the traditional concept of remedy for sin, the friendship-model could be said to exploit the Augustinian idea of excess sexual energy as venial sin, unnecessary to the logic of the relationship and to that extent unhelpful, but, when accepted with patient good humour by the partner, unharmful too. This approach, though capable of accepting, perhaps, that in some sense a homosexual act was both 'intrinsically disordered' and 'not to be approved', would be inclined to protest against the opinion (again from the Vatican) that 'to judge homosexual relationships (i.e. sexual ones) indulgently . . . goes against the . . . moral sense of the Christian People'. *Indulgentia* is precisely the term used by Augustine in relation to this excess of sexuality, and, indeed, perfectly characterises the view that the whole anxiety of the Christian tradition over sexual *acts* has been overdone. This view, indeed, since it has no interest in emulating the exclusive lifelong bond of marriage, is prepared to view 'indulgently' even what the advocates of the marriage-model are inclined to deplore as 'promiscuity'. Yet at the same time it would de-emphasise the importance of a sexual element to a serious relationship.

This is one of those disagreements of gays among themselves that the Church has to listen attentively to. I welcome the alternative model, in that it seems to take seriously, and, indeed, even make a virtue of, an often-observed feature of male homosexual relationships, their episodic character, and so brings a rather wider range of homosexual experience into the discussion. Consider what happens if we think of homosexual relations as para-marriages, and perhaps introduce some kind of Church recognition of them. After some years' cohabitation, a male couple may say to each other, 'We will always be grateful and always love each other; but for each of us to pursue his life's goals at this point it is better for us to part, not from incompatibility or breakdown, but simply in pursuit of new horizons.' The marriage-model requires the Church to frown on this. But would it be right to do so? Could it be certain that the arguments which would apply to a marriage would apply here also? I, certainly, am not certain; and so I welcome the opportunity to engage with an account of the gay consciousness that treats the homosexual dynamic as simply different.

The third concept of vocation is the strongest. May we discern a special gift that the gay Christian has to offer the Church? This notion could, I think, be intelligible if we were to frame it in terms of prophecy, and ask whether there is some message that is offered for our common upbuilding – something, that is, more than a demand for accommodation, something about the authenticity and integrity of Christian living. It is easier to envisage such a message, I would think, emerging from that side of the gay movement that advocates an affective dimension of friendship, for there it is more evident how what it has to say would touch us all. One might, building on suggestions in their writings, conceive the message as follows. The Church made a mistake when it swallowed the uncompromising critique of Eros which was developed in the first half of this century out of Kierkegaard by figures such as Anders Nygren and Denis de Rougemont, riding on the anti-idealist wave that swept through Christian thought at the time. Eros, the quest for the ultimate, mediated through earthly beauty and its hold on our desires, is essential to the joy and delight of the Gospel. It liberates the energies evoked by sexual imagery for transference to the higher cultural, moral and spiritual goods, commuting the yearnings of the body into the heroism of the soul and the visionary rapture of the spirit. To be a fellowship of Agape, the Church must at the same time be a fellowship of Eros. The homosexual, with a special gift for affective friendship, serves to cultivate Eros in the Church, to renew its sensitivity and its instinctive responsiveness to beauty, and so to attest the beauty of God.

There, at any rate, is a thesis worthy of debate, the more interesting in that it has parallels with other theses that have emerged from quite different quarters. I do not know where the debate could lead us. One thinks at once, of course, of counter-theses and counter-questions. How could a Christian Eros acknowledge the critique of idolatry, such as arises from Deuteronomy or Deutero-Isaiah, with its strongly anti-iconic bias? How seriously will a gay eroticism take the ascetic disciplines which are associated with the erotic ladder of ascent? My point is not to pursue the debate here and now, but merely to point to it as the road by which we might move out from the present stalemate to discover something together. Will that happen? Well, it depends considerably upon how the Christian gay movement addresses the Church. So long as it is content to present itself in the guise of injured protest, armed with a list of rights it has been denied, then, whatever does happen, a meeting of minds will not happen. The language of rights is completely impotent to resolve this kind of issue. 'Right', it used to be said, 'flows from the spring of righteousness'. Rights are not foundational; they derive from that fabric of right (in the singular) that belongs to the network of relations that constitutes reality. Until there is agreement upon what is *real*, any discussion about what is *right* remains floating in the air. The rights that some claim to be deprived of appear to others as no more than the moral furniture of a fantastic and make-believe world. If, however, the gay movement conceives its role theologically, and assumes, not only in rhetoric but in substance, the task of speaking to the Church out of the word of God, then, whether what it says is what I have projected for it or something else, the Church will have something it must listen to. Only, one word of caution for those who speak and those who listen when God's word is abroad. The first, and surely the hardest demand that it makes on them is: patience.

Notes

1. 'Das natürliche und die Moral', *Zeitschrift für Evangelische Ethik*, vol. 38, no. 3, 1994, pp. 168–89.
2. 'The Decade of the Last Chance: An interview with Scott Symons', *The Idler* (Toronto) vol. 23, 1989, pp. 21–30.
3. Michael Vasey, *Strangers and Friends* (Hodder & Stoughton, 1995). Elizabeth Stuart, *Just Good Friends* (Mowbray, 1995).

3

Call to
Biblical Values

Gerald Bray

THE CURRENT DEBATE about homosexuality in the Church has provoked a number of comments, among which the St Andrew's Day Statement must be considered one of the more balanced, thoughtful and conciliatory of those which have appeared. However, it will soon be quite clear to anyone who reads it carefully that its authors are concerned to uphold the exclusive legitimacy of traditional Christian teaching and practice in this area, and therefore cannot be described as neutral in their approach. On the whole, the Statement is carefully worded, and has been helpfully divided into Principles and Applications, which complement one another quite well. The authors recognise that they have not said all that there is to say, and they appreciate that others of equally deep Christian conviction may (and probably will) disagree with them at different points. The St Andrew's Day Statement is an invitation to dialogue, not a definitive pronouncement, and it is in this spirit that the Church of England Evangelical Council commissioned it and has now made it available to the wider public.

In responding to this Statement, it is only fair to begin by accepting the authors' intentions and the limitations which they recognise in their own work. Their main concern, expressed in the first paragraph of the Introduction, is to find a starting-point of common faith in the Gospel, on the basis of which further discussion can proceed with those who differ on this particular question. This is a laudable aim, and it is hard to see how any Christian could take exception to it. However, there is one slight snag, which is that the authors of the Statement do not define what they mean by the 'Gospel'. Presumably they are referring to the main message of the New Testament (if not of the entire Bible), and not merely to the Four Gospels, but even if we can assume that much, it is still not clear what the word actually means.

This is not a minor point, because different understandings of what the Gospel is frequently cloud debates of this kind, and ensure that dialogue partners pass each other like ships in the night. It is possible to express the Gospel in positive terms (e.g. salvation, redemption, resurrection life) which will attract broad agreement, but if the negative side is not clearly expressed as well, misunderstanding is sure to result. What are we redeemed from? To what extent is a resurrection life possible in this fallen world? What sort of community is the Church, which is supposed to be the locus of the Gospel witness? The authors need to give more attention to these questions, in order to avoid the kind of impasse which will inevitably result if fundamentally incompatible presuppositions are hidden under a catch-all label like 'Gospel'.

A second difficulty, which also arises in the Introduction but which recurs throughout the Statement, is that the authors quite clearly have a preconceived idea of what marriage is (and perhaps even more importantly, of what it is *not*), but they merely assume that others will accept this and do nothing to defend their point of view. They regard it as self-evident that 'marriage' means the contractual and in some sense 'sacramental' union of one male and one female, in what is intended to be a lifelong bond. However, it is precisely at this point that homosexual activists are currently challenging the Church's traditional teaching. These people agree with traditional Christians that marriage should be between two individuals (there is no suggestion of polyandry on their part), and that in principle it should have a lifelong intention and be of a quasi-sacramental character. What they question is why this institution should be confined to two people of different sexes.

This is a point which the authors of the St Andrew's Day Statement have not even begun to discuss. What is the purpose of marriage? In keeping with much modern thought on this subject, they would probably be keen to emphasise such things as 'companionship' and so on, and to de-emphasise the once traditional insistence on the procreation of children (which would obviously demand heterosexual union), but if procreation is left out of account, why should marriage not be extended to homosexual couples? There are plenty of homosexual activists who will argue that marriage provides them with a structure of commitment which helps them to stabilise their relationships, and which cuts out the promiscuity which so many people assume to be intrinsic to homosexual relationships. There are some homosexual couples who have stable, long-term unions which are just as happy as most heterosexual ones, and a good deal happier than some. Why should they not call their relationship a marriage, and enjoy the kind of legal advantages and responsibilities which matrimony entails? The authors of the Statement do not want to accept this, but it is not altogether clear why, and they need to spell this out if they are really going to connect with the current debate.

The St Andrew's Day Statement is strong on the need for fundamental theological principles to guide their thinking, and here the authors are to be congratulated for setting the homosexual question within the broader context of Christian theology as a whole. Unfortunately the three principles which they outline are so broad that they could be used in any situation, and if they were to be taken out this document and stated independently, it would be impossible to guess what their original context was. Perhaps the authors could be encouraged to add one or two more principles, which would relate what they are saying more specifically to the issue of homosexuality, or even to human relationships in general. The closest we come to this is in Principle III, which among other things, says: 'The Spirit gives us strength and confidence to live as men and women within the created order, finding peace and reconciliation . . .'. We need to come a bit closer to home than that, surely?

As far as the principles themselves are concerned, the main difficulty comes with affirmations like: '[in Christ's] resurrection our human nature was made new' (Principle I), and 'the Father of Jesus Christ restores broken creation in him' (Principle III).

What exactly is meant by statements of this kind? The renewal of human nature and the restoration of creation are basically eschatological concepts, a fact which the authors of the Statement implicitly recognise in their Application sections, where they speak about spiritual warfare, taking up the cross, and so on. In this present life our human nature, like the rest of creation, remains unchanged – that is the whole problem! We cannot live as resurrected people when we are not; the *eschaton* cannot be advanced into our present life.

This is a major problem with all statements of this kind, and the authors need to reconsider the implications of what they have said very carefully. Why do I, as a Christian, continue to have disordered or misguided desires, if I have some sort of renewed humanity? Christ became sin for us in his earthly body, but in his resurrection body he had already triumphed over sin. Why is this not also (and equally) true of us? If my human nature has died and risen with Christ, and I still have homosexual desires, what could possibly be wrong with them? Is this not an indication that for some people at least, homosexuality is just as 'natural' as heterosexuality is for the majority?

I suspect that behind statements of this kind there lies a deep-seated unwillingness to face the duality which is inherent in the Christian life, and which cannot be ignored if the biblical witness is to be taken seriously. Christians are people who have been redeemed eschatologically, and who enjoy the first-fruits of that redemption in a personal relationship with Christ, which is brought into our hearts by the indwelling presence and power of his Holy Spirit. But it is that very presence which illuminates the darkness in which we live, and which forces us to combat it with all the weapons of spiritual warfare which God gives to us. The authors of the St Andrew's Day Statement know all this of course, as their Application section makes clear, but they ought to think more closely through the relationship between the *now* and the *not yet* (to use a popular expression), and rephrase some of their principles in a way which is less idealistic and truer to actual human experience.

It would also be good if they could edit their text and remove (or at least clarify) some of the nice-sounding abstractions to which they are rather prone. These sound wonderful, but it is very difficult to see quite what they mean. An example of this, taken from Principle III, which we have already quoted, is the statement that men and women have the strength and confidence, in the power of the Holy Spirit, to find 'peace and reconciliation'. What exactly does this mean? Peace and reconciliation with whom? On what basis? The Bible tells us that we have peace and reconciliation with God, and that we are to seek to maintain it with our fellow Christians. Over the centuries we have been very bad at that, and the Church has been divided for reasons great and small almost from the very beginning of its history. Are we supposed to find peace and reconciliation with those who reject Christ? And why should peace and reconciliation not include tolerance of practising homosexuals within the Christian fellowship, given that we all live in an imperfect world?

Perhaps the authors of the Statement will reply that they could not say everything in such a short space, and they are undoubtedly right about this. But they should be encouraged to be more precise in what they affirm, in order to avoid the kinds of misunderstandings which such generalities expose them to. Here, it must be said, the Application section provides an important (if perhaps unintended?) corrective to the open-endedness of the principles. It becomes clear in the Applications, for example, that the authors of the Statement recognise the continuing presence of sin in the Christian believer, and this helps to narrow the focus of the principles, which (interestingly enough) do not mention this point. There is a welcome emphasis on self-denial, and a clear recognition that personal fulfilment does not mean the exhaustive expression of every human desire – something which is obviously impossible in any case.

It is implied, though not explicitly stated, that the best option for homosexuals is celibacy in the context of singleness, which is a legitimate option offered by Scripture to those who are not married. Of course, the Statement does not say that the single life is a gift from God to those who are called to a particular ministry; nowhere does the Bible even so much as hint that it is an answer for those tempted by homosexuality! Those who are single for the sake of the Gospel surely do not need to be burdened with the suspicion that they must be homosexual if they have chosen such a lifestyle. Single Christians know only too well that this suspicion already exists in too many cases, and it is sure to be encouraged by statements of this kind.

The third Application raises the question of friendship, which the Statement regards as legitimate, but does not deal with very satisfactorily. To suggest, however obliquely, that friendship can be a homosexual substitute for marriage is dangerous and potentially destructive of the whole concept. The authors of the Statement need to pursue this question further, and consider more carefully than they have done what the implications are. They recognise that it is possible, and even desirable, for heterosexuals to have deep (same-sex?) friendships as well, but it is not altogether clear what this means in practice.

In many cultures, for example, it is quite acceptable for men to hug and kiss each other in greeting, but not for men to treat women in that way. In our culture, men may sometimes be seen hugging and kissing women to whom they are not related, but not other men. Similarly, in our society it is possible for an unmarried heterosexual couple, or for two women to live together without arousing comment, but not for two men. We already live in a situation in which affection or closeness between males is regarded as homosexual, whether it is or not, and as C. S. Lewis remarked in *The Four Loves*, this casts a pall over the whole notion of friendship. To offer 'friendship' as a way out of sexual intercourse for homosexuals may sound both kind and practical, but the danger is that it will only reinforce this impression, with the result that true friendship will be even harder to find than it already is.

Finally, something should be said about the Statement's welcome, but somewhat ambiguous, recognition that pastoral practice does not always coincide with theological principle. As the second Application puts it: 'Pastoral care . . . needs a certain flexibility.' This is true, as any good pastor knows, but how flexible can we be? Can I say, for example, that it is better for a homosexual couple to live together in 'matrimony' than to burn with desire for others? This may not be God's ideal, or the Church's official teaching, but in the circumstances do we have to be flexible and accept that a worse condition is being prevented by this less than perfect solution? The authors of the Statement may not realise it, but they are running the risk of seeing their whole position undermined by an appeal to expediency of the kind at which the Church of England excels. Do we want a Church in which everybody pays lip-service to the principle of heterosexual marriage, while in practice they accept that this is an unattainable ideal? That sounds more like popular Roman Catholicism than like evangelical Protestantism!

In conclusion, let me say that the issues which the Statement raises and seeks to deal with are not ones to which an easy or readily agreed answer is likely to be found. To their credit, the Statement's authors have recognised this. But in the course of debate, they may discover that their well-intentioned approach will have to harden considerably if the position which they are trying to defend is to be maintained. If this does not happen, they are liable to discover that dialogue will lead to compromise, which in turn will lead to surrender. After all, those who advocate a liberalisation of the Church's teaching and practice on this subject are not looking for pastoral care and sympathetic understanding from evangelicals. They are far more likely to be wanting to make a political statement justifying and supporting what they are perfectly content to go on doing, regardless of what anybody else thinks about it. Evangelicals might as well be realistic about this, and learn to present their own case accordingly, without losing the note of compassion which this Statement is so concerned to sound.

4

Christian Same-Sex Partnerships

Jeffrey John

THE ST ANDREW'S DAY Statement was put forward, no doubt in good faith, as an attempt to seek common ground in the debate about homosexuality. It is not hard to see, however, why many of its readers have felt that the Statement's content and tone belie that claim; and why since its publication it has been widely used for propaganda purposes by ultra-conservative groups who have little interest in reasoned theological debate on the issue. The Principles which open the Statement are common ground, certainly; but the subsequent 'application' of these Principles is highly tendentious, doing little more than restate the traditional hard line against all same-sex relationships in an unequivocal fashion. This is indeed a Statement and not a discussion document. In particular, the bald assertion that 'there is no place for the Church to confer legitimacy on alternatives to [marriage or singleness]', if taken at face value, simply closes debate before it has begun. What follows therefore cannot be said to build on much common ground in the Statement; it is a defence of Christian same-sex partnerships against its conclusions.

Identity

The point made about identity in the first paragraph of the Statement seems at first sight uncontroversial. Of course we find our ultimate identity in Christ; and our sexuality is no more ultimate, ontologically speaking, than our race or other personal characteristics. 'In Christ there is neither male nor female, Jew nor Greek, slave nor free' – nor, one might add, straight or gay. I imagine no homosexual Christian would wish to argue otherwise. But it is unclear why this leads the authors to feel (as they seem to) that those who, as a matter of unavoidable fact, have an exclusive or predominant attraction for their own sex are wrong to call themselves 'homosexuals'. We may agree that at the deepest ontological level of identity there is no such thing as an Englishman; but we do not usually object, in the conditions of this life, to Englishmen describing themselves as such and making the best of the advantages and disadvantages their state entails.

If what lurks behind this paragraph is the claim that 'there is *really* no such thing as a homosexual', or that at some deeper level we are all *really* heterosexual, for most homosexuals that claim will have as much force as the proposition that there are no *real* Englishmen. It is an idea which may express an ultimate ontological truth – a truth about heaven, 'where there is neither marriage nor giving in marriage, but we shall be like the angels' – but it is one which has little practical or spiritual consequence for the present life. Certainly one can agree (if perhaps this is what is being suggested) that no one should imagine that their sexuality defines the most important thing about them; and it may well be true that in modern life sex has come to play too dominant a role in the self-perception of us all. Nor is it always desirable to be labelled, whether by oneself or by others. Nevertheless it is simply the case that a large minority of people find themselves overridingly, unchangeably and often exclusively attracted to their own sex. That is a very important part of their personal identity in this life and they are not being foolish or misguided when they choose to say so. On the contrary, saying so is part of their Christian responsibility to deal with the truth. We are all called to face the facts about ourselves, and to make the best and most positive use of the potentials and qualities God has given us.

Self-Denial

Paragraph 2 reminds us that we are all 'called to various forms of self-denial' and to 'struggle against our disordered desires'. That is true, but it begs the question: *what* should we deny ourselves, and *which* desires are disordered? For a Christian homosexual, as for the Christian heterosexual, the question is always 'What for me is the way of holiness? How is God calling me to fulfil the purpose of my creation, to grow in love and self-sacrifice, and so in his image?' To find the answer to that question in a call to a faithful, lifelong, same-sex partnership (and let me be clear that I am defending no other kind of homosexual practice) is no more or less self-indulgent than finding it in a call to marriage or celibacy. A covenanted homosexual partnership involves no less demand for self-denial than a heterosexual marriage (arguably rather more in the face of social and ecclesiastical hostility), and is no less a school for sacrificial love. Even the Bishops' Statement on Sexuality, grudging as it is, has acknowledged that there are homosexual couples 'who grow steadily in fidelity and mutual caring, understanding and support, whose partnerships are a blessing to the world around them, and who achieve great, even heroic sacrifice and devotion'.[1] In practice it becomes extremely hard for those who have known partnerships which bear these fruits of the Spirit to persist in arguing that they are simply sinful – or that the people concerned have somehow mistaken their own true identity. Experience tends to expose the impertinence of the suggestion. And once it is conceded that a same-sex partnership can be a blessing and a means of grace, why should those who feel called to find their happiness and fulfilment in such a relationship be asked to resist that call on the grounds of self-denial? There is nothing good about self-denial for its own sake (on the contrary, it generally has a warping effect), nor does God demand pointless and arbitrary sacrifices.

The inference in this section of the Statement that to be homosexual is the same as to be called to celibacy is frankly demeaning to genuine celibates. A vocation to celibacy is a positive calling, not a *pis aller* or bolt-hole from the truth about oneself. When freely embraced by homosexual or heterosexual Christians a celibate life can be immensely fruitful for the individual and for the Church. But it is quite illegitimate to argue that to be homosexual must mean being called to celibacy, and so to impose it, negatively as it were, against the profound instinct in most human beings to find fulfilment in union with another as well as in union with God. Of course some people who do not feel called to the celibate state are temporarily or permanently forced into the single state for various reasons – the death of a spouse, divorce and separation, reasons of health and temperament, or simple failure to find a partner. We regard such reasons as unfortunate and unavoidable accidents; but there is no ground for counting homosexuality among them.

Disordered Desires

In what sense, if any, is homosexual desire disordered? The so-called natural-law argument against homosexual practice starts from the observation that our genital equipment exists primarily for procreation, and of course in gay sex procreation is not a possibility. More fundamentally, bodies of the same sex simply do not fit together in the same way as a male and female. So one may accept that homosexuality is 'disordered' to the extent that it does not fit the generally observed order of nature. 'Generally' needs underlining, however. Homosexual behaviour is common to many classes of animals, so at least one form of the natural-law argument – that because animals do not engage in homosexual behaviour neither should humans – is clearly wrong.

There is however a far more important consideration that tells against the basic assumptions of the natural-law argument. The truth is that in other matters we do not regulate our behaviour or derive our moral precepts from simple observation of what nature does or does not do. Civilisation itself depends on our disobeying many instincts and urges which might be termed 'natural'. We are constantly reinventing, adapting, manipulating and often reversing the ways of the natural world in order to serve what seems to us to be a higher good, a better 'law'.

More specifically, in managing nature we do not usually have qualms about adapting, altering or reversing natural bodily processes and functions in order to prolong or enhance life. Medicine and surgery are obvious examples. We intervene to maximise the capacities of our bodies and the health and wholeness of our lives. Even if one were to accept the description of a homosexual orientation as a 'disorder' or 'handicap', those who suffer other forms of disorder and handicap are not normally condemned for adapting and using the gifts and capacities they still possess in the most creative way possible. We rather applaud and support them. Those who claim to be repelled and disgusted by homosexual forms of intercourse might ask themselves whether they would be disgusted by a painter who expresses his creativity by painting with his feet; or by an author who expresses himself by blowing down a tube to operate a typewriter. (They should also of course ask themselves whether they would object to acts of manual, oral and anal sex between heterosexuals, and if not, why not?) I would resist applying the terms 'disorder' and 'handicap' to homosexuals – except in so far as homosexuals are handicapped by other people's prejudices – but I believe there is a true analogy between the homosexual's 'unnatural' use of his or her genital equipment to make love, and these examples of the 'unnatural' use of the body to make art.

As the Bishops noted in their Statement,[2] the long and unresolved 'nature versus nurture' argument about the origin of homosexuality has little bearing on discussion of the morality of homosexual practice. Campaigners for the acceptance of gay relationships have tended to insist on a genetic origin, on the grounds that it would seem to confirm that homosexuality is a 'given' of creation, and therefore 'natural' and willed by God. Opponents have wished to see it as a psychological disorder, due to parental or other 'mistakes', and therefore attributable to human failure and not to the will of God. However, even if the origin of homosexuality could be clearly shown to be genetic or psychological (and it is just as likely to be both, to different degrees in different cases), how would that tell us whether the phenomenon of homosexuality is good or bad, willed by God or not? Genetic conditioning produces good things and bad things: the wonderful diversity of races and features and capacities, which we believe is part of God's will in creation; and congenital disease, which we believe is not. Equally our psychological conditioning or early parenting works in highly unpredictable ways to help shape our adult character for good or ill. But what matters morally for all of us is not so much how we came to be what we are, but what we do with it. God takes us where we are, as we are, and helps us make the best of what we have.

Scripture: Romans I

Of the passages quoted in section II, paragraph 1, only Romans 1 supports any particular link between homosexual behaviour and human rebellion against God. It is important to see, however, that homosexuality is by no means the focus of Paul's interest in Romans 1. From Romans 1:18 to the end of the chapter Paul is engaged in an attack on Gentile idolatry. He argues that all people could have deduced knowledge of God from observing his creation, but they chose to reject God and turn to idol worship (vv. 20, 21). Because of this perverse rejection of him, God abandoned them to their lusts and impurity (v. 24), to dishonourable passions exemplified in the exchange of heterosexual intercourse for homosexual (v. 25), and to a base mind and improper conduct, exemplified in a long list of sins which closes the chapter (vv. 28–32). This completes the attack on the Gentiles. The tables are then turned at the start of chapter 2, where Paul rounds on the Jews in his readership (who may well have been smugly applauding up to this point) to condemn them equally for the same sins, although they had even less excuse, having the Law. The rhetorical pattern is carefully constructed, and reaches its climax in chapter 3 with the fundamental proclamation that Paul wants to impress on Jews and Gentiles alike: that all have sinned, none is righteous, but all can be justified through the atoning sacrifice of Jesus Christ.

The rhetorical force of the exercise lies in Paul's quoting back at the Jews their own conventional propaganda against the Gentiles. Both Palestinian and Hellenistic Judaism portrayed homosexuality as an exclusively Gentile vice. In Hellenistic Judaism especially, the homosexuality to which the Gentiles are supposed to incline is conventionally related to their idolatry, the moral 'exchange' of one sex for another being seen as the direct result of the religious 'exchange' of the true God for an idol. Paul repeats this standard argument. Several verses in Wisdom 13 and 14 are sufficiently close to make borrowing a real possibility, and there are also parallels in Philo, Josephus and the Testament of the Twelve Patriarchs.

Of course the fact that Paul borrowed a piece of conventional anti-Gentile polemic need not undermine the authority of what he says; but there is another point to be made about the presuppositions of his argument. When Paul argues that homosexuality is 'against nature' he does not only mean that it is against the order of nature itself, but that it is against the person's own nature. Like all earlier and contemporary Jewish (but not all classical) writers on the subject, Paul does not recognise a category of homosexually orientated people, but only homosexual acts. He takes it for granted that homosexual behaviour is a free, perverse choice on the part of 'naturally' heterosexual men and women. This assumption is clear in his statements that homosexuals 'gave up' or 'exchanged' heterosexual relations in verses 26 and 27. It is also essential to the portrayal of homosexuality as a reflection of idolatry. Paul must believe that homosexuals wilfully choose their unnatural perversion in the same way that he must believe that idolaters wilfully suppress the truth about God that must be known to them from observing creation. Otherwise, as he says, God would not be just in his condemnation, and Paul could not say they are without excuse (vv. 19–20).

Yet we know that this fundamental assumption on Paul's part is false. His belief that homosexual acts are committed by naturally heterosexual people is untrue. There are quite clearly those whose exclusive or predominant inclination – whether for genetic reasons or reasons of upbringing – is unarguably and unchangeably towards their own sex. And as Paul himself admits, if men and women had no choice in the matter, God would hardly be just in condemning them. We may well agree with him, and conclude that this false assumption on his part undermines any blanket condemnation of homosexual practice on the basis of Romans 1.

It is also fair to point out that in the society in which Paul lived prostitution (cultic and secular) and pederasty (in the sense of the Greek practice of a temporary pupil–tutor relationship between a teenager and an older man) were the standard models of homosexual practice, and these are the forms which are likely to have been uppermost in Paul's mind when he refers to homosexuals. One can hardly make a fair ethical transfer from the likely assumptions behind Paul's use of the terms translated 'homosexual' here (or in the sin-lists of 1 Cor. 6:9 and 1 Tim. 1:10) to the situation of two adult Christians in a lifelong, faithful partnership. The chances are that Paul never envisaged the case of such a relationship – and he certainly was not doing so in these passing references.

Why is such weight put on these verses? A number of writers, mainly evangelicals, seem to regard the acceptance of homosexual relationships as entailing apocalyptic consequences for Christian tradition and biblical authority. Gordon Wenham for example has written that 'to accept homosexual acts by inverts would be to deny the doctrine of creation . . . the whole biblical teaching on creation, sex, marriage, forgiveness and redemption will be fundamentally altered'.[3]

Will it? What, scripturally speaking, is the purpose of sex? Childbirth, of course; though in the Genesis story itself the only *stated* purpose of God's creating a companion for Adam is not procreation but because 'God said, "It is not good for man to be alone" '. Complementarity and intimate companionship are as much part of God's plan in creating sex as childbirth. It seems significant that Paul, and Jesus himself, while referring to the creation story, never mention procreation or physical sexual difference in their teaching about marriage, but rather the spiritual meaning of two people becoming 'one flesh'. The stress is entirely on the quality of the relationship, and in particular that it should be a covenant of sexual fidelity and indissoluble union, in the image of God's covenants with us. Furthermore the insistence on fidelity is not explained, as we might expect, with reference to practical considerations of childrearing and domestic stability, but always with reference to the personal, spiritual implications of sexual union itself.

For Paul, it is clear that sexual union always has spiritual consequences, whether for good or ill. Promiscuous sexual activity involves desecration of the body, which is a temple of the spirit and itself a member of the body of Christ (1 Cor. 6: 15–20). But where sex expresses mutual love and commitment, that relationship becomes a μυστηριον (Eph. 5: 32), a holy mystery or sacrament which reflects the covenant union between Christ and his Church and becomes a channel of love and grace in the world. For a human being to enter such a relationship is to realise an important part of what it means to be made in God's image. It means to further God's purpose in creation by reproducing the kind of creative (but not necessarily procreative) self-giving love that is basic to God's own nature. Accepting and supporting faithful homosexual relationships does not mean jettisoning this fundamental biblical teaching about the sacramental, covenantal character of human sexuality. On the contrary, it affirms and extends it.

Those who cling to a supposed natural-law argument against homosexuality in Romans 1 would do well to remember that Paul appeals far more clearly and frequently to a theory of natural law and to the creation story in order to justify his now largely abandoned teachings about the veiling and silencing of women. Paul wrote that women must be veiled because man was created first and it is primarily man who is the image of God (1 Cor. 11: 7–8). He believed it was shameful for a man to wear long hair and a woman to wear short hair because 'nature itself teaches us so' (1 Cor. 11:14 – a much clearer teaching from 'natural law' than anything in Rom. 1). No woman is permitted to teach or to hold authority over men, and women are commanded to be silent 'because Adam was formed first, then Eve; and Adam was not deceived but the woman was decieved and became a transgressor' (1 Tim. 2:12–14). All these teachings rest on theological arguments which appeal to God's plan in creation no less than Romans 1: 18 ff. Indeed Paul is much clearer about their authoritative status and the practical rules he intends to deduce from them, even to the point of saying that the silencing of women is a command of the Lord, and if anyone disputes it he is to be rejected (1 Cor. 14: 33–8).

Paul lays far more weight of doctrine and authority on his teaching about the place of women in the Church than on his incidental references to homosexuality. Yet the fact that today this teaching is consistently ignored, even in the most so-called biblical churches, is not felt to 'alter fundamentally the whole biblical treaching on creation, sex, marriage, forgiveness and redemption'. The truth is that in questions concerning the place of women, even hard-line fundamentalists have now been forced by the pressure of social change to recognise that certain biblical teachings must sometimes be weighed against other biblical principles (notably justice and charity) and must sometimes be set aside. The reason this change has come about in the case of women but not in the case of homosexuals does not relate to any systematic concern for obedience to biblical authority. It is simply that, whereas prejudice against women is now much less tolerated in society, prejudice against homosexuals is still widely approved.

Legitimacy

The Statement asserts that 'there is no place for the Church to confer legitimacy upon alternatives [to heterosexual marriage or singleness]' (s. II, para. 2). Again the question is begged. Why? What legitimates a sexual relationship? We are long past arguing – unless we are extremely conservative Roman Catholics – that sex is only right and good when there is a possibility of conception. In any case, the idea that openness to procreation was a necessary condition for moral sexual union was never logically or rigorously applied, since even the most conservative churches have generally accepted that sexual relations are legitimate in marriages where one or both partners are infertile or past the age of childbearing. This is clearly because within marriage sexual activity has always been perceived as a good thing in itself.

If we ask what the legitimating purposes of marriage are, the Book of Common Prayer laid down three: first, the procreation of children; second, 'a remedy against sin, and to avoid fornication'; third, for the 'mutual society, help and comfort that the one ought to have of the other, both in prosperity and in adversity'. The ASB puts the same thing rather more positively (with procreation last). Marriage is

a gift of God in creation and a means of his grace, a holy mystery in which a man and a woman become one flesh. It is God's purpose that, as husband and wife give themselves to one another in love throughout their lives, they shall be united in that love as Christ is united with his Church. Marriage is given that husband and wife may comfort and help each other, living faithfully together in need and plenty, in sorrow and in joy. It is given that with delight and tenderness they may know each other in love, and through the joy of their bodily union, may strengthen the union of their hearts and lives. It is given that they may have children, and be blessed in caring for them and bringing them up in accordance with God's will, to his praise and glory.

With the exception of childbirth all these purposes of marriage can be fulfilled in a permanent, stable, faithful same-sex relationship, and are being fulfilled in many. The case of infertile heterosexual couples demonstrates that the absence of the possibility of procreation does not mean that the attempt to achieve God's other purposes in creating sexual love thereby becomes immoral or illegitimate. We may, it is true, feel that a childless marriage is 'second best', and not exactly the equivalent of a childbearing marriage, because it does not offer all the possibilities of fulfilment that a fertile marriage does; but we do not say it is wrong. On the contrary, we still call it a way of holiness, a framework for learning God's kind of love, because it is a covenant between two persons in his image which reflects the covenant of love between him and his people.

The case of a same-sex couple is closely, if not exactly, analogous. It too may be regarded as 'second best' because of the impossibility of childbirth. But in personal, spiritual and sacramental terms, it may be as much a vocation, as much a way of holiness, as much a covenant reflecting God's kind of love as a heterosexual marriage. Let it be said again: this is a matter of experience, not merely of theory. There are many such Christian partnerships, even if social and Church hostility means they largely remain invisible. The onus therefore lies on those Christians who reject them to show where the difference lies *in moral status* between a childless marriage and a same-sex partnership based on the same quality of faithful commitment. The Statement itself offers no ground for discerning such a difference, and I do not believe that such a difference can be shown.

Clergy in Homosexual Relationships

The St Andrew's Day Statement, section II, paragraph 3, approves the Bishops' Statement on the incompatibility of ordained ministry with a same-sex relationship. The conclusion of this section of the Bishops' Statement runs:

> We have, therefore, to say that in our considered judgment the clergy cannot claim the liberty to enter into sexually active homophile relationships. Because of the distinctive nature of

their calling, status and consecration, to allow such a claim on their part would be seen as placing that way of life in all respects on a par with heterosexual marriage as the reflection of God's purposes in creation. The church cannot accept such a parity and remain faithful to the insights which God has given through scripture, tradition and reasoned reflection on experience.[4]

Again the issue focuses on what is meant by the 'imparity' between homosexual and heterosexual relationships, and why this is seen as a deciding factor in respect of the clergy's 'exemplary' function. The bishops earlier in the report make it clear that they do not consider a faithful homosexual relationship a vicious or morally inferior way of life; otherwise they could not recommend the acceptance of such couples into congregations, nor describe their relationships as 'a blessing to the world around them'. The imparity cannot reside in the impossibility of childbirth, since there is no bar on clergy in infertile marriages. If the bishops regard homosexuality as a handicap, there is no bar on handicapped clergy who are otherwise able to perform their clerical functions. Nor are celibate clergy debarred in the Anglican Church, despite the fact that such a state arguably flies more directly in the face of 'God's purposes declared in creation'. So why, having concluded that for lay homosexuals a faithful, permanent relationship may be their way to holiness, do the bishops say this cannot be so among the clergy?

The ruling is linked to the statement that clergy are called to exemplify an ideal, but that (in this mysterious and unspecified way) clergy in a homosexual partnership fall short of the ideal and therefore cannot be an good example. Of course for the majority of people heterosexual marriage is the ideal – and there are faithful married clergy to exemplify it. For those who are called to celibacy, faithful celibacy is the ideal, and there are faithful celibate clergy to exemplify that also. I have argued that for homosexuals who are not called to celibacy a faithful covenanted partnership is the ideal (and in the case of lay people the bishops, at least in certain paragraphs, seem to accept it) – and there are in fact many clergy partnerships to exemplify it too.

The situation of a person in a committed, lifelong same-sex

partnership is not analogous (as is sometimes argued) to that of a divorced and remarried person, who (depending on the Anglican province) may also be denied ordination or, if already ordained, removed from office. In the case of a divorced and remarried person the covenant has been plainly and publicly broken. That is not the case with homosexual partnerships which remain faithful and unbroken, in the image of God's covenant with us. Where such a relationship does break down, one would could reasonably expect the same discipline to apply as after a broken marriage. However, as things now stand in the Church of England, a priest or bishop who is divorced and remarried (even more than once) is considered more acceptable than a priest who has remained faithful to one person of the same sex for a lifetime. This is despite the fact that, by contrast with the doubtful scriptural testimony against homosexual relationships, remarriage after divorce is unequivocally forbidden by the teaching of Jesus himself as reported in three Gospels and by St Paul. Again, it is hard to avoid the conclusion that popular prejudice and politics count far more in determining these attitudes than genuine scriptural or theological considerations.

The current situation is the more depressing because same-sex couples need more than almost any other category of people to be offered an 'ideal' by the Church – a positive theological framework within which to conduct a holy life – and to have it exemplified for them. It is the experience of many clergy in a same-sex relationship who have allowed this to be known that they generally draw a large pastoral clientele of other gay Christians who cannot find the kind of positive Christian counselling they need anywhere else. In this situation the example and role-model of the priest really is an indispensable source of hope, and a rock on which others can build. But of course it is intolerably hard for clergy to fill this need if they receive no support from the Church.

The position outlined in the Bishops' Statement is unstable for another reason. Many (probably most) of the bishops who subscribed to it know perfectly well, and in private fully accept, that some of their clergy are in same-sex relationships. Many homosexual clergy have insisted on being honest about their private lives with their ordaining and employing bishops, with those who selected them for training, with their training college principals and with others in authority. Almost all such clergy have been retained and supported. It is extraordinary that so many bishops under the cloak of collective anonymity have allowed this private support to be publicly withdrawn, presumably for the sake of political pragmatism. In the aftermath of the Bishops' Statement, a number of bishops contacted their homosexual clergy to assure them it did not mean what it said. Other clergy who offered their resignations were persuaded to stay with the advice not to be 'naïve'. The position has been described as ludicrous by some of the bishops themselves, and inevitably leaves them hostage to the charge of hypocrisy, which in the public eye damages the Church more gravely than the phenomenon of clerical homosexuality itself, and within the Church fuels cynicism and suspicion. Integrity demands a decision: either to change the ruling, and apply the same criteria of acceptance to lay and clerical relationships alike; or else to retain the ruling, and make arrangements for the honourable release and compensation of homosexual clergy who have hitherto been found acceptable. There is no other honest option.

Fulfilment

Section III of the St Andrew's Day Statement repeats the point that 'a life may be fulfilled without occasion to employ the power of sexual expression, just as it may without occasion to exploit the potential for education, parenthood or mobility'. Of course it may. But we normally try to maximise these human potentials, not to restrict them, unless there is compelling cause to do otherwise. In a moving passage of their own Statement the bishops write of marriage:

> A true marriage reflects Christ's love for us all. He too gave himself to others 'for better, for worse, till death'. In it we learn to break down our pride and self-concern, to be open to our partner as he or she really is, to treasure what is good, and forgive faults, to sacrifice ourselves for the sake of the other, to be loyal whatever the price ... A good marriage creates for each partner the same kind of environment that we recognize as promoting growth to maturity in the case

of children: a combination of love and challenge within an unbreakably reliable relationship.[5]

Would we deny that means of fulfilment to two heterosexual people who wished for and were capable of it? Why then would it occur to us to deny it to two homosexual people? It is crucial to grasp that the framework of hope that this passage describes is equally applicable to a same-sex couple as to a man and woman. It is not a heterosexual hope, or a homosexual hope, but a human hope: this is the way that the great majority of human beings will find their path to maturity – personal and spiritual – and towards their ultimate fulfilment in Christ. The St Andrew's Day document tries to suggest that for a gay person compulsory celibacy will be more conducive to holiness – and thus ultimately more fulfilling – than such a relationship, but fails to explain how or why this should be. My own observation of the gay subculture inside and outside the Church convinces me of exactly the opposite: that enforced celibacy for homosexuals is widely conducive to personal disintegration and loneliness, punctuated by more or less frequent lapses into promiscuous and furtive sex with all the spiritual damage and degradation it entails.[6]

For many years I have ministered to young Christians in secular and theological colleges, many of whom were lesbian or gay, many of them desperately struggling to reconcile their sexuality with their faith, and with membership of a hostile or uncomprehending Church. Almost all rejected promiscuity, or the futile prospect of a series of abortive relationships. What they hoped for was precisely the same as their heterosexual friends: finding someone to love and be wholly given to, someone to grow together with, someone to be there at the end of the day and to the end of their life. It seems to me inhumane and un-Christian (in a profound, not trivial sense) to deny that hope to so many men and women whom God has created for ultimate fulfilment – yes – but a fulfilment which will only be reached through our learning in this life to love one another in his way. That is why I believe we have an absolute duty in the Church to offer homosexual couples, clerical and lay, not merely a grudging admission, but a positive theological understanding of their relationship, just as we do for heterosexual couples in marriage: to help them realise the same hope, the same ideal, of secure, faithful, lifelong love.

Notes

1. *Issues in Human Sexuality: A Statement by the House of Bishops* (Church House Publishing, 1991), p. 33, para. 4.6.
2. *Issues*, p. 31, para. 4.2.
3. 'Homosexuality and the Bible', in T. Higton (ed.), *Sexuality and the Church: A Way Forward* (ABWON, 1987), pp. 37–8.
4. *Issues*, p. 45, para. 5.17.
5. *Issues*, pp. 20–1, paras. 3.3, 3.4.
6. See Dr Ben Fletcher's similar findings in *Clergy under Stress* (Mowbray, 1990).

5

Travelling Together?

Michael Vasey

THE THEOLOGICAL SERIOUSNESS of the St Andrew's Day Statement runs counter to the mood of much current discussion about gay people and gay lifestyle. Although this makes it inevitable that discussion will continue in other places and other styles, I share the apparent judgment of its authors that disciplined theological reflection is essential if the Church is to respond adequately to the phenomenon of the gay movement. Much vocal evangelical opposition to gay people confidently, even abrasively, claims the authority of God in Scripture. This claim will be tested not only by the demanding criteria of St John in 1 John 4:20 ('those who do not love the brother whom they have seen, cannot love God whom they have not seen') but also by whether evangelical Christians can rise to the theological tasks and priorities articulated in this Statement.

I recognise in the Statement a very similar theological stance and methodology to that which governed my own approach in *Strangers and Friends*. For this reason, I have attempted with some precision to tailor my response to the categories and concerns that govern the Statement itself. Although I have some evidence of serious reflection on my book, there has been much less indication that evangelical Christians in or outside the Church of England are willing to engage with the careful listening, or the possible redefinition of categories, to which both *Strangers and Friends* and the Statement point.

The Statement's essential rationale emerges in its opening words:

'Faced with practical questions which arouse strong and conflicting passions, the church has only one recourse: to find in the Gospel a starting point from which those who differ can agree to proceed in their discussion.' While it begins by focusing on the question of 'how we should respond to those, including clergy, seeking to live in quasi-marital relations with a partner of the same sex', it plainly sets out to provide a broader framework for discussing homosexuality. I warmly welcome the method and thrust of this Statement although they are unlikely fully to be understood either by evangelical Christians wanting an uncompromising assertion of traditional values or by gay Christians looking for security and acceptance within the Christian community. The careful and nuanced attention given to the subject by this group and their desire to identify an agreed starting-point for such controversial questions represent a deeply Christian response to current controversy.

In *Strangers and Friends* I saw my role as guide, interpreter and exegete: as providing a map for a discussion which has often been damaging, polarised and confused, and also giving some leads for the many different questions raised by the contemporary phenomenon of homosexuality. Although the mood of the St Andrew's Day Statement is more sombre almost to the point of distaste, I am delighted to note many points of convergence between *Strangers and Friends* and the Statement.

A. Strengths

1. It recognises that the subject of homosexuality requires further reflection

The Statement is entirely correct in saying that, 'The interpretation of homosexual emotion and behaviour is a Christian "task", still inadequately addressed' (p. 8). This reflects a modesty that has not characterised recent public evangelical discussion. At various points in the Statement there are welcome attempts to recognise the openness which such an assertion implies – note, for example, the reference on p. 6 to 'more than one interpretation of present disputes'.

The use of the term 'homosexuality' in this context, although understandable, is less than helpful. The term originates in a precise context in the nineteenth century and already imports into the discussion significant ways of organising Christian thought that do not relate directly to biblical or classical categories and which often confuse theological discussion.

2. It sets the discussion within the context of credal orthodoxy ·

The Statement begins with credal principles and hopes thereby to serve 'all who do not intend a decisive break with orthodox Christianity' (p. 6). This represents a very constructive response to the current debate. For myself, I am entirely happy with the principles set out on pp. 6–7. In particular I welcome the affirmation about 'understanding all human life and experience through the Scriptures . . . [and] guided by the Spirit of God' (p. 6); the application of this on p. 8 that, 'the church must be open to empirical observation and governed by the authority of the apostolic testimony'; and the warning against 'being lulled by the vague idea that there is a transparent and necessary progress of thought working itself out in history' (p. 8). This last warning, of course, needs to be heard as much by cultural conservatives as by those tempted to go 'with the flow of history'.

The phrasing 'open to' and 'governed by' is accurate and helpful. In discussions about *Strangers and Friends* I am often asked whether I am attempting to set 'culture' over Scripture. I certainly do not recognise this as a description of my method and do not see myself as doing more than 'being open to empirical observation'. At a discussion sponsored by the *Church of England Newspaper* on 24 February 1996, Oliver O'Donovan and I were in agreement that such empirical observation is a necessary part of proper theological reflection and an appropriate preliminary to bringing an area of human life under the judgment of Christ through Scripture. (Disagreements may remain about whether accounts of social and personal experience distort serious theological discussion by their emotional content or compensate for a lack of understanding of gay people's experience and perspectives. Any use of such experience must allow for the possibility that people's self-understanding may be distorted and should be brought to the bar of Scripture.)

The approach taken by the Statement means that current

disagreements should be seen as second-order issues in theology so long as there is no intention to challenge the sort of central doctrinal tenets referred to in the principles of the Statement. In terms of Reformation thought we are dealing here with adiaphora (non-essentials). As Oliver O'Donovan puts it in *On the Thirty Nine Articles*. 'The moderation [of the English Reformers] consisted rather in a determined policy of separating the essentials of faith and order from adiaphora . . . Anglican moderation is the policy of reserving strong statement and conviction for the few things that really deserve them' (p. 14). This does not rule out passionate debate and disagreement. However, it does effectively contradict the position taken by Wallace Benn at the Evangelical Anglican Leaders Conference in January 1995 that the acceptance of 'homosexual practice' should be treated (along with the uniqueness of Christ) as a defining point for authentic evangelical Christianity.

3. It affirms the context of grace and sanctification

Strangers and Friends (pp. 60; 220 ff.) and the St Andrew's Day Statement (p. 10) make similar use of Titus 2:11–15. Behind this coincidence lies a rarely recognised measure of common ground in the pastoral responses to individual need adapted by groups with different views of genital activity. In the light of this emphasis on grace, one should note two sentences on pp. 8–9: 'The primary pastoral task of the church in relation to all its members, whatever their self-understanding and mode of life, is to re-affirm the good news of salvation in Christ . . . In addressing those who understand themselves as homosexual, the church does not cease to speak as the bearer of this good news.' There is a considerable contrast between these welcome challenges and the reality as experienced by gay people in, or on the margins of, the Church.

4. It respects the context and particular circumstances of individuals

There are a number of references in the Statement which recognise that the particular requirements that God or the Christian community make of individuals are properly affected by the particularities of their lives, i.e.

> principled pastoral care which is more responsive to particular individual circumstances (p. 5)

> In any individual case, the form which this struggle takes may be determined by circumstances (wealth or poverty, illness or health, educational success or failure). (p. 7)

> Pastoral care, however, needs a certain flexibility, taking note of the circumstances which make each individual case different from every other, and discerning ways in which the Gospel touches people in different situations. (p. 9)

> The church, then, will give constant encouragement in following Christ not only to those who conform to one of these two vocations, but to all who seriously intend discipleship in fellowship with the body of the church. (p. 9)

These statements appear to justify a measure of ethical pragmatism that will live with certain patterns of behaviour which seem to contradict the 'ideal' affirmed elsewhere in the Statement and will provide effective congregational support for people whose lives embrace such patterns.

This is not very far from the positions that I suggest in *Strangers and Friends*. However, both the term 'pastoral' and the notion of an 'ideal' cause me anxiety. The first because it easily implies a Church which stands above the individual Christian in his/her following of Christ. The second because it fails to acknowledge the particularities of life and of our obedience to God. God calls me to conform to the call of Christ and not to some broader social norm (cf. John 5:44). Although there may be different ways of articulating the role of ethical pragmatism it is significant that its necessity is recognised in the Statement.

5. Other points of agreement
There are, of course, many other positions taken in the Statement with which I agree. For example, the Statement is correct to assert the ethical coherence of the distinction that *Issues in Human Sexuality* draws between clergy and laity (p. 9). My difficulty with the Bishops' Statement at this point is not that it is theoretically defensible but that it is simply unworkable (cf. *Strangers and*

Friends, pp. 207–9). Many of the finest clergy are gay and a number of them are in stable and supportive relationships of various sorts. Integrity in Christian ministry is hardly helped by a Church culture that requires subterfuge and denial. Effective clergy serving in situations of some difficulty should not lightly be deprived of appropriate close supportive relationships.

B. Disagreements

1. Implied criticism of the assertiveness of gay people

Some people may understand the remarks about constructing any other ground for identities outside Christ on p. 7 (and possibly the allusions to 'political meanings' etc. on p. 5) as implying that gay people are to blame for the current 'disagreements' – what one might call the 'uppity nigger' reaction to gay self-assertion. It is easy to treat those who are trying to give their own view of their lives and experiences as troublesome and misguided intruders to the established discourse of right-minded individuals. I am not persuaded that the Statement entirely avoids this danger.

2. The legitimacy of gay 'identities'

The first paragraph of p. 5 (Application) accurately sets out the dangers implicit in treating any human characteristic or social location as a source of personal identity. However, it does not give sufficient consideration to the social reception or character of various human characteristics. 'Class, race, nationality' (p. 7) may not have the ontological character of what is to be human, but they are part of how individuals participate in and negotiate the societies to which they belong. While such 'identities' can lead to a distorted understanding of the self or become a way of defending oneself against one's neighbour or God, they can equally be seen as a way of celebrating the particularities of one's humanity. For all their ambivalence, social identities (and their partial internalisation) are intrinsic to how human beings live out their vocation as social beings, and express the corporate aspect of our humanity.

It may be helpful at this point to summarise from *Strangers and Friends* two separate factors that have operated in the emergence of the modern gay movement. (*a*) One is the process of social definition that arises from not conforming to the particular way in which one's society receives the created duality of gender. The Bible's teaching that God has made us male and female provides a mandate for the social order as well as for marriage. (This is the general thrust of the Bible and underlies the fascinating passage 1 Cor. 11:2–16 which I discuss at various points in *Strangers and Friends*, cf. pp. 31, 34–5, 39–40, 130–2, 196–7.) It is intrinsic to the social processes by which individuals assimilate this created duality of gender that some individuals will respond atypically and will then have to negotiate their society in a different way from the majority. A gay identity is fundamentally an alternative social identity that arises out of the way in which a particularly structured imagination is received by, and forced to negotiate, its society. It is part of the argument of *Strangers and Friends* that under the Old Covenant non-normal aspects of the creation received a negative symbolism which the different dynamic of the New Covenant tends to reverse.

(*b*) Gay movements can also be seen as part of a complex movement in the wider culture which originates in the late medieval identification of desire (eros) and marriage, the triumph in the eighteenth century of the idea that society is properly ordered around competition between men rather than affection and bonding between men, and then the entrenchment of these intuitions in the new social order created by industrialisation and technology. So, for example, Cassius, in Shakespeare's *Julius Caesar*, addresses Brutus in terms of a love which we would only use within a very restricted 'romantic' context. The organisation of desire and affection which we find in Shakespeare (a late medieval figure in my view) disappears at precisely the moment at which something like gay subcultures emerge in Protestant Britain, the Netherlands and Switzerland. The gay identity therefore emerges not only as the way in which certain imaginatively non-conforming individuals negotiate (or are pigeonholed) by society but also as the bearer of certain broader human intuitions that are being suppressed in the wider culture.

Social identities (including a gay or lesbian identity) on this view are not to be seen as ultimate or ontological realities – but they are to be respected or affirmed for the social mechanism that they represent. They provide social space for an aspect of life and vocation. It is intriguing to ask whether the social identities of gay and Christian have the same status. *Strangers and Friends* attempts to draw out similarities in the way in which the two social identities operate (cf. pp. 189–94). Classically the core Christian identity has a liturgical character, being formed around public reading of Scripture, baptism, eucharist and Sunday assembly (cf. Article XIX). The evangelical movement is often alienated from these identity markers and tends to locate authentic Christian identity in certain secondary shibboleths – of which being pro-family and anti-gay is one. An interesting New Testament example of the way in which social pressure and exclusion can contribute to a separate social and religious identity occurs in the recipients of the letter to the Hebrews (cf. *Strangers and Friends*, pp. 249–50).

3. The simplifications involved in the Statement's notion of two vocations

The Church of England Evangelical Council, in commending the Statement for study, singles out for endorsement two sentences from p. 9: 'It [i.e. the Church] assists all its members to a life of faithful witness in chastity and holiness, recognising two forms or vocations in which that life can be lived: marriage and singleness (Gen. 2.24; Matt. 19.4–6; 1 Cor. 7 *passim*). There is no place for the church to confer legitimacy upon alternatives to these.' I have three quarrels with these assertions.

(*a*) In history the Church has sanctified or legitimated alternative forms of affectionate relationship. The obvious and major examples lie within the complex social phenomenon that we call monasticism. Another more disputed example is that of the liturgically legitimated same-sex unions studied by John Boswell. It may be that these should be seen as forms of quasi-kinship association and he may exaggerate the genital 'potential' of the practice – but it is clear that these were seen as a different form of affectionate relationship from monastic association.

(*b*) They limit the application of loyal and affectionate faithfulness (and the social recognition and support of the same) to marriage. This seems to me bizarrely narrow. It fails to take account of the concept of the household which provides a pervasive background to the New Testament. It does not do justice to the reality of many people's lives – including celibate gay people. One might note the following answer from Martin Hallett in *Conduct Which Honours God: The Question of Homosexuality* by Simon Vibert (p. 31):

> Secondly, I do quite a lot of speaking on the subject of 'Singleness' and at times I feel a bit of a hypocrite because I do not feel like a single person! That is not because I have 'heavy', in depth relationships, but it is because there are people in my life who are special to me and for whom I am special. The sense of commitment in those relationships makes me feel that I am not alone.

(*c*) While these sentences in the Statement do not actually mention genital acts, they appear to conflate uncritically affectionate relationships, intimacy, eros, touch, physical affection and genital acts. Disentangling and uncoupling all these is an essential prerequisite to coherent ethical discussion. As a summary these assertions effectively ignore a variety of important forms of human association and direct the modern Church's hostility and suspicion against particular individuals. This is part of a process by which the Church, in the name of a certain view of the purpose of genital acts, stigmatises certain forms of supportive friendship.

Furthermore these sentences disguise the considerable diversity in the moral evaluation of genital acts that exists within the Christian tradition. The current outrage about the 'quasi-marital' character of certain gay relationships is fed by an erroneous sense that the rest of the Church believes what Christians have always believed about genital acts. As I have attempted to show in *Strangers and Friends*, such a conviction will not stand up to serious examination. The recent acceptance of contraception is simply part of a much larger shift. One form of common advice to struggling gay people is to rely on friendship and masturbation; there is little awareness of how far this departs from either the view of genital acts held by Philo and Aquinas or from the attitude to bodily emissions to be found in Leviticus.

The shorthand summary of the tradition represented by these two sentences obscures the question of the legitimacy of a range of practices (such as oral or anal sex – as well as masturbation) also used by straight people. In *Strangers and Friends* I have argued that the key to scriptural teaching on genital acts is that they derive their meaning from the society's self-understanding and are evaluated in terms of the social order (and the socially recognised value of individuals) that they support. This is not intended to justify unbridled and unprincipled individualism nor is it an overt or covert attack on marriage. However, a general Christian ethic does not require the rejection of non-marital forms of social affection and association. Nor does it require the same ethical evaluation of genital acts for those who are able and those who are not able to conform to the gender patterns prevailing in the culture.

C. Omissions

The Statement's explicit aim of establishing 'the extent of common ground available to the church' over homosexuality leads to this disclaimer. 'It is not intended to cover every issue that must be considered in this context, and nothing should be inferred from what the statement does not say' (p. 6). However, any attempt to articulate an orthodox framework must show some awareness of the situation into which it speaks. This can be seen in the way the Statement focuses on 'quasi-marital relations with a partner of the same sex' and remains strikingly reticent over genital acts. Some matters need more explicit acknowledgement.

The Statement's tentative recognition that some people may have a different 'interpretation of present disputes' without intending 'a decisive break with orthodox Christianity', challenges the way these issues have been discussed within the evangelical community. Currently this effectively excludes gay evangelicals – and particularly gay evangelical clergy – from participating. One celibate evangelical gay incumbent said to me about the *CEN* dialogue mentioned above, 'you must explain why I cannot be there'. Wrestling with this is an essential part of establishing an orthodox framework for theological discussion. A social process that silences orthodox evangelical gay people contributes to a wider sense that being gay or pro-gay is nearly identical with being theologically heterodox. The present regrettable state of the discussion arises in part from the effective exclusion of gay evangelicals from the public process of reflection on Scripture.

It is naïve for any statement from an evangelical group to fail to acknowledge the part that the Christian tradition, and within it the evangelical movement, has played in the stigmatising of gay people in society. A deeper repentance is required than admitting having overdramatised the issue (cf. p. 6).

The assertion on p. 7 of the essential humanity of gay people not only has implications for how we articulate our personal identity or live out our discipleship. It equally challenges Church and society to acknowledge and defend the common humanity that gay people share precisely at those points at which it is attacked or denied. This must involve an active concern for justice as it affects gay people and a willingness to be identified with the particularities of this quest. My own conviction is that, after individual friendship, this remains one of the most important areas for reconciliation and for growth in understanding.

This welcome assertion of common humanity also requires a humble willingness to respect and support the particular perspectives and concerns of those who see themselves, or whom society identifies, as gay. This should include allowing gay people to identify issues that are important to them. It also has particular implications, as I try to show in chapter 12 of *Strangers and Friends*, for the process of discerning an ethic for gay people. This needs to respect rather than violate the humanity and Christian discipleship of those concerned. It should focus on finding appropriate social scripts in society rather than on genital acts. It must take into account the way in which a contested social identity shapes people's starting-point and also changes some of their ethical options.

6

Dancing in the Spirit

Elizabeth Stuart

I AM GRATEFUL for this invitation to respond to the St Andrew's Day Statement. It is a welcome and unusual opportunity for Christians from different standpoints and backgrounds to engage in measured dialogue. Often the only place that we meet is in radio studios or in front of cameras, pitted against one another for someone else's sport and entertainment. There is a great deal in the Statement with which I am in agreement, a fact which should be unsurprising since we are all members of the body of Christ, but which nevertheless surprised me and reminded me how easily and almost unconsciously we fall from neighbourly love (which will never obliterate difference or disagreement) into structured enmity and mutual demonisation. Nevertheless, I do have some problems and profound disagreements with aspects of the approach and content of the Statement. I draw out and examine these differences in a spirit of humility, acknowledging freely that I might be wrong, you might be right, or none of us may be right. It is to a theology of humility that I wish to turn first.

Not Knowing for Sure or Dancing with the Spirit

I have no argument at all with your three theological principles except that the full implications of these principles are not fully worked out. In the Christ-event we have the fullest revelation of the nature and being of God, indeed, we experience the embodiment of God. But as you note, that event is not yet complete. There is at the heart of the Christian tradition a belief that God's self-revelation continues, that there is and there always will be more to come as the same Spirit which was incarnate in Jesus continues the process of unwinding the rich tapestry of the being of God (John 16:12–13). The Church's claim to the truth therefore can never be absolute. And whilst I agree entirely with your warning that 'the church must avoid being lulled by the vague idea that there is a transparent and necessary progress of thought working itself out in history', it is also equally true that the Spirit is at work in our world, unfolding and enticing us further into truth.[1] We are dealing with 'such a fast God, always before us and leaving as we arrive', as R. S. Thomas has put it.[2] This is the frustration and delight of Christian discipleship, to be engaged in something much more creative than the application of static principles to present situations, to be involved in the Christ-event as intimately as the apostolic community was. It is in a real sense to be ever early Church, revelling in the world-transforming presence of the divine but also nurturing the headache that comes with such revelry. The headache is caused by the fact that the Spirit incarnates itself in the midst of the mess and muddle of human fragmentation, historicity and contingency, to be pursued by human beings whose eyes and ears are focused through lenses of class, race, gender, social position and conditioning, and so on. It is therefore difficult to discern who is dancing the dance of the Spirit and who is following other steps, without either seeking to lock the Spirit in the past or equate the revelation of the Spirit entirely with one's own position (which would be idolatry). The Scriptures certainly provide us with the maps our ancestors in faith charted as they danced with the Spirit. They are invaluable as guides for us as we attempt to distinguish between which steps dance in time and which do not, but as we have seen they refuse to co-operate with our attempts to confine revelation to their words. They point beyond themselves. Nancy Wilson, theologising out of her experience as a resident of Los Angeles, notes that maps however useful and reliable give a false impression of the way the world is, for they suggest a static world. In fact the earth is in movement and every so often seismic activity reminds us of this fact and forces us to redraw our maps and rebuild our lives.[3] Similarly, the maps we inherit from our ancestors in faith may prove to be generally reliable but we have to allow for the possibility, indeed the probability, that there will in our time and context be at least some activity by the Spirit which will shift our perception of the world and demolish some of our theological structures, forcing us to do some creative rebuilding and remapping.

It will be obvious by now that I am not a postmodernist. I believe in the Christian metanarrative and I believe in its fundamentally eschatological character, i.e. that God is drawing creation towards a final redemption and liberation. However, some of the insights of postmodernism resonate deeply with the incarnational nature of Christian faith, in particular the insight (most clearly articulated by Habermas and Gadamer) that there is no such thing as neutral, objective interpretation, that we bring to our hermeneutical endeavours value–laden subjective assumptions. This has led to a growing recognition in theology of the way in which the white, male, 'first world' perspective has been privileged, and indeed associated with 'the truth' for centuries, and that space must be made for other perspectives in the collective Christian search for the Spirit. At the moment we are experiencing a kind of Pentecost in Christian theology as various groups of people find their theological voices and reflect upon their faith from the perspective of their experience. Among these are lesbian and gay Christians, of course. Perhaps you interpret this phenomenon as part of the 'Babel of confused tongues' which plagues the Church. With Rebecca Chopp, I would associate this eruption of undoubtedly disruptive Christian voices with the work of the Spirit (Acts 2).[4] What is clear is that with the emergence of new voices, the task of discernment becomes an extraordinary complex matter. The argument for 'epistemological privilege' to be given to those who have so far been deprived of a voice in theological discourse, on the grounds not only that they deserve equal voice but that it was to such that the good news was revealed, is a forceful one and one which has validity for the historical moment. In the future Christian theology may find itself forced to ground its strategies of discernment in praxis rather than in proposition, perhaps in the building up of human friendship which you recognise as one of the primary activities of the Spirit.

What all of the above necessitates is that those of us engaged in theological reflection ground that reflection in humility, or what Carter Heyward has called a theology of 'not knowing for sure',[5] which involves acknowledging one's non-neutrality and situatedness and therefore the possibility of being wrong. This in turn serves to create a space for genuine mutual encounter, dialogue and friendship and perhaps revelation. And so, before I go on and address issues more specifically about homosexuality, I want to make clear that I approach the subject as a lesbian who has been in a partnership with another woman for fifteen years. I am white, middle-class and a Christian of the Roman Catholic tradition. I am also a feminist, which means that I am concerned with the liberation of women (and indeed men) from the complex structures which we name 'patriarchy', a stance which I believe to be entirely compatible with Christianity and indeed largely inspired by the Gospel. All of these aspects of myself come into play when I do theology and when I respond to your Statement. I am disturbed by the fact that as authors of this Statement you did not feel it necessary to acknowledge your own situatedness and your own non-neutrality, because a failure to acknowledge these things restricts the possibility for genuine dialogue. It gives the impression (which may well be utterly erroneous) that you identify the principles and applications set out in the Statement as 'the truth' and that you invite responses from people like me because you want somehow to prove that in fact my theology represents 'a decisive break with orthodox Christianity', which you equate with the theology of the Statement. In my experience the only lesbian or gay theologians who 'intend a decisive break with orthodox Christianity' are those who cease to identify as Christian. Most of us are, however, suspicious of the orthodoxy/heresy dualism, which we associate with what Charles E. Winquist has named as the 'debilitating smallness' of a Church that has attempted to identify divine truth with the interpretations of a particular group of people. It is sometimes thought by people who have had little to do with lesbian and gay Christians that we unthinkingly assume that our sexuality and faith are mutually compatible. This is simply impossible as at every turn we are told by fellow Christians and by society at large that our love is 'sinful'. Therefore all of us who feel able to proclaim ourselves joyfully lesbian or gay and Christian do so because we have been through intensive theological reflection. This of course does not make us right but it should earn us respect as people who genuinely seek to follow Christ and as loyal members of the Church, our loyalty being all the more remarkable since we are often made to feel so unwelcome. Therefore before responding to specific points in the statement I would want to warn all of us involved in this debate against identifying our own theology with 'the truth' and categorising those who differ from us as unorthodox Christians. I may be wrong, you may be wrong, we may all be wrong and it is right for us to engage with and challenge one another, but we are all members of the body of Christ, genuinely and sincerely struggling to keep up with the dance of the Spirit.

Anthropology

You state that

> we must be on our guard . . . against constructing any other ground for our identities than the redeemed humanity given us in him . . . Our sexual affections can no more define who we are than can our class, race or nationality. At the deepest ontological level, there is no such thing as 'a' homosexual or 'a' heterosexual; there are human beings, male and female, called to redeemed humanity in Christ . . .

On the one hand, as one who stands on the social constructionist side of the debate on the origins of sexual orientation, I would agree that homosexuality and heterosexuality are not universal truths grounded in the created order but very recent human concepts and constructions designed to interpret and order human relationships, as even a cursory review of understandings of same-sex (and indeed, opposite-sex) attraction through history and in cultures different to our own reveals.[6] On the other hand, I am uncomfortable with your statement that 'our sexual affections can no more define who we are than our class, race or nationality' because this seems to imply that our historical circumstances are of no interest to God, that I exist in the vision of God as an ahistorical, asexual and colourless being – a being to which I have no access – because I do have a class, race, sexual orientation and nationality.

One of the lessons of the incarnation, and before that of the history of the Hebrew people, is surely that God engages with people in the midst of their historical context, that the fragmentation, contingency and instability of history is the site of revelation and redemption. There is also a danger, as black and liberation theologians have so clearly demonstrated, that any theological down-playing of human social, racial and sexual difference can result, and indeed in the past has done so, in an interpretation of the Gospel which offers no critique of the oppression and marginalisation of whole groups of people and reduces redemption and liberation to 'pie in the sky when you die'. Thus the Gospel becomes good news only for those who enjoy social and economic privilege and power, for they are able to enjoy the insignificant accidents of their birth and still look forward to eternal life. The praxis of Jesus demonstrates that historical circumstance does matter and the reign of God makes different demands upon people according to their historical circumstance (so compare the story of the rich man in Mark 10:17–22 with the story of the Syrophoenician woman in 7:24–30). I do not believe that God has 'made' me white, middle-class, British or lesbian. These are historical accidents, but the good news is that God dances in historical accidents and the Gospel addresses them. Because I enjoy social and economic privilege over the majority of the rest of the world's inhabitants (and indeed only enjoy that privilege at the expense of the autonomy and flourishing of those people) the demands of the Gospel on me are going to be significantly different from the demands on them. However, the fact that I am female and a lesbian complicates matters, for through and in these parts of my embodied self I experience and have the potential to experience marginalisation, violence, economic and social inequality, and the Gospel addresses me in the midst of this reality too. Redemption is worked out in different ways in my life. In recent years womanist theologians like Alice Walker have exposed the extent to which modern Western culture has conceptualised difference as a problem and therefore of no ultimate significance.[7] We like to believe that 'underneath we are all the same' but what that can often mean is that we believe that underneath everyone is like us, because to be like us is to be truly human. This allows us to isolate our cultural assumptions from criticism and to associate all difference which challenges those assumptions with 'falling short' or sin. Difference and diversity are not antithetical to God, whom we worship as Trinity and in whose image we are made, who takes historical contingency into the heart of the divine being.

Therefore I do not think we can say that in God's eyes there is no such thing as gay and straight, white and black, rich and poor etc. without losing something deeply significant about the incarnation. What then are we to make of St Paul's declaration that 'there is no longer Jew or Greek, there is no longer slave or free, there is no longer male or female; for you are one in Christ Jesus' (Gal. 3:28)? Here we encounter Paul drawing out the implications of Jesus's abolition of the whole priestly symbolic system of purity. The world is no longer ordered on the basis of one group enjoying divinely ordained superiority over another, difference is not abolished but its significance in terms of purity and access to the divine is. I am fascinated by the fact that you do appear to attribute the deep ontological meaning you deny to heterosexuality and homosexuality to maleness and femaleness. Why? Most of us (but significantly not all of us) are born with one of two possible sets of sexual organs, we are born embodied in a gender which creates difference but study after study has shown that the interpretation and social ordering of that difference is a social construction.[8] To attribute a significantly deeper ontological significance to gender than to sexual orientation or race is to risk being drawn into the theory of complementarity so beloved of recent Church documents on sexuality and yet shown by theologians such as Gareth Moore and Alison Webster to be grounded more in Jungian psychology than in biblical tradition and to reflect patriarchal thought-patterns: 'men and women turn out to be complementary; they fit each other socially because women occupy the space defined and left for them by men.'[9] And when this theory is taken to its logical conclusion as it was by Barth, single-sex friendship and community living must be condemned as 'disobedience', which has rather embarrassing repercussions for any analysis of Jesus's lifestyle![10]

I would therefore suggest a slightly different anthropology to your own. Human beings are created with the ability to mirror and co-operate with God in the activity of creation – we make and remake our world, as we interpret and order it. None of our creations have universal, eternal, ontological significance but they are nevertheless real and serve to make us who we are. God enters into this process of creation, not to abolish or override it nor to provide an escape route, but to warn us against defining groups of people dualistically against one another in terms of right/wrong, pure/impure and so on and to summon all to live out of compassion, justice, mutuality and radical vulnerability and to co-create out of those values. This is what it means to live in Christ (Matt. 25:31–46). In as much as our created categories prevent the living out of this vision they must be changed (as we have seen our current understandings of what it means to be male and female changing). We have to be engaged in a constant interrogation of our culture from the perspective of the reign of God, but to be human is to be incultured and it is there that God meets us. At the moment in Western culture one of the ways in which we define ourselves is in terms of our sexuality, therefore we have to believe that God meets us in that 'reality'. Furthermore there seem to be good theological reasons for welcoming this development inasmuch as it involves an understanding of human beings as fundamentally relational and embodied.

Desire

I find your discourse on desire overly pessimistic. You speak of desire in entirely negative terms as something to be struggled with and finally overcome. The Brazilian theologian Maria Clara Bingemer has argued that if Christians wish to assert that 'God is love' then, 'in the beginning God can only be the object of desire – not of necessity nor of rationality. Theology – which seeks to be reflection and talk about God and God's word – must therefore be moved and permeated in its entirety by the flame of desire . . . Born of desire, theology exists as theology only if it is upheld and supported by desire.'[11] A Christian therefore has to begin with an optimistic view of desire as grounded in the human longing for God. Desire must be a starting-point for theology and sexual desire is part of that. Indeed, there is a strong biblical tradition of locating the presence of the divine in the midst of human desire for mutual intimacy (see the Song of Songs, 2 Sam. 1:26 and Ruth). This recognition that desire may constitute a royal road to God renders the centralisation of self-denial in Christian discipleship somewhat problematic, for within this paradigm self-actualisation not self-denial can be grace-led and filled. We see this clearly in the story of Jesus and in the lives of Christian martyrs. It is far too simplistic to read these lives as lives of self-denial. They are lives of true self-actualisation, of authenticity and truthfulness, in which there is a congruence between belief and behaviour. Certainly all these men and women faced and rejected the opportunity to be less than themselves, to take easier courses, and the choices that they made undoubtedly caused pain and hardship but it is dangerous to classify this as self-denial, for we can end up saying that if we desire something we must be wrong. This can have the effect of further marginalising, silencing, disempowering and diminishing those who up until very recently had no sense of self, for they were defined by others – among these are many women, black people, disabled people and gay people. A theology of self-denial might conclude that the movements for liberation amongst these people is sinful because it involves self-interest. Yet the Scriptures teach us that one of the ways the Spirit of God moves in history is to call marginalised, oppressed and despised peoples together and form them into communities of justice and mutuality. The Jesus-movement was more about the voiceless finding a voice than it was about self-denial. The discourse of self-denial also assumes the existence of an autonomous self unconnected to others. Liberation and feminist theologies amongst others have recalled us to the biblical witness that we are not isolated selves but interconnected. We find both God and our sense of self in the midst of community. As you so rightly point out, in Jesus we know human nature as it truly is and is meant to be. In him we know what it is for humanity to flourish in right relationship with God and therefore we know the object of our desire. In him we see one whose sense of self and self-fulfilment was extremely strong and who indeed rejected the conventionally religious path of self-denial (Mark 2:18) in favour of food, drink, fun and intimacy, because in these human desires he located the possibility of the reign of God. The discourse of self-denial, then as now, isolates people from one another. Others and our bodies become potential enemies which we learn to fear and avoid. We end up denying the goodness of creation and the presence of God within it.

This is not, of course, to say that desire cannot be perverted by sin. To a large extent desire is socially constructed, as Foucault demonstrated, and used to bolster certain economic and social systems. Desire when perverted becomes lust, the sin of possessiveness and objectification (Matt. 5:27). It involves the treating of another person as an object for one's own use and it can be as evident in our desire for a particular pair of shoes without concern for who made it and in what conditions as it is in sexual relations. It is also evident in the unthinking assumption that one's personal way of being and relating is 'right' and 'holy' and any alternative must be 'sinful', without any mutual engagement with the person or persons one is condemning. Desire longs for another but within the context of mutuality and the web of relationships in which we already exist. It recognises our mutual interdependence and therefore at times may require personal sacrifice in order that others (and therefore we ourselves) may flourish. Because lust is a perversion of desire, and because we are born and schooled and structured into sin, it is often difficult to distinguish between the two. Here we have to judge our longings by their fruits. If they lead to justice, mutuality, compassion and friendship more than they lead to objectification and diminishment (because all our efforts will be tainted by sin) and not only in our private judgment, then we can recognise them as products and sacraments of grace and locations of revelation.

Lesbian and Gay Love and the Church

Turning now to your specific statements on homosexuality, it is in your handling of Scripture that I become most acutely aware of our radically different starting-points. It is obvious to you that the biblical authors condemn homosexual behaviour 'within the broader context of human idolatry'. Nothing could be less obvious to me. To begin with, I think it is misleading to give the impression that the biblical authors talked about homosexuality at all, since the concept and reality of homosexuality as we experience it now in twentieth-century Britain is barely a century old. I have similar problems when it comes to talking about heterosexuality. Marriage as lived out in the first-century Palestinian and Hellenistic worlds bears precious little resemblance to marriage as it is understood and lived out today. When we are seeking to discern the movement of the Spirit in the muddle of human relations, using the maps of the Scriptures to point us in the right direction, we have to look for what we might call family resemblances between our terrain and that of Scripture. We have to ask if the apparent (and we are all, I am sure, acutely aware of the difficulties of translating the Corinthian passages) condemnations of same-sex sexual activity in the passages you cite, grounded as you note in the context of human idolatry, bear any resemblance to the lives of the majority of lesbian and gay people today. In other words, does same-sex love necessarily manifest itself in the symptoms of idolatrous behaviour clearly laid out by Paul in Romans 1:18–32?

Of course humanity is never free from the sin of idolatry, and we can recognise our own and every society that has ever been in Paul's description, but if we are to apply these biblical condemnations to contemporary lesbian and gay people as a class then we have to prove that there is something in their way of being that necessarily makes them behave in these ways. And I believe it is simply impossible to prove such a thing. On the contrary, the chief reason why we are having this discussion is that homosexuality has been revealed to be an issue not so much for the Church as *of* the Church. To a large extent the Church is as gay and lesbian as it is heterosexual. Richard Cleaver speculates on what would happen if one day just the gay people were spirited away from the Church, 'organists vanish from their benches, singers from their choir lofts. Readers, preachers, priests, and altar servers – even an occasional bishop . . . what would it mean to have no liturgical specialists?'[12] It would mean that orthodoxy, which in its primary sense is 'right worship', would be plunged into crisis. Our ability to worship God 'rightly' would be diminished. We would all be in danger of succumbing to idolatry. The point rather mischievously put is that lesbian and gay people are to be found in the heart of the body of Christ. We know them as good, faithful servants of Christ. It is an odd sort of idolater that seeks to serve the real God with such devotion, that longs to serve the Church and to have the Church recognise and bless their love. It is an odd sort of idolater that serves and longs for open acceptance in a Christian community which has too often committed the sin of Sodom against her/his people, denying them hospitality, demonising their difference and condoning by silence violence against them.[13]

'You will know them by their fruits. Are grapes gathered from thorns, or figs from thistles?' (Matt. 7:16) If anything good can come out of the appalling AIDS pandemic it is that many came to know lesbian and gay people by their fruits rather than through stereotypes and heterosexist eyes. It revealed the extraordinary love, devotion and sense of connectedness and kinship that exists in the lesbian and gay community. Sociological studies have revealed that lesbian and gay partnerships tend to be consciously structured on models of equality and mutuality and that there is a determined effort within lesbian and gay communities to bind people together in ties of friendship and kinship which bears fruit in mutual help and support.[14] The obvious involvement of lesbian and gay people in liberation movements of all sorts also cannot be ignored. We are not dealing here with a people who as a group are characterised by 'wickedness, evil, covetousness, . . . envy, murder, strife, deceit, craftiness', nor are they God-haters. As a people their love for one another seems to bear fruit in a desire for beauty, justice and friendship. Whatever kind of same-sex sexual behaviour Paul had encountered, it bears little resemblance to contemporary lesbian and gay life (which is not of course to deny that lesbian and gay people are capable of idolatry, and the evil and brutishness which are its fruits, but then so are heterosexual people). This is why when lesbian and gay people look into the Scriptures we do not recognise ourselves in the mirrors normally held up to us. We see more distinct family resemblances in the passionate devotion of David and Jonathan, Ruth and Naomi, Jesus and the Beloved Disciple – which is not in any sense to claim these characters as gay or lesbian but simply to say that, in the passionate friendship (which certainly in the case of David and Jonathan may have included an explicit 'sexual' element) between these people in which God's presence dwelt, we recognise something of our own experience, a kind of tribal identification. This tribal identification is not based upon intimate relationship alone. Lesbian and gay people have found in the story of the Passover and Exodus a family resemblance to their own experience of being formed into a self-affirming people after the Stonewall Riots of 1969. Perhaps it takes lesbian or gay eyes to perceive the theme of sexual subversion that runs through the Hebrew and Christian Scriptures, in which the story of salvation is often only furthered by the positive agency of the sexually marginalised, particularly eunuchs who contrary to popular supposition, were not *de facto* celibates and indeed were regarded in ancient times as a third sex who generally engaged in sex with other men.[15]

Perhaps it also takes sexually marginalised eyes to see that there is in Jesus's teaching something much more radical than an endorsing of 'two forms of vocations in which life can be lived: marriage and singleness'. Jesus's attitude to marriage as it was constructed in his day is rather negative – it has no place in the reign of God (Matt. 22:30) – and he demonstrates a similar attitude towards blood family. He appears to call people not to marriage or to singleness (one could hardly characterise his life as the life of a single man, lived as it was in intimate community) but, as you yourselves note, to friendship in which we experience a foretaste of what is to come in the glorious reign of God. It is a sad fact that heterosexual marriage, in the manner in which cultures have structured it up until very recently, has often prevented friendship between men and women developing, which may be why Jesus could see no place for it in the resurrection. Celibates, married people, single people and lesbian and gay people can manifest friendship in their lives and in their different ways of being sexual. I want to suggest that it is to this friendship that Christians are called in all aspects of their lives and therefore it is on the basis of the manifestation of friendship that sexual relationships should be judged and not the sex of the people involved. As a community of friends the Church should help herself to become holy by condemning those relationships which do not manifest the justice, equality, mutuality, faithfulness and compassion that are the heart of friendship. That will include speaking up on issues upon which it has been strangely and shamefully silent, like marital rape and domestic violence. But it should also hold up and celebrate those relationships which do manifest the qualities of friendship, which must include lesbian and gay relationships.[16]

You will, I am sure, disagree profoundly with what I have said, which raises an issue which is perhaps prior to the issue we are discussing, which is how Christians who disagree with one another establish and maintain holy friendship. In your opening remarks you regret the 'highly dramatised' nature of the debate so far. It is hard not to dramatise a debate which touches the lives of people so centrally and personally, and people, as I have pointed out, who are not outsiders but insiders. It is right that Christians should open their lives to mutual examination and criticism but grounding our lives in a theology of humility perhaps would encourage us to tread less heavily upon each other's souls. I humbly submit that in the modern lesbian and gay liberation movement we see the seismic activity of the Spirit unfolding something of the revelation promised by Christ, recalling us to the vocation of friendship and extending it to our sexual relationships. In the glorious diversity and difference of the children of God we all may thereby be united in the common project of proclaiming and living out the Gospel.

Notes

1. For a more fully worked theology of incompleteness see Gareth Jones, '"What is truth?" Rehabilitating Pontius Pilate', in Frances Young (ed.), *Dare We Speak of God in Public: The Edward Cadbury Lectures, 1993–94* (Mowbray, 1995), pp. 115–32.
2. R. S. Thomas, 'Pilgrimages', *Frequencies* (Macmillan, 1978).
3. Nancy Wilson, *Our Tribe: Queer Folks, God Jesus, and the Bible* (Harper SanFrancisco, 1995), pp. 182–96.
4. Rebecca S. Chopp, *The Power to Speak: Feminism, Language, God* (Crossroad, 1989).
5. Carter Heyward, *Staying Power: Reflections on Gender, Justice and Compassion* (Pilgrim Press, 1995), p. 7.
6. Michael Vasey provides an excellent analysis of some of these developments in *Strangers and Friends: A New Exploration of Homosexuality and the Bible* (Hodder & Stoughton, 1995), pp. 72–161.
7. Alice Walker, *In Search of Our Mothers' Gardens: Womanist Prose* (Harcourt Brace Jovanovich, 1983).
8. Elaine Graham, *Making the Difference: Gender, Personhood and Theology* (Mowbray, 1995).
9. Alison Webster, *Found Wanting: Women, Sexuality and Christianity* (Cassell, 1995), p. 123. See also Gareth Moore, *The Body in Context: Sex and Catholicism* (SCM, 1992), pp. 117–39.
10. Karl Barth, *Church Dogmatics*, part 3, vol. 4 (Edinburgh: T. & T. Clark, 1961), pp. 164–6.
11. Ursula King, *Feminist Theology from the Third World: A Reader* (SPCK and Orbis, 1994), p. 311.
12. Richard Cleaver, *Know My Name: A Gay Liberation Theology* (Westminster/ John Knox Press, 1995), p. 134.
13. Wilson, *Our Tribe*, pp. 167–70.
14. See e.g. Kath Weston, *Families We Choose: Lesbians, Gays, Kinship* (Columbia University Press, 1991).
15. Wayne R. Dynes, *Encyclopedia of Homosexuality* (St James Press, 1990), pp. 376–8.
16. For a fuller working out of my theology of friendship see my *Just Good Friends: Towards a Lesbian and Gay Theology of Relationships* (Mowbray, 1995).

7

Christ, Creation and Human Sexuality

John Colwell

I AM NOT a homosexual. I do not make this denial through any sense of defensiveness or embarrassment. I make it rather to clarify that there are perspectives on this theme in which I cannot possibly share. I cannot participate in feminist theology because I am a man. I cannot participate in black theology because I am white. I may sympathise with many of the aims, methods and conclusions of such theologies, but I cannot fully participate in their activity because of my particular identity. Feminist theology is not identified primarily by its agenda but rather by the particularity of its female perspectives on theological issues. These are perspectives which I can hear, appreciate and affirm, but they are not perspectives in which I can share. This is, of course, without prejudice to whether or not such perspectives are appropriate to the work of theology – I happen to believe that they are both appropriate and inevitable – but that is not the point. I am not a woman, I am not black, and I am not a homosexual: there are perspectives which I can hear and (maybe) appreciate and affirm, but in which I cannot participate. I do have friends and acquaintances who identify themselves as homosexual. I can listen to them. I can try to empathise with their perspectives. But I cannot share in them any more than I can share in the particular perspectives of a female theologian or a black theologian.

All this presupposes that the underlying comparison is valid, that being homosexual is comparable to being a woman or being black, that being homosexual is 'given' in the same way that being a woman or being black is 'given'. In recent years the validity of these comparisons has increasingly been assumed in anti-discrimination policy: many local authorities, charitable organisations, and even private companies seek to outlaw any form of discrimination on the grounds of sexual orientation as also on the grounds of sex, race, religious persuasion and disability.

The latter two categories in such formulae, of course, raise other possibilities concerning the manner in which homosexuality might be considered as 'given' since, while they may not be 'given' in the same sense as sex and race, there are other senses in which both religious persuasion and disability can validly be considered to be 'given'.

The inclusion of the category 'religious persuasion' is problematic for a number of reasons. Is it really intended that all religious persuasion, no matter how bizarre, should be equally tolerated, especially when religious persuasion is so inextricably intertwined with religious practice? This relationship between belief and practice will be considered towards the end of this paper. Of more immediate relevance at this point is the comparison between homosexuality and religious persuasion in terms of 'givenness': while there is a sense in which religious persuasion can be considered as something adopted or chosen there is also a sense in which it can be considered as something 'received', though the manner of 'receiving' is different from that which pertains with sex and race. Therefore if, at least to some degree, homosexuality is 'received' is it so in the sense that sex or race are 'received', or is it rather 'received' as is religion, through participation in the tradition and life of a certain kind of community? Moreover, if homosexuality is received in this latter sense, is it at all appropriate, at the same time and without prejudice to its 'givenness', to consider it also (like religious persuasion) as something adopted or chosen?

The remaining comparison between homosexuality and disability is deeply offensive to many who identify themselves as homosexual. The comparison immediately implies that there is something wrong, or at least something less than ideal, in being homosexual.[1] By contrast, the increasing response from some sections of the homosexual community is to suggest that it is those who wish to suppress homosexuality, rather than homosexuals themselves, who have a problem: homosexuality is to be perceived as being received as a gift rather than as a disability. Notwithstanding this response, the issue of whether or not the comparison between homosexuality and disability is appropriate will be the central concern of this paper. Disability, after all, is itself something 'received'. One may be disabled through birth, one may be disabled through accident or sickness, but one is rarely disabled through choice: disability, generally, is something 'given'. But what are the theological implications of disability being something that is 'given' and do these implications, to any degree, inform a theological response to homosexuality? I need theological categories of both createdness and fallenness to account for the 'patriarchy' which is the corruption of maleness and femaleness and against which feminist theologians so rightly protest. However, I do not need a category of fallenness to comprehend maleness and femaleness; maleness and femaleness are positively 'given' in creation even if the corruption, in which they are generally comprehended, is not so. But, unlike the distinction of maleness and femaleness, I cannot account for disability without a theological category of fallenness. Therefore, the question which this final comparison raises is whether homosexuality is 'given' in a sense that is similar to maleness and femaleness or whether it is given rather in a sense that is similar to disability: can I account for homosexuality theologically without a category of fallenness as well as a category of createdness? It is at this point that my difficulties with the St Andrew's Day Statement begin.

The St Andrew's Day Statement, privately published on 30 November 1995 in response to the request of the Church of England Evangelical Council and reproduced in *Churchman*,[2] states its aim as being 'to find in the Gospel a starting-point of common faith from which those who differ can agree to proceed in their discussions'.[3] In order to fulfil this aim the Statement seeks firstly to affirm a series of credal principles and secondly to apply those principles to the issue of homosexuality. Both the aim and the method are laudable, indeed, it would be hard to imagine any other method suitable to the aim. If Christians differ over issues of practice and morality those differences must be set within the context of that which is held in common. Nor, without inappropriately anticipating the conclusions of this present paper, would I want to distance myself from the implied conclusions of the Statement: my problem is rather with the manner in which these conclusions are reached; my difficulty is not so much with what is said within the statement as with what is not said – despite the protest that 'nothing should be inferred from what the statement does not say'.[4]

In the course of a private conversation with one of the authors of the statement it was likened to the Barmen Declaration. While this may be a somewhat ambitious comparison, it is an apt comment on an identity of theological method, focusing on the significance of the incarnate Christ and refuting rival claims to authoritative revelation derived from reflection on culture or history. The Barmen Declaration, of which Karl Barth was the key author, was adopted by the first Confessing Synod of the German Evangelical Church on 31 May 1934. Its intention, in response to the German Christian movement and its support of Hitler, was to declare that 'Jesus Christ, as he is attested for us in Holy Scripture, is the one Word of God which we have to hear and which we have to trust and obey in life and in death'. Alongside this affirmation was set the corresponding rejection of 'the false teaching, that the church could and should acknowledge any other events and powers, figures and truths, as God's revelation, or as a source of its proclamation, apart from and besides this one Word of God'.[5] It was later in that same year that Barth responded with his vehement *Nein!* to Emil Brunner's *Natur und Gnade*,[6] rejecting his argument that 'the task of our theological generation is to find a way back to a legitimate natural theology'.[7]

Now if I had to make the choice between aligning myself with Barth or Brunner concerning these issues, and especially within the particular context of the struggle against Nazism, I hope that I would side with Barth every time – but not without the protest that there must surely be an alternative. With Barmen, Barth and the St Andrew's Day Statement, I want unequivocally to affirm the exclusively Christological focus of revelation, but with Brunner, or at least with what I suspect underlies his quest, I want to enquire as to how this one Word is spoken and heard in a world which, as yet, does not acknowledge unanimously the Lordship of Jesus; I want to enquire more specifically concerning how this one Word resonates within creation and identifies our createdness and fallenness in the light of our chosenness. This is precisely the issue which Barth himself seems to be addressing in his discussion of Jesus Christ as 'The Light of Life'[8] though whether he does so effectively and persuasively is perhaps to be doubted – it is difficult not to conclude with Colin Gunton that Barth's pervading reticence concerning the person and work of the Spirit issues in an account of revelation that presumes its immediacy.[9] A doctrine of revelation expressed in terms of its immediacy militates against the possibility of a general (or 'common') revelation: God is encountered immediately in Christ or not at all; there is no coherent means of accounting for the Spirit mediating Christ's presence through creation and human history. And, with fatal consequences in the sphere of moral theology, reticence concerning the commonality (and universality) of the possibility of a mediated knowledge of God through the Spirit forfeits any coherent category of human accountability.

But at least Barth does offer an account of a doctrine of creation alongside his doctrine of reconciliation, and at least his doctrine of creation includes a description of ethics.[10] The authors of the St Andrew's Day Statement are right to affirm that '[t]here can be no description of human reality, in general or in particular, outside the reality in Christ' and that therefore '[w]e must be on guard . . . against constructing any other ground for our identities than the redeemed humanity given us in him', and that '[o]ur sexual affections can no more define who we are than can our class, race or nationality',[11] but a definition of humanity in Christ must be related explicitly to a definition of humanity in creation. Other than in explicit relation to a doctrine of creation, a definition of humanity in Christ gives no account of maleness and femaleness and no account of human sexuality and, since this is the point at issue, this does seem to be a disastrous omission. If, without reference to a doctrine of creation, Christ is the comprehensive definition of our humanity then it would surely be reasonable to conclude that celibacy is the only valid response to human sexuality that conforms with this definition. I suspect that this is not the conclusion which the authors of the St Andrew's Day Statement wish to be drawn.

That humanity is ultimately defined in Christ should be recognised as confirming the fallenness and perversion of patriarchal expressions of maleness and femaleness; it may well reveal the created provisionality of this distinction, it certainly should be seen as the denial of any determinative significance for this distinction in our relatedness to God and to one another, particularly within the Church, but it ought not to be interpreted as a denial of the givenness and goodness of maleness and femaleness. That humanity is ultimately defined in Christ should be recognised as affirming that human fulfilment is not dependent upon sexual fulfilment, but it ought not to be interpreted as a denial of the givenness and goodness of human sexuality. That human fulfilment is not dependent upon sexual fulfilment is rightly recognised by the authors of the St Andrew's Day Statement as of relevance to the issue of homosexuality but, of itself, it is an insufficient response. Human sexuality may not be ultimate but, as that which is created and therefore given and good, it is appropriate. Consequently, if a particular expression of human sexuality is to be perceived as inappropriate this can only derive from a qualification of its givenness and goodness and it is difficult to see how this qualification can be derived Christologically.

All this brings us back to the possible comparison between the givenness of sexual orientation and the givenness of disability. When Jesus encountered a man born blind, his disciples, reflecting a not uncommon assumption concerning the relation between sin and disability, asked whether the man's blindness was caused by his own sin or that of his parents (John 9: 1ff.). Jesus doesn't just respond by denying that the man's blindness was the outcome of any particular sin, he also responds by healing him. Disability, whether it derives from birth or from subsequent illness or accident, may not be the outcome of any particular sin but it is none the less an outcome of the fallenness of creation. By healing those who are disabled Jesus identifies disability as an aspect of creation's fallenness and 'frustration' rather than as an aspect of creation's goodness and, in doing so, he also anticipates the future liberation of creation 'from its bondage to decay' (Rom. 8:18ff.). Understandably those who are disabled protest against the dehumanising effects of patronising pity. We rightly respect those who strive to accept their disability as the context in which life must be lived.[12] But attempts to redefine disability as something other than disability lack conviction: overwhelmingly those who are blind would prefer to see; those who are deaf would prefer to hear; those who are lame would prefer to walk. To attempt to redefine disability as something good in itself is to deny the ultimate goodness of creation by denying its present fallenness. The failure to admit the reality of present fallenness is a refusal to believe in the future liberation defined in the Gospel. Disability may be given but it is not given in the same manner that maleness and femaleness are given; it is dissonant; it is not given as an aspect of creation's goodness but as an aspect of creation's fallenness, distortion and corruption.

By anticipating the future liberation of creation Jesus exposes its present fallenness and affirms its intended goodness. To believe the Gospel is not just to hope for this future liberation, it is also as a consequence to admit the present fallenness of creation and its distinction from the goodness that is intended. This understanding of the world is revealed. It is apprehended by the Spirit through the Gospel story. It is not a conclusion derived from any independent and universally accessible rationality. But it is not incoherent. The Gospel definition of the world by its future resonates with our deepest instincts concerning what is wrong with the world and what is to be hoped for. It coheres with what we generally (though perhaps mistakenly) term 'nature'. Most of us do not need the Gospel to tell us that disability isn't 'good'. But we do need the Gospel to explain this common 'instinct', to reassure us that disability is not ultimately 'intended', and to reveal to us that the basis for the abolition of disability has been accomplished in history and that we can therefore hope for its abolition with confidence. This does not imply a natural theology but it does imply a coherence of the Gospel with the way things actually are and a resonance of the Gospel with the way we instinctively feel. We are created in God's image and his omnipresent but often unrecognised Spirit speaks to us through our story in a manner that echoes the story of Christ which is the Gospel. When we hear the Gospel we should recognise the echo for what it is.[13]

If it is understandable that those who are disabled protest against the dehumanising effects of patronising pity it ought similarly to be understandable that some pronounce themselves 'proud to be gay'. Sexual orientation, like disability and like maleness and femaleness, is an aspect of received identity. For this reason it is not something to be apologised for. Without prejudice to a doctrine of original sin I am no more directly culpable for my sexual orientation than the man born blind was culpable for his blindness. But I am accountable for what I do with my sexual orientation, just as I am accountable for the way I live with my masculinity and the man born blind was accountable for the way in which he lived with his blindness. And, since the manner in which a person lives with their sexual orientation will be an outworking of the manner in which they understand that sexual orientation, it is crucial that we explore the manner in which sexual orientation is received: is it received as maleness and femaleness are received, or is it received as disability is received, or is it received in some other way?

I am certainly not suggesting that the comparison between homosexuality and disability is exact but I am suggesting that, in the light of a doctrine of createdness and fallenness, it is more appropriate than the comparison with maleness and femaleness; that homosexuality, like disability, evidences the dissonance of present creation. Notwithstanding the dogmatic claims that often are trumpeted from both sides of this debate, there is, as yet, no finally convincing scientific theory concerning the causes of homosexuality. It may be genetic. It may be developmental. It may be a combination of both factors. In this respect at least the comparison with disability has potential since disability too can be the outcome of various factors. But this, while possibly helpful, is not the primary intention of the comparison.

Even if the distinction between maleness and femaleness is provisional (Matt. 22:30)[14] it is none the less positively given in creation and positively affirmed within the Gospel story. Jesus himself may not have married. By his singleness he affirms celibacy as a valid response to human sexuality, but he does not by his singleness affirm celibacy as the only valid response to human sexuality. As the traditional marriage service affirms: he attended a wedding at Cana in Galilee and consequently 'adorned and beautified' marriage 'with his presence'. The humanity of Christ defines and includes all humanity but it does not thereby abolish maleness and femaleness or qualify the sense in which maleness and femaleness are created and 'good', rather both maleness and femaleness are equally affirmed in the single humanity of Christ. This is where being male or female differs from being slave or free, a Jew or a Greek: the first category is 'given' in creation, the latter categories are consequences of the fallenness of that creation. The intention of the comparison between homosexuality and disability is to recognise that homosexuality, like disability, is a consequence of creation's fallenness rather than creation's goodness.

There are certainly those who would reject the comparison by affirming the goodness of sexual expression whether it be with partners of the same sex or of the opposite sex. But I suspect that there is something hollow in this claim (and this is the point where I must acknowledge that I cannot speak from personal experience). Those known to me who identify their orientation as homosexual do so by identifying their sexual feelings as being, in some sense, dissonant with their physical form.[15] Some may respond to this dissonance by remaining celibate, some may respond to this dissonance by marriage notwithstanding their sexual attractions, some may respond to this dissonance by affirming the appropriateness of homosexual expression – but the sense of dissonance remains. One might try to deny this sense of dissonance by attributing it solely to 'brainwashing' by a received tradition, but the denial lacks conviction: it is not just one's tradition with which one is in conflict, it is one's own physical identity. Whether one gives priority to one's physical form or whether one gives priority to one's sexual feelings there is an underlying sense of disorder: in an ideal world one's body and one's feelings would cohere.

This sense of dissonance resonates with the Christian account of creation and fallenness. God created male and female. The appropriate companion for Adam was Eve. A person's body and a person's sexual feelings are intended to cohere. But the world is not yet as it is intended. The world is fallen. Dissonance is ubiquitous. There is disability. There is homosexual orientation. To deny the dissonance of homosexuality, just as to deny the dissonance of disability, is to deny the intentionality of creation by denying its fallenness. One cannot deny the dissonance of homosexuality without denying the Gospel. Consequently it may be one's attitude to sexual orientation, rather than sexual orientation itself, which is 'given' in the sense that religious persuasion is given. The degree to which homosexual orientation may derive from developmental factors is at least as comparable to disability as it is to the acquiring of religious persuasion, particularly if an element of choice is admitted in relation to the latter which doesn't always appear to be present with respect to homosexual orientation. But it is through participation in the tradition and life of a certain kind of community that one comes to view homosexual orientation in a particular way. It is here also that an element of conscious choice is more likely to occur, especially when that persuasion tends to deny or to repress an inner sense of dissonance. To deny the dissonance of homosexual orientation is a religious statement and, as such, it coheres less effectively than the Gospel with one's experience of living in the world and with one's own innermost instincts.

But what are the consequences of recognising homosexual orientation as an aspect of the dissonance that issues from the world's fallenness?

Christian character and behaviour ought not to be determined (indeed, cannot be determined) merely by conformity with rules. For this reason alone arguing about the specific meanings of biblical words which may (or may not) relate to homosexual behaviour is of limited worth. Christian character and behaviour are determined by what it means to live truthfully, trustingly and hopefully, as well as lovingly, in the light of the Gospel. Other than in the general sense of our shared culpability for the fallenness of the world we may be no more culpable for our sexual orientation than we are culpable for disability. But we are culpable for the manner in which we live in response to the Gospel with our sexual orientation and disability.

Those who are blind and who recognise their blindness as dissonance (and who doesn't?) may certainly seek to be healed.

But if healing doesn't occur those who are blind but who live in response to the Gospel may know that blindness is not their future nor the ultimate determining factor of their present; in the light of their chosenness they can live hopefully within the world's present fallenness; they can continually strive to see their identity defined by their being in Christ, rather than by their blindness; they can trust the indwelling Spirit to enable them to live even now in the light of who they will be, which is who they already are in Christ.

Similarly those who are homosexual in orientation and who, in the light of the Gospel, recognise that orientation as dissonance, may also seek healing in some form.[16] But if no change in sexual orientation occurs those who believe the Gospel are called to live truthfully: they need not live in pretence but neither need they live as though their identity were determined by their sexual orientation. Since they recognise their sexual orientation as an aspect of dissonance they will seek neither to compound that dissonance nor to gratify it, rather they too will strive to live in the light of who they will be and who, in Christ, they already are. They can certainly live trusting in divine mercy, but they can also live trusting in the power of the Spirit to remake them in the light of the character of Christ.

This can be glibly said but it is not glibly intended. I have no conception of what it means to be blind and therefore I need the grace (I hope without patronising pity) to understand when someone can only respond to their blindness with anger, bitterness and frustration. Somehow I need to be loving without ceasing to be truthful and truthful without ceasing to be loving. If I fail to be this I too am failing to live in the light of the Gospel. Similarly I have no conception of what it means to be homosexual. I may have sexual desires which I recognise as dissonant and which therefore must remain unfulfilled but I cannot conceive of what it means for every sexual desire to remain unfulfilled. I acknowledge that there are those, both heterosexual and homosexual, who have led celibate lives, but I also acknowledge that this too is beyond my comprehension. And because I can think of no other circumstance that, in the same manner and to the same degree, calls for such sustained sexual discipline, the Church here supremely must be a community of mercy and grace. But again it is called to be such truthfully. The Church ceases to be a truthful witness to the Gospel if it ceases to be a community of mercy and grace. But the Church also ceases to be a truthful witness to the gospel if it ceases, mercifully and graciously, to testify to the fallenness as well as the chosenness of men and women, if it ceases to recognise the consequences of this fallenness as dissonance, if it ceases to call the compounding of this dissonance sin.[17]

The context in which this debate presently occurs is increasingly with relation to its implications for the 'clergy'. To the question of whether a different standard of behaviour is to be expected from men and women who serve and lead the people of God the honest answer is 'Yes'. Christian leadership is, at least partly, a matter of being an 'example'. This does not mean that anyone who recognises their orientation to be homosexual should be excluded from Christian leadership. It certainly does not mean that those in Christian leadership have attained spiritual perfection. It does not even mean that those in Christian leadership are less prone to temptation (quite the reverse may be the case). But it does mean, or at least it ought to mean, that the character and behaviour of those in Christian leadership exemplifies what it means to live in coherence with the Gospel. The man or woman in Christian leadership will be especially concerned to live truthfully as well as lovingly, trustfully, hopefully and, perhaps above all, thankfully.[18]

Notes

1. While it may be valid to contest the comparison one must be cautious lest one does so in a manner which is itself offensive to those who suffer some form of disability.
2. *Churchman*, vol. 110, no. 2 (1996), pp. 102–6.
3. St Andrew's Day Statement, p. 3.
4. Ibid.
5. 'The Barmen Confession on the Identity of the Church' quoted in Alister E. McGrath (ed.), *The Christian Theology Reader* (Blackwell, 1995), p. 278.
6. Karl Barth with Emil Brunner, *Natural Theology*, tr. Peter Fraenkel (Geoffrey Bles, 1946).
7. Quoted in Eberhard Busch, *Karl Barth: His Life from Letters and Autobiographical Texts*, tr. John Bowden (SCM, 1976), p. 248.
8. Karl Barth, *Church Dogmatics*, vol. 4, part 3, tr. eds. G. W. Bromiley and T. F. Torrance (T. & T. Clark, 1961), pp. 38–165.

9. Colin E. Gunton, *A Brief Theology of Revelation* (T. & T. Clark, 1995), p. 5 *et passim*. Note also Gunton's comment in response to Berkeley: 'it is in the Spirit of truth that we find the reason for our being able to understand what is there', p. 37.

10. Though note that Charles Curran criticises Barth's discussion of homosexuality within this context on the grounds that Barth's 'Christomonism' effectively blinds him to the validity of insights to be gained through psychology and psychiatry: Charles Curran, *Catholic Moral Theology in Dialogue* (University of Notre Dame Press, 1976), pp. 190 ff.

11. St Andrew's Day Statement, p. 5.

12. If some homosexuals object to the comparison with disability it should be noted that many who are disabled themselves object to the label since it so often has been used in a belittling sense. I hope that I have made it clear that this is not the manner of its use in this discussion.

13. 'What allows us to look expectantly for agreement among those who do not worship God is not that we have a common morality based on autonomous knowledge of autonomous nature, but that God's kingdom is wider than the church.' Stanley Hauerwas, *Christian Existence Today: Essays on Church, World, and Living In Between* (Labyrinth, 1988), p. 17.

14. Why on earth didn't the disciples ask Jesus the meaning of this enigmatic response?

15. While I recognise the distinction between homosexuality and transsexuality, the latter perceiving this dissonance as absolute, a sense of underlying dissonance is difficult to evade and is evidenced by an unease concerning penetrative sex amongst some homosexuals.

16. While I certainly accept that someone can be healed in respect of their 'affections' and orientation, I also suspect that this and other forms of healing are more rare than some elements of the contemporary Church would have us believe. In this area especially, pretending that something is other than it actually is can be exceedingly dangerous and damaging.

17. Gerald Bray, in an editorial introducing the St Andrew's Day Statement, refers to 'the forces of chaos and destruction which are trying, often in the name of love and compassion, to destroy our society'. *Churchman*, vol. 110, no. 2 (1996), pp. 99–101, p. 101.

18. 'It is not enough that the clergy do not lie, cheat, or behave promiscuously, but ministers must have a character capable of sustaining their peculiar responsibility of performing the official acts of the Christian community. Ministers are not "better" than any other Christian, but they have made themselves open to a call from others that may well make them different.' Hauerwas, *Christian Existence Today*, p. 142.

8

Questions of Clarification

Dave Leal

To BEGIN WITH, a general word about the approach. It is certainly good to see an attempt being made to define more precisely the nature of the disagreements which lead to such 'strong and conflicting passions' where Christian reflection on questions relating to homosexuality is concerned. The Statement explicitly, if slightly ambiguously (am I reading the words 'the issue' in line 8 of paragraph 1 correctly?), restricts itself to the question of 'how we should respond to those, including clergy, seeking to live in quasi-marital relationships with a partner of the same sex'. This is, of course, only one in the range of questions which are being asked under the general heading of 'the Homosexuality Debate' (see subtitle of the Statement).

There is also, for example, the question of whether relationships which are 'sexual' but not 'quasi-marital' might be appropriate between people of the same sex. Readers ought to respect the fact that questions such as this are not, or at least not directly and explicitly, being addressed in the Statement. The authors of the Statement might, however, reflect on the logic of their more restricted attention. It has this much in its favour: many 'pro-gay' writers *do* appear to reject what might be termed 'casual' homosexual relations, whilst wishing to promote the 'quasi-marital' relationships which lie at the heart of the question the authors wish to address. However, it may also and easily be the case that the very selection and isolation of this question within the more general range of questions which might be asked generates a set of concerns of its own. Has anything of *theological* significance been conceded by imagining it possible to isolate the question in this way? This issue of homosexual 'quasi-marital relationships' is often isolated by those supporting such relationships, citing the criterion of fidelity as a kind of independent and self-justifying basis upon which theological evaluation may be accomplished. The intention of the Statement's authors in isolating their particular question might usefully be clarified if it were to be made explicit whether this is (for example) regarded simply as *the most practically pressing issue*, rather than one which can *ultimately* be viewed in isolation from answers to a range of other, but related, issues.

Introduction

Apart from the concern just raised about interpretation of 'the issue' in paragraph 1, little more needs to be said. It is probably deliberate that the Statement should speak of 'the issue' having become 'so highly dramatised', without spelling out further what is meant by this. This is a reminder that not all writing need be absolutely specific to achieve its end. It is open to the reader whether this calls to mind general or specific instances of (for example) 'anti-gay' propaganda, or the way in which interest in the topic of homosexual character and relationships has become so consuming that the churches have been distracted from other, more serious, concerns. However, it is less clear that the strategy offered in the later sentence should be quite so readily or straightforwardly commended: 'If its assertions should prove susceptible of being accommodated within more than one interpretation of present disputes, that will be an advantage, since it hopes to include all who do not intend a decisive break with orthodox Christianity.' It obviously depends what 'susceptible of being accommodated' amounts to. If this is simply a search for a 'form of words' which may be read with satisfaction by both parties to a dispute, each accepting them in some sense significant for their own side but distinct from the sense taken by their opponents, then we seem to be some distance from the desire of the authors. If the strategy of credal principles and application is to be taken at face value, one suspects that the agreement on and acceptance of 'credal principles' is to be looked for in a fairly precise and unambiguous fashion. That those who 'find that they cannot agree' are asked to 'be precise about their disagreements' suggests this is the correct interpretation, so the invitation to suspect the authors of aiming at a 'fudge', and an unworthy purchase of apparent agreement today at the expense of uncovering hidden division tomorrow (all the harder to bear when significant agreement *appeared* to have been reached), ought to be dismissed before we proceed.

It might be worth noting that the desire to identify relatively fundamental and secondary matters in theology is one which could be challenged, though it appears to be acceptable in the minds of the authors of the Statement. Challenges could be offered at a variety of levels. One might, for example, hold that no properly theological conviction is entirely logically independent of any other, so that the denial of even the most apparently 'secondary' matter would commit one to a rejection of some matter which may appear to have much more intuitively fundamental status. It might also be appropriate to mark a deep distinction between matters which are theologically undetermined, and which are therefore exempt from the categories of 'true' and 'false', and those matters which *are* true or false but where their truth or falsity is undetermined by (logically, neither truth nor falsity is entailed by) the particular context of discussion with which one happens to be engaged at the time. If all 'subsets' of theological truth are mutually logically dependent, of course, there will never be a case where the latter of these has any practical purchase. Allowing for the possibility that this 'mutual dependency thesis' is false, we might imagine that (for example) we can regard the truth of claims about the theological significance of animal suffering as of secondary importance with respect to investigation of the truth of the *filioque* statement in the creed. Yet this 'with respect to' is obviously no signal that we can regard the duty to investigate the claims of the significance of animal suffering as of secondary importance in itself. If questions of human sexual existence are theologically secondary matters with respect to *some* questions which might be asked, this does not make them unimportant, or their resolution necessarily non-urgent, or their truth or falsity any the less true or false.

Principles

I have very little to say on this section. The words 'made new' (s. I. l. 5) might be spelt out, for all that this may be unwelcome to the authors. The precise meaning of these words may be theologically controversial, but the significance which they (and their interpretation) bear for discussions of human sexual existence is obvious. The issue is the distinction between *redemption* on the one hand and something which might be termed *recreation* on the other.

Application I

'. . . there are human beings, male and female, called to a redeemed humanity in Christ' (para. 1, l. 13) This assertion apparently serves to write 'male' and 'female' into human being at the deepest ontological level. This may create difficulty for some readers, even when correctly understood, but my initial purpose here is rather to draw attention to possible misunderstanding, based around a misreading of sex as gender. What 'male and female' means here *has to be disclosed in Christ*, so that even about the appropriation and comprehending of the categories of male and female we can be mistaken. There is 'a complex variety of forms of alienation' which threaten us even in receiving the nature and significance of such an apparently obvious thing as the truth of our existence as 'male and female'.

Paragraph 2 reflects upon varying forms of relative passivity and the necessity of patience. Its theology of baptism might well be thought through a little more. I'm not sure if all of the authors are Anglican (some certainly are), but perhaps the question of who exactly is being thought of when the words '*consciously* undertaken in baptism' (l. 4; emphasis mine) are used might be raised! The context of discussion here ('part of *every* Christian's life') makes this suggestive of a somewhat surprising baptismal theology. Perhaps 'consciously' could be dropped without too much damage to the authors' intentions.

This paragraph raises a range of questions about the precise location of the self after the resurrection of Christ. The self which is spoken of here as denying itself, and also the criteria by which we judge whether our 'struggle' has been 'successful at every point', are relativised by precisely those truths which the principles of the previous page sought to make explicit. It is not entirely clear what might usefully be added at this point. Perhaps simply that this paragraph seems to invite deep reflection upon the relationship of self and Christ if one is to permit the precise understanding of the authors to be made clear. What exactly was the significance of the word 'alienation' in the previous paragraph? Should one ask 'alienation from *what*?', or 'from *whom*?' The 'truth' of who I am – the deepest ontologically significant facts about me – are, even when I have the right words to indicate them, matters from which I am apparently at least in some measure epistemically distanced. I do not know what these facts mean, precisely, nor do I fully understand their implications. The phrase 'self-denial' should serve, even once the word 'consciously' is dropped because of its unhappy association with baptism, as an indication that the authors mean by 'self' here the self alienated from 'a character . . . like Christ's'; and if this character has indeed the character of a promise we might even be so bold as to speak of an epistemological alienation from the truth of the self. Or do the authors imagine the 'deepest ontological level' to be open to flux and change through the process of formation of Christlike character?

Application II

Paragraph 1: it might be asked, in the light of the final paragraph of Application I, why the 'interpretation of homosexual emotion and behaviour is a Christian "task" ' at all. Perhaps, though, all that is intended is that the interpretation of homosexual emotion and behaviour is a task which under present circumstances Christians might reasonably be expected to address.

Two avenues guiding interpretation are opened up: openness to empirical observation, and governance by apostolic testimony. These are dealt with in order, after a preliminary reminder of the context within which 'the phenomena of homosexual behaviour' are treated by the biblical writers. I have no complaint with the presentation of this context, which appears entirely correct: the area which is likely to provoke comment is the ascription of the word 'homosexual' to such 'behaviour' (as in, "homosexual acts' and so forth). There is, of course, a legitimate (and usually badly mishandled) discussion regarding what is actually meant by the relevant vocabulary in the New Testament epistles. Briefly, one may approach the matter of 'homosexual behaviour' as referring to a particular range of actions characterised entirely 'externally' by an account of the physical happenings as 'empirically observed'. Or one may seek to interpret these happenings by engaging them with their logic in the subjective life of the individual, and seek to comprehend their relevance accordingly. Given that nothing which is likely to count as an action with any relevance to our present discussion could be characterised without loss entirely externally, and that the charge of idolatry appears to imply some connection with a (perhaps merely negative) internal logic or significance, the 'either – or' may not be as sharply focused as all that, but more might be and needs to be said at this point to elaborate what of the variety of interpretations of these passages is being accepted and what rejected. (By 'merely negative' I intend to include the possibility that a critique of certain actions might focus on what they fail to evidence, as much as on their positive elevation of false deities.)

Paragraph 2: this constitutes a reflection on the nature of being 'open to empirical investigation'. The warning concerning belief in a 'transparent and necessary progress of thought' is obviously appropriate, and is well-founded here, though sadly it might be heard as no more than a fashionable conviction. The authors hold that the criteria for discrimination of the competing voices seeking to direct empirical investigation belong primarily 'to the understanding of human nature and its redemption that the Gospel proclaims.' I am not entirely clear how the authors would wish to spell out (if indeed they imagine that it can be spelt out in general terms) how the interaction of theological commitment and empirical investigation under the guidance of scientific or quasi-scientific theory is to be achieved, or what is to be achieved by it. It appears that the Gospel is viewed as operating as a kind of ideal 'closure principle' which may both *rule things out*, discerning certain forms of life outside the bounds of redeemed humanity, and *rule in*, by criticising any too-restrictive interpretation of the limits of good human living. It would be good to know whether this *is* what is intended, and if it is, how it may operate in practice.

Paragraph 3: by the careful way in which it is phrased, this raises again the issue of self-understanding and self-designation, and therefore once again the question of the defining of self. See comments at the end of Application I above. Two other matters are raised, the practical question of the limits of that which 'the church' can 'confer legitimacy upon', and the question of conscientious dissent.

In my own discussions with those who have read it, it is the first of these that has actually appeared to be the most arresting element of the whole Statement, so it will be worth seeking some degree of clarity from the authors on this point. What exactly are the 'alternatives'? It might be claimed with some justification that the alternative of 'singleness' is not really regarded as a vocation as such in Scripture, or at the very least that there are two senses of 'vocation' being played out here, only one of which can be at issue. (I restrict my attention to Scripture not least because this is the apparent ground for justification recognised in the Statement itself.) There is an important distinction between the 'vocation' to be human in the light of the resurrection of Christ, a vocation which may indeed constrain us to live within a patterning or ordering of human life in some way for which a general (but, be it noted, not at all 'vague') set of parameters are given within which some particular course will need to be mapped out, and the more specific *vocation to* . . . which constitutes the particular calling of each of us within these parameters. 'Singleness' cannot be a determinate vocation in this latter sense, because it is common both to the celibate for whom singleness is a genuine vocation or 'form', and to the person who has not yet acknowledged – has not yet been required by the Lord to acknowledge as his or her own – the 'form' of marriage or the 'form' of celibacy.

Does it matter that we get this right? I suspect that in the context of discussing homosexuality it probably does, if only because of the importance of the theme of celibacy in current debates. Such issues as whether celibacy can be commanded or required have surfaced, albeit in ways which often betray serious misunderstanding of the context within which they are asked. A proper 'placing' of the respective language of vocation appropriate to singleness and to celibacy would be helpful.

Even once this is resolved, it remains to be asked whether the two 'alternatives' (of marriage, and of celibacy/singleness) are correctly understood. What is it, for example, to understand marriage rightly in the context of redeemed humanity in Christ? It may well be that this question is one deliberately left open by the authors, and one which is offered as a ground on which work towards further clarification can proceed. Yet obviously for the Statement to achieve the sought-for agreement, some parameters are required and must be supplied. Is it appropriate, for example, for a reader to feel that he or she is remaining open to the possibility of common dialogue with the authors of the Statement on the basis of a belief in (say) polygamy, or a legitimate extension of the concept of marriage to include same-sex marriage partnerships?

It is for such reasons that the phrase '[t]here is no place for the church to confer legitimacy upon alternatives to these' is properly problematic with respect to its interpretation. (There is a sense in which it is *unproblematic* with respect to its interpretation, namely the assumption that the Church is not entitled to expand the range of legitimate forms of life in the area of human sexual existence beyond those sanctioned by 'apostolic testimony'. The interpretation is unproblematic, and many readers will simply suggest that under this interpretation it is false, placing a restriction on God's freedom in regard to creation and revelation. The authors are, one supposes, operating with a belief that God has deliberately engaged in a strategy of self-limitation with regard to the disclosure of new legitimate forms of life; or, rather, that God has engaged in a fecund strategy of complete revelation of all legitimate forms of life within the confines of a certain revelatory context, namely that of 'apostolic testimony'.) The problem in interpreting the phrase in question concerns the boundary conditions for what is to count as an 'alternative' when the norm against which alternatives are being measured is itself under-characterised. In short, how are we to work with such a criterion in practice?

Leading in to the second major issue, that of conscientious dissent, we note especially the phrase 'no place for the church to confer legitimacy'. The word to note is *confer*. What picture are the authors working with here? The 'norms' of marriage and 'singleness' (however the latter is intended) are not norms *because* the Church 'confers' them. Presumably the point is that there is no possibility for any body (not even the Church, the body to whom the Statement is addressed) to confer legitimacy on alternatives which lie outside the bounds of apostolic testimony for human sexual existence, and maybe for other areas of life too.

This issue of 'conferral' is presumably of relevance because of the legislative relationship which ecclesial authority may exercise over the life of its ministers. If this is the pattern of thought, the language is carefully chosen as directed towards the question of clerical sexual discipline. And as, surely, the clergy do have 'a particular commission to expound and exemplify the teachings of the church', the expectation that they will conform to this teaching is a perfectly proper one. Dissent from this may well focus on the extent to which conscientious disagreement by a Christian minister may be 'in the name of the Church', and may therefore even issue in practices contrary to Church teaching on precisely the basis of living a life more properly authentic to 'church teaching'.

In any event, it is correct to recognise this matter as a debate at least intelligibly distinguishable from the issue of lay people 'who seriously intend discipleship in fellowship with the body of the church' but who 'conscientiously dissent from the biblical teaching as the church understands it'. The Statement stops short of saying anything at this point about the issue of how far any person may 'seriously intend discipleship' and yet 'conscientiously dissent from the biblical teaching as the church understands it'. The willingness to accept that a person may belong to both of these categories simultaneously may constitute an acknowledgement of a particular stage on the way to fullness of Christian discipleship, a phase in the individual's spiritual growth. It may also, however, constitute a recognition of one way in which reform of understanding may be offered to a Church currently lacking in right understanding. Perhaps the authors hold either of these to be potentially valid in particular cases. They do not say this, though, and request their readers to infer nothing from what is not said (Introduction, para. 3).

As a footnote to these reflections we might reflect upon the basis of the distinction between clerical and lay discipline in such areas as homosexual relationships. One useful tool here will be to apply the distinction (common to many Christian denominations) between 'order' and 'ministry'. (The Statement uses the word 'clergy'.) Now, the ordination services make it clear that certain ministries are properly associated with ordination, so that when the Statement says that 'clergy . . . have a particular commission to expound and exemplify the teachings of the church', the authors can affect disinterest in the 'ministry or order' question.

However, many Christians who are not formally ordained are none the less exercising ministries which, though not formally *characteristic* of lay Christians, are perfectly proper tasks for them. Some of these tasks are explicitly recognised and validated (the status of 'reader' or lay preacher). Some are recognised by the explicit statement in the Canons of the Church of England that a person may be 'ordained to' such a task, that is, may 'serve his or her title' in such a post. Examples are a tutorial fellowship in an Oxford or Cambridge university college, or a lectureship in a theological college. In the light of this, we might ask whether the logic of 'special considerations' can be articulated more fully. It may be that the authors of the Statement will point to the word 'commission' as crucial, though the commission to order is, of course, explicitly regarded by the Church of England as something to be *discerned* rather than simply *conferred*.

It should be added that the authors develop their approval of 'arguing that special considerations affect the behaviour of the clergy' only within the context of an affirmation that 'this teaching [that is biblical teaching as the church understands it] applies to all'. What matters more, then, than the precise interpretation of the basis and significance of any 'special considerations', is the extent to which Church teaching can be properly challenged by dissenting behaviour.

Application III

Here again there is an interesting duality in the 'vocations' of marriage and singleness, which invites some clarification (see comments on celibacy and singleness above).

Paragraph 1: this is a very welcome paragraph which affirms the meaning of individual life in community, and thus properly relativises the private agendas of sexual fulfilment which often appear behind contributions to theological debate over human sexuality.

Paragraph 2: this expands somewhat the understanding of legitimate forms of sexual life discussed at Application II, paragraph 3. It appears that these forms are properly *permissive*, in that they set the bounds within which human (including sexual) character and conduct may develop and flourish. The conception of freedom and exploration is a significant one. It needs to be held alongside an adequate conception of human dependence on God and his creative and redemptive will for humanity, which is precisely what the authors, by placing their reflections on this theme at the *end* of their presentation, have done. Detached from this context, and losing the primary sense of the necessity of 'obedience' to the forms of life offered as properly human, the vocabulary of freedom and exploration can too readily become incitements to inhumanity.

It might be worth noting the use of the word 'friendship' in this section and in discussions of sexuality more generally. The authors speak of marriage and singleness as 'in their different ways' (a phrase used in each paragraph) contributing to human existence, first of all in pointing forward to the 'fulfilment' of all creation in Christ; and secondly to 'the blessing of human friendship'. There is a danger of misunderstanding here. The insistence on the words 'in their different ways' might imply that the authors are aware of this, and certainly there is insufficient content in these paragraphs to be clear what their line would be on the precise nature of any distinction which may be drawn.

It appears that there are two vocabularies at stake, that of 'friendship' and that of sexual states (that is, under the criteria for legitimacy adopted in the Statement, of singleness and marriage), and there is a long tradition (Christian and pre-Christian) of regarding marriage in particular as a special kind or particular species of what is commonly translated as 'friendship'. It is obviously the case that the current everyday English use of words like 'friend' and 'friendship' map pretty badly on to marriage. This may betoken a certain impoverishment in our contemporary understanding of the 'grammar' of friendship, of course. Yet the species-of-friendship' view may also have its impoverishing potentiality for the understanding of marriage. There is no absurdity, nor is there any humour, in the phrase (I quote from a recent magazine article in which a man discusses his relationship with his ex-wife) 'and after a while it was fine again; we sort of downgraded to friendship'. One might question this use of language, too, because 'downgraded' might already beg the question of whether marriage is on a kind of 'common scale' with friendship.

One suggestion which may help to resolve our thinking about these matters along the right lines is an encouragement to look with more astonishment than we ordinarily do on the character of marriage as taught in Christian Scripture and tradition. In marriage we see the possibility of a God-ordained pattern of human relating which is *voluntarily* and *irrevocably* submitted to, where the irrevocability stems from the character of the relationship which is bestowed upon the couple. This raises, of course, a variety of practical limitations on the two people as 'individuals' if the marriage is to have any effect upon them. I take it that this is what Paul has in mind when he expresses concern that marriage imposes a variety of obligations, obligations which make those who are married less freely available for 'the things of the Lord' (1 Cor. 7:32–4) than those who are not. It is not, we may note, the welfare of children, or even especially the care for one's husband or wife when ill, that he seems to be concerned with!

These practical limitations stem from the very nature of each marriage as a self-giving of each person to the other. What can we learn from this about the theological evaluation of the 'quality' of relationships other than marriage which might be called friendships? First of all, that friendship would be subject to all the same concerns about availability for 'the things of the Lord' if it, too, imposed the same quality of duties and responsibilities of care and concern which marriage does. This is not intended as a first step towards denial of the good in human friendship, an extreme relativising of friendship by the demands of God. Friendship is not something which exists *alongside* Christian being, as a hobby might exist alongside a profession; Christ, as the Statement reminds us, calls us his friends. And a relationship which simply takes pleasure in another person when it is convenient to do so, without any form or sense of duty or commitment to that person, is not good friendship. *Good* friendship obviously and thankfully has a commitment which does transcend the more fleeting emotions of transitory liking and disliking, and carries on in its commitment to the other person through differences and disagreements about ecclesiology or music or football.

We are, of course, surely called to enjoy our friendships, and to discover our humanity in and through them. What seems much less clear is whether we can regard friendships as offering the possibility of a quality or a kind of commitment of self which is significantly equivalent to marriage. It is entirely intelligible that friends might wish to mark a bond of permanent commitment to each other, might seek to covenant with each other in friendship, which may in Christian hope be extended beyond the grave. In response to such an impulse a couple of remarks may be offered. The first is that between Christians no deeper and more permanent mark of relationship can be given than the status of *brothers* and *sisters*. This is a status which moves us beyond the affective bonds, of whatever depth, which 'friendship' may conjure up, and forces a realisation that the relationship is *given* rather than *chosen*. The second is that whilst there might be no divergence between my desire to commit my energies to the delights of relationship with friends, or to the meeting of their needs, on the one side, and my primary duty of service to God on the other, it is certainly possible that these may diverge. To promise my time and my energies, whether specifically or in open-ended ways, beyond what I may later be freely available to offer in the Lord, is to promise too much.

This is not at all to say that we should hold our friendships lightly (which would be a likely outcome of seeing them as an aside from Christian vocation). It may be in these very contexts of relationship that Godly service can be offered, and that we may find some practical experience of the joy of Christ. We must guard against infecting our friendships with a similar sad absurdity to that which has replaced marriage with cohabitation, where for fear of being hurt commitment is refused, and thereby the relationship is robbed of the very potential which may have been sought in it. Yet marriages, in so far as they display a particular character of open-ended self-giving, do so with the horizon of that self-giving firmly rooted in this world. Marriage *qua* marriage is until death. Christian friendship is friendship already experienced *beyond* death, and can thus hold less tightly to any pathological necessity to be in the constant company of friends, or to be the immediate source of practical provision for them. Baptism is amongst many other things a permanent covenant of friendship with Christ and with all Christian people, an opportunity to demonstrate to those outside the Church what friendship can really be. Marriage has this capacity too, but the manner in which it does so, its consenting closure of the couple from relatively free availability to Godly service until death, makes it importantly distinct. To speak of marriage and of other forms of human relating as species of some overarching concept, and then to label it 'friendship', is to expect a great deal from those accustomed to hear the word in its common contemporary usage. Even were they to begin to grasp the point, there would still be a significant potential for them to be misled.

It is, I suppose, possible that this would be the kind of spelling out which the authors might give to their phrase 'in their different ways'. It constitutes a relativising of the good of marriage, making it utterly 'of this world', albeit carrying a special vocation in this world which points beyond it to the relationship of Christ and his Church. This relativising may be picked up in Paul's remarks in 1 Corinthians (see especially 1 Cor. 7:29–31); it may also be noted in the Gospels (as at Luke 14:20, 26). Perhaps by understanding the special character and horizon of the marriage relationship more fully we might be enabled to distinguish sexual affection more clearly from other aspects of human affection than is common, and to understand what constitutes right order and what disorder in our affections. At that point we may also be able the more fully to distinguish between what is ultimately, and what only penultimately, significant in our human relating.

9

Divine Order and Sexual Conduct

Simon Vibert

IT IS WELCOME that in responding to the call for clarification in the emotive issue of homosexuality the authors of the St Andrew's Day Statement have produced a document which is theological rather than expository/exegetical in style. Undoubtedly the authors would not deny that there is work to be done in the area of hermeneutics. The challenge of Michael Vasey in his *Strangers and Friends* that the '7 knock down arguments' (consisting of the biblical texts: Lev. 18:22; 20:13; Deut. 23:17–18; Rom. 1:18–32; 1 Cor. 6:9–10; 1 Tim. 1:8–11; Jude 7) do not help the modern debate about homosexuality needs to be addressed.[1] However, the outcome of the debate on human sexuality in general, and homosexuality in particular, is not only dependent on the interpretation of seven Bible passages. Although a clear case against same-sex sexual relationships can be inferred from them, my point is that even if these texts were removed, the theological panorama of the biblical teaching on God, humankind and the created order consistently affirm our deductions from apparently isolated texts.[2]

Nevertheless, there are broader brushstrokes on the canvas. The credal style of this statement makes up the background, with the horizons and landscape clearly marked. This theological foundation stimulates further exegetical precision as well as itself being the outcome of careful exegesis. The individual texts in the foreground of much of the modern debate have this two-way relationship, of both challenging and confirming the received theological wisdom and putting detail in the overall theological picture.

The St Andrew's Day Statement is set in a credal genre not unlike the historic doctrinal creeds of the third and fourth century. It would also be fair to say that, like those creeds, the Statement is not accessible to a popular audience without an appreciation of the history of the debates surrounding their publication. It may be that the Statement will be helpful as a touchstone of orthodoxy, but it is largely inaccessible to the majority of people whose theological education is reduced to evangelical soundbites. Some of the words used in the statement are loaded with contemporary significance and need 'unpacking' – 'alienation', 'quasi-marital relationships', 'conscientious dissent from biblical teaching'. For example, while it is helpful to allude to scientific debates and different interpretations concerning the intended audience Paul has in mind (in Rom. 1:26–7), or precise terms of the nature of the challenge to the Church, without a detailed knowledge of the current state of the debate, those allusions will be lost on most readers.

The three theological principles which the Statement builds on are: (i) the life and death of Jesus Christ; (ii) the work of the Holy Spirit in applying the work of Christ and fostering a life of holiness; (iii) the final hope of recreation in Christ (see next section). These three themes can in fact be reduced to one: Jesus Christ through his incarnation, his Spirit and future coming and consummation, is the central theological focus of Christian ethics. He is the Word made flesh, revealer of the Father. Through his death and resurrection new life is made available to all who are adopted into his family. His work is continued through his Holy Spirit who guides our understanding and through Scripture brings about encouragement towards holiness, which is Christlikeness. The eschatological fulfilment of Christ's work will be when broken creation is restored and renewed at the end of time. This Christocentric summary is helpful. In its ethical discussion the Church needs to affirm the centrality of Christ's work begun in the incarnation and his atoning death, and awaiting consummation at his return.[3] The working party should be congratulated in succinctly outlining Christ-based ethics. As most writers know, it is far harder to be brief than verbose!

However, if we are to build a working framework around 'fundamental agreements', is this theological foundation sufficient? Is enough said about the natural order? Can it be assumed that people have any conception of 'our created intention'? Do people have an awareness of the effect of the fall upon our inter-personal relationships, our understanding of God, or our ability to think clearly? Can we assume that people recognise in Christ the humanity they long for, and yet at the same time find repulsive?

On p. 8 the Statement refers to the Church's task of interpreting scientific discoveries. The scientific community needs to be reminded that ethical behaviour is not determined genetically. To that extent, as we shall explore further in a moment, even to talk about orientation can be misleading. The definition of modern homosexuality has more recently turned on the sociological phenomena of the modern 'gay movement'. The consequences of this have been that the rights of the gay community and issues of justice have overshadowed ethical discussions. However, the Church's task of interpreting the times involves bringing biblical theology to bear on our understanding of humanity and God himself. For these reasons we believe the Statement spends too little time speaking about creation.

God and Creation

The authors do well to remind us that the fallen mind is darkened and subverts the truth about God and creation: by nature we suppress the truth rather than welcome it. (The meaning of *katechein*, Rom. 1:18, is that whenever truth is presented to the human mind our natural instinct is to want to stifle and snuff it out rather than welcome it.) We turn to Scripture to interpret and understand who we are and what is expected of us by our creator. Without the light of Scripture we will not even begin with the same basic understandings about how this world works and the place of humanity within it. Returning to our analogy of the painted landscape, whether we even notice the horizon or background is in fact determined by what may appear in the foreground.

In one sense there is no greater theme in the Bible than that of idolatry, the worshipping of the false, the no-god, the self. The problem of false worship is frequently the context of Paul's ethical discussion of homosexuality (Rom. 1:18 ff.; 1 Cor. 6:8 ff.). This may not be narrowed down to an issue of cultic prostitution in the context of pagan worship. For Paul, idolatry is the turning upside down of the created order. It is the substituting of creation over the creator. In other words idolatry is bigger than wrong thinking about God, it has to do with the misuse and abuse of creation.

It is in this broader creation context that the biblical condemnation of homosexuality takes place. There are sinful acts which are said to be against nature. Surely these are not against *human* nature (i.e. the perceived sexual 'orientation') but our created nature? In other words the debate does not surround the displays of the pervert (as opposed to the invert) involved in pagan false worship. Such a distinction is ultimately irrelevant. Rather the acts are sinful because they go against the way in which we are created. This is amplified further in 1 Corinthians 6. Paul speaks of two types of homosexual partners: male prostitutes (*malakoi*) meaning, 'Soft/effeminate', thought to be the passive partner in a homosexual relationship; and 'homosexual offenders' (*arsenokoitai*), literally 'male + intercourse', thought to refer to the active partner in the relationship.[4] Paul is clear: all such behaviour is contrary to nature. However, since coming to Christ (being washed, sanctified and justified) their former lifestyle has been repented of and change is the evidence that something real has happened. Verse 11 makes plain that it is their conduct which now marks them out as being different. Later in this letter Paul outlines the created distinctions between men and women (ch. 11) from which he deduces that within the created order complementarity, co-equality and authority coexist.

The important point I infer from this Pauline teaching is that created distinctions remain the basis upon which Paul builds his ethical teaching. This basis needs to be restated and not assumed. In the context of the homosexuality debate this most obviously resonates with the need to define who we are. It seems rather weak of the statement to dignify the difficulties of individual circumstances when the Bible seems to make no concession for the degree of temptation felt (1 Cor. 10:13). In what way is it fair to judge 'individual cases differently' (p. 9)? Are we defined by our circumstances? Our genes? Our 'orientation'?

Defining 'Personhood'

The Statement raises the important question of how to define human reality. Who are we as people? 'In him we know both God and human nature as they truly are' (p. 7). Indeed the authors are right to affirm that we are not to be defined by our feelings, social grouping, or filial relationships. 'Our sexual affections can no more define who we are than can our class, race or nationality' (p. 7).

Human reality is found 'in Christ' (p. 7). It is true to say that Christ exemplified human perfection as well as full divinity. 'He is the image of the invisible God' (Col. 1:15), unlike the imperfect image found in fallen humanity. To be sure if we want to see what it is like to be human we look at the man Christ Jesus. The process of change in the life of a new believer is that of being transformed into his likeness and being renewed in his image (2 Cor. 4:1–18; Rom. 12:2). In our glorified state we will continue to be 'in Christ', because only through him is broken creation restored (p. 7).

However, is it sufficient to define human reality solely in terms of the reality we find in Christ? Does the Bible not also teach human reality in creation? The Statement makes many references to the restoration of broken creation, its fulfilment, its redemption of creation and its richness (pp. 7, 10). But it seems to assume that the original intent and perfection of created humanity, and the effect of its subsequent fall, is either part of the existing knowledge of the reader or irrelevant.

The Bible recognises human reality in Adam and Eve

If we look at the paradigm of how God relates to men and women, we see that the Bible unashamedly uses the marriage model, traced right through Scripture. Yes, it would be simplistic and culturally blinkered to see Adam and Eve as being a model for the isolated nuclear family. However, Genesis 1 and 2 are foundational in terms of what they say about divinely created models of how God relates to his people (see Hosea, Revelation 22, etc. as examples). Moreover, these Genesis passages are quoted by Jesus speaking to Jews in the Gospels and Paul speaking to Gentiles in Ephesians with no attempt to retranslate into the very different Jew/Gentile social settings. In other words, it is heterosexual monogamy which is set up as the model, not nuclear family life.

Adam and Eve are said to be made in the image and likeness of God (Genesis 1:26–7). It is important to appreciate that the image refers to the man and the woman jointly. The context implies that to be made in the image of God includes at least further multiplication of the image of God throughout the world through procreation, and domination of the world as vice-regents under God. It would be unfair to infer that procreation is the only aspect of the image of God. Indeed Genesis 2:24 implies that the union of man and woman in marriage is primarily a social, rather than a sexual one. Woman is given to man for companionship and friendship, such intimacy within marriage is part of the created intention of human beings. The implication is that man and woman together corporately image God.[5]

The Bible recognises human reality as continuing post-Genesis 3

How are we to define the kind of relationship with God into which every human being is born? All Christians would agree that we are not born *tabula rasa*. The doctrine of total depravity is sometimes misunderstood. Human beings are not all as bad as we could possibly be; degrees of wickedness are manifested in our society.

Perhaps it is too obvious to state that there is no part of humanity that is untainted by the fall. The pronouncement of God's curse upon the rebellious couple in the garden affected procreation and the relationship between the sexes (Gen. 3:16); it affected human fruitfulness and enjoyment of all the created order (3:17 ff.); and it created a distance between God and his people (3:24).

However, despite the severity and pervasiveness of God's judgment, human beings remain in relationship with God. It is a mistake to assume that we only come into relationship with God through new birth (e.g. John 3:1 ff.), although clearly the doctrine of the new birth is foundational. It is consistent with the analogies of Scripture to talk about a relationship of either obedience or disobedience.[6] The prodigal did not cease to be his father's child even though he had taken his inheritance, brought the family name into disrepute and actively distanced himself from his father's household. The implication behind the word *metanoia* (repent) is that a change of direction and change of mind (indeed a radical change) is needed if we are to see the kingdom of God.[7]

It seems to me that the St Andrew's Day Statement needs to spell out the implications of this continuing relationship with the Father. For even a hostile relationship affects the way in which all other relationships are to take place. If we are to concede that the only true definition of personhood is 'redeemed humanity in Christ', what can we say about those who are not 'in Christ'? Surely they are manifesting *human* behaviour? If they are in hostile relationship with their Father, how might this understanding help us appreciate the way in which human sexuality is expressed? We remain, to a greater or lesser extent, God's image in this world.

Indeed the teaching elsewhere in the Bible is both positive and negative about the whole of creation's witness. 'The heavens declare the glory of God' affirms the psalmist (Ps. 19:1). Paul also says: 'Since the creation of the world God's invisible qualities . . . have been clearly seen, being understood from what has been made . . .' (Rom. 1:20). We may infer that the Bible assumes that, though the witness of creation is to some extent stifled, nevertheless it continues its eloquence in declaring God's glory. The manifestation of the revelation of God began at creation and has continued *since* creation, including the present! In much the same way, even fallen humanity continues to image God. Alec Motyer argues that the composite picture which makes up human beings in the image of God includes physical, matrimonial, governmental, spiritual, moral and rational attributes.[8]

Christ is the 'image of the invisible God' (Col. 1:15). He perfectly mirrors God. He is the second Adam. The St Andrew's Day Statement is right to point to his perfect humanity as the prototype of what our lowly bodies will become as we are renewed in his image.

But it is also clear that the image of God remains, even in fallen humanity. The Christian apologetic task will include encouraging people to recognise the dignity with which human beings are born, calling upon them to understand their present relationship with their creator, and recognising the future restoration of creation (Principle III).[9] Paul says that God calls men and women to account on the basis first of the witness of creation; second from the voice of conscience; and third, to those with Judaeo-Christian privileges, from the teaching of Scripture (see Rom. 1–3).

The Deepest Ontological Level?

'At the deepest ontological level . . . there is no such thing as "a" homosexual or "a" heterosexual; there are human beings, male and female, called to redeemed humanity in Christ . . .' (p. 7). Let us consider this statement as a biblical approach to defining 'personhood'. In Christ we meet perfect humanity; and in Christ we will be made fully human once his work is complete. To this extent the Statement's denial of any other ground for our identity is well put.

Such a definition of humanity has important implications. Neither the homosexual nor the heterosexual may define their identity (or 'orientation') on the basis of genetics, culture or socialisation. The current trend is to assume that a person's sexual 'orientation' is something which they either have no control over (denying any influence from 'nurture'); or to assume a necessary right to express that 'orientation' (on the grounds of 'nature'). This suggests that human ethical conduct is determined by factors beyond our control. We believe that this rests very uneasily with the biblical teaching. We are not convinced that the Bible writers would put any weight behind the current debates over sexual 'orientation'.

The difficulty with using the phrase 'at the deepest ontological level there is no such thing as "a" homosexual' is determining what exactly is meant, and whether those whom we would hope to persuade will be disposed to grapple with it and to understand it. If we are to sustain such a radical definition of personhood it needs to take into account our created nature, as well as our redeemed nature in Christ. 'At the deepest ontological level' we are, first, human beings created in the image of God. Secondly, we are marred by the fall; and thirdly, we are a new creation in Christ (2 Cor. 5:17).

If the Church is going to win this apologetical argument then we have to offer some hope of understanding this present complexity in addition to presenting the goal of perfect humanity in Christ in the future. To be sure, the creation waits in expectation for future consummation (Rom. 8:19); is presently subjected to frustration (v. 20); and indeed the whole creation groans in anticipation (v. 22). Despite that frustration the Bible does call for dogged discipline in participation with the sanctifying work of the Holy Spirit – both to live up to our created potential and anticipate our future glory. Hence whenever there is a focus upon future consummation, the injunction is also given that we live in the light of that day. So 'putting off the old self' and 'putting on the new self' is described both as 'being renewed in the image of the creator', and as the abolition of all human distinctions – Greek/Jew, circumcised/uncircumcised, barbarian, Scythian, slave or free (and surely one would want to include sexual 'orientation' in this list?) – for Christ is all and is in all (Col. 3:9–11).

In a nutshell, our identity at the deepest ontological level is *given* in both creation and Christ. The implications for our ethical conduct are great. We appeal to (created) human nature as well as redeemed human nature in Christ. We appeal to the world around us to recognise the damaging effect of ignoring biblical standards. General revelation dictates a degree of awareness of the wisdom of creation standards. So, we appeal: homosexual practice is wrong – not just because it offends God, but because it is damaging psychologically, physically and socially. Psychologically, homosexuality is not a journey into 'wholeness'; physically, human beings do not procreate through same-sex sexual relationships; and anal intercourse can result in life-threatening diseases; and socially, despite protestations to the contrary, homosexual practice contributes to the undermining of the moral and ethical foundation of the society.

To what kind of lifestyle does the Bible call people? What does it mean to live as those who are 'called to follow in the way of the cross'? The life of self-denial and discipline spelt out on p. 7 badly needs to be heard in contemporary Christian circles. What does the Bible say about the 'single' person (see p. 9)? Or indeed the person struggling with sexual temptation?

Church is family

The statement reaffirms the two vocations traditionally recognised within the Church: fidelity within marriage; chastity without. Are these vocations described here as 'singleness' and 'marriage' (p. 9)? It may seem like splitting semantic hairs but in fact the Bible does not use the word 'single' in the way we do. Christians sometimes wrestle with the question of whether they can call their 'singleness' a 'vocation'. When do they cross over from expecting marriage in the future to believing themselves 'called to singleness'? Perhaps this is the reason why the Bible uses the term 'unmarried'. The word 'unmarried' appears in 1 Corinthians 7:8 ff.; in 7:34 Paul appears to be distinguishing between two groups of people, the 'unmarried' (*agamos*) and the 'virgin' (*parthenos*).[10] It may be that Paul saw one state of singleness as being voluntary, the other as involuntary. In the context of the argument in 1 Corinthians 7 Paul sees a distinction between celibacy and a spurious asceticism which neglected responsibilities within marriage. Barrett comments 'we might take *virgin* in the ordinary sense, to denote a woman unmarried and without other sexual experience, and *unmarried* to mean a woman . . . who had renounced marriage'. Given the difficulties with the passage, he qualifies this statement with a caution: 'But this is guesswork; evidence cannot be cited to prove this meaning of *unmarried* (*agamos*).'[11]

If there is some uncertainty as to how a Christian in Corinth could discern whether God was 'calling' them to celibacy, the same could be said to be true for the experience of modern Christians. People do not readily use Paul's vocational language to describe inter-personal relationships. The Bible implies that the unmarried person is no 'island', but remains in relationship with the family until, or if, he or she gets married.[12] Such was the Ancient Near East's understanding of the bonds that unite what we would call 'extended families' that the 'single' person remains intimately related to that family. This has many implications in our fragmented social environment in which families are more often than not separate geographically and socially. Paul sees the principles of headship and household applying in two particular ways in the New Testament: the household of God (the Church), and the household itself (the family).[13] Regaining a sense of corporate solidarity would help this process. It has to be stressed that, however poorly many churches may exemplify this, there is a wider family to which every believer is called to become a full member.

Unmarried does not mean unfulfilled

The Statement has some positive things to say about the value of human friendship. The Church has to say to those whose desires for sexual relationships with members of both the same and opposite sexes are very strong that there is more to the Christian life than abstinence from certain conduct. 'The primary pastoral task of the church in relation to all its members, whatever their self-understanding and mode of life, is to reaffirm the good news of salvation in Christ, forgiveness of sins, transformation of life and incorporation into the holy fellowship of the church' (p. 8). Indeed in Christ we do have exemplified healthy same-sex and opposite-sex, non-erotic friendships. It is helpful to remind ourselves that not every desire may be reasonably fulfilled, whether as unmarried or married people. Both paths call for discipline and self-denial.

A Radical Agenda

My hope in this chapter has been to affirm the Statement and encourage the authors to continue along the helpful path which they have begun. The definition of our ethical conduct must arise out of the model found in Christ and his life-transforming work still being continued. Our quibble, if anything, is that they need to be more radical.

First we would hope that the people of God can begin to explain the biblical perspective on this world. We have answers to many of the important issues of life. Why did God make this world? What may we expect of people made in his image? What effect has the fall had upon our ability to mirror God, and know God? What may we expect from the offer of redemption in Christ, both now and at the end of the age? To the world this sounds radical. This is nothing less than a call to ethical conduct which is normative irrespective of whether people have yet come to agree with our theological presuppositions.

Secondly, the Anglican Church must be more radical. On a couple of occasions the Statement has, in our opinion, been overly charitable to our current state of confusion as a denomination. The Bishops' Statement on Human Sexuality has been interpreted by many as being double standard and endorsing a two-tier ethic.[14] It is a mistake to assume that the pastoral epistles espouse two standards of ethics, one for clergy and the other for lay people. Surely what Paul is calling for is a greater exemplification of the one standard amongst those who are going to lead the flock, not a lower standard for the *laos*?

One of the reasons why the 'Bishop' is called to higher standards is in order that he may model the Christian life. But the other reason is in order that bishops may exercise pastoral discipline. Surely nowhere in the New Testament are they called to 'respect the integrity' of those who dissent in such a way that does not call sinners to repentance and a chaste lifestyle along the lines of 1 Corinthians 6 (p. 9)? The frustration for many evangelicals is that 'respecting the integrity' has come to mean an almost total lack of Church discipline. Robert Runcie, the former Archbishop of Canterbury, has recently admitted that he had knowingly ordained practising homosexuals, and the present Archbishop recently referred to those who protested against the 'celebration' held by the Lesbian and Gay Christian Movement in Southwark Cathedral as a 'pressure group' and 'bullying, loud-mouthed controversialists'.[15] 'Gay' ordinands have testified to introducing their live-in partners at the bishop's palace. If the pastoral care which the statement calls for (pp. 8–9) is to happen then it needs to challenge the attempt to find a conciliatory line which allows mutually exclusive conclusions to be drawn from a statement intended to clarify ethical conduct. Surely the pastorally sensitive will want to speak out about the damaging effect of endorsing unbiblical same-sex sexual relationships? Surely, the Church must take up the prophetic challenge and call people to recognise the damage which is done by ignoring biblical principles? To fail to do this is far from compassionate, it is weak and dishonouring to God.

Thirdly, the challenge for the Church of God is that we live up to our calling in Christ. If we are to be a radical alternative community for those who struggle with their sexual identity, how real is our welcome to them? Are churches 'nuclear family' orientated or 'biblical family' orientated? If we are to offer hope to those who call themselves homosexual, do they find manifested in our Christian communities people whose lives have been changed by Christ? Do they find those who exemplify the grace of God continually at work in their lives, and extend that grace to others?

We still wait for the radical reordering of heaven and earth, and until that moment arrives we are called to live as people hoping for and anticipating the glory of that day. We continue to grapple with the full significance of that day of the Lord's return, and await the future restoration of creation. We look forward to both continuity with this age (Heb. 12:26–7), and yet also try to grasp the changes that will affect the very way in which men and women relate to each other (Matt. 22:30).[16]

The watchword of the Christian Church in this age is 'hope'. By so saying we recognise that we live with creation – fallen creation – until Christ's work is complete, as the apostle Peter affirms (2 Pet. 3:11b–14):

> What kind of people ought you to be? You ought to live holy and godly lives as you look forward to the day of God and speed its coming. That day will bring about the destruction of the heavens by fire, and the elements will melt in the heat. But in keeping with his promise we are looking forward to a new heaven and a new earth, the home of righteousness.
>
> So then, dear friends, since you are looking forward to this, make every effort to be found spotless, blameless and at peace with him.

Notes

1. Michael Vasey, *Strangers and Friends* (Hodder & Stoughton, 1995), pp. 124 ff.
2. See my exegesis of these passages in *Conduct which Honours God? The Question of Homosexuality* (The Fellowship of Word and Spirit, 1995); also *A Different Kind of Circle? A Review of Strangers and Friends.* FWS File 1, 1996.
3. See K. Barth, *The Humanity of God* (Fontana, 1961).

4. See D. F. Wright, 'Homosexuals or Prostitutes: The Meaning of *arsenokoitai* (1 Cor. 6:9; 1 Tim. 1:10)', *Vigilae Christianae*, vol. 38, 1984, pp. 125–53; William K. Peterson, 'Can *arsenokoitai* be translated by "homosexual"? (1 Cor. 6:9; 1 Tim. 1:10)', *Vigilae Christianae*, vol. 40, 1986, pp. 187–91; David F. Wright, 'Translating *arsenokoitai* (1 Cor. 6:9; 1 Tim. 1:10)', *Vigilae Christianae*, vol. 41, 1987, pp. 396–8.

5. It is sometimes objected that we should not make deductions about family life from these two chapters. Adam and Eve are the first family, the first society and the first Church. How can we take principles applied to a theological type and apply this to modern families? The problem with this objection is that the Bible itself, via Jesus and Paul, do just that in the passages mentioned above. The normative nature of what Gen. 1–2 teaches is so significant that it permeates the whole of the biblical corpus.

6. In fact this strand is even there in John 3:18.

7. The Bible teaches both that we are alien from God, needing new birth and adoption into the family of God; and that we are born into a rebellious relationship with our heavenly Father.

8. A. Motyer, *Look to the Rock* (IVP, 1996), pp. 68–74.

9. It is from the creation accounts of Gen. 1–2 that we seek guidance *economically* (i.e in the sense of speaking about our function/role) as well as *ontologically* (i.e concerning our being). 'In Christ' does not imply anything about gender distinctions in humanity.

10. However there are complications with this passage. The word order is inconsistent in the manuscript traditions, which raises the question as to whether the two words are synonyms; whether one modifies the other; or whether Paul is talking about two distinct groups of people. See G. Fee, *The First Epistle to the Corinthians* (Eerdmans, 1991 edn), pp. 334–5 n. 4, for an outline of the main alternatives.

11. C. K. Barrett, *The First Epistle to the Corinthians* (Black's New Testament Commentaries, 2nd edn., 1971), pp. 180–1.

12. J. B. Hurley in *Man and Woman in Biblical Perspective* (IVP, 1981), cites the Babylonian culture *c.* 1775 BC and Assyrian culture 1450–1250 BC as examples of the way in which Israelite family structures and marriage laws emerged (pp. 22 ff.); there are radical differences between these cultures and twentieth-century lifestyles (and indeed some attitudes in later Judaism, from AD 70 onwards). The headship principle which Paul affirms in 1 Cor. 11, must have some resonance with the picture Hurley builds up of ancient Israelite custom:

> Men and women alike grew up in a nation which thought of itself as an extended family, with profound commitments to the 'father's house', which terminology might point to immediate family, the clan or tribe, or even to the nation as a whole. The laws of Israel both presume and inculcate such commitment and ancestry and corporate identify. The consistent identification of individuals by ancestry and by family units reflects the depth to which such thinking had penetrated. A person did not think of him or herself as an individual, but as so-and-so, of the

tribe of so-and-so. Existence was corporate existence. (p. 34)

13. Hence the Overseer is called to demonstrate his 'management' in both his own family and God's Church (1 Tim. 3:1–7).

14. *Issues in Human Sexuality: A Statement by the House of Bishops* (Church House Publishing, 1991), e.g. 5:20–2.

15. The Archbishop of Canterbury's address at Great St Mary's church Cambridge, Sunday 24 November 1996.

16. e.g. what is the significance of Jesus's statement about the transitory nature of marriage? Is Jesus saying that, because in the next life there will be no need of procreation, relationships will be carried on in a less exclusive manner?

10

Truth and Love in Our Sexual Feelings

Martin Hallett

I BELIEVE THE St Andrew's Day Statement is a very important contribution to the homosexuality debate in the Church of England. Perhaps this is one of the most important issues the Church has to face? The implications for ethical teaching are enormous. We have stern reminders in Scripture of the need for the Church to give moral guidance. Strong action seems demanded against those who encourage behaviour which is sinful or against God's ideal (e.g. 1 Cor. 5; Rev. 2:20). This surely puts an awesome responsibility on Christian leaders seeking to find God's ideals in sexual morality, especially in the context of a society where sex simply within marriage seems abnormal. Perhaps modern society is no more sexually immoral than in the past, but the communicating influences are certainly more powerful. A Church longing to relate to God's world will almost inevitably absorb some of its thinking, either directly or indirectly. Some Church leaders react strongly against sexual immorality and see celibacy as the unmarried Christian's choice. Some actively seek deliverance and healing for homosexuality. Others may be tempted to conform by setting less rigid boundaries for sexual behaviour, especially in the context of a loving relationship, hetero or homosexual. I wonder if responses from both the liberals and conservatives are trying to conform to standards in a society which is saying everyone needs sex: the liberals by moving the traditional Christian boundaries of no sex outside marriage, whilst conservatives want to enable us to be married or deny our sexuality.

I am very grateful that the St Andrew's Day Statement makes it clear that sexuality is the issue in the Church, not simply homosexuality. I applaud the encouragement to understand ourselves as human beings with emotional and sexual needs rather than with a 'homo or heterosexual' label.

Are Single Heterosexual Christians More Privileged than Homosexuals?

When I became a Christian, about twenty-four years ago, I was still very much aware of strong emotional and sexual feelings towards some people of the same sex. Many of my Christian friends were aware of this and accepted it. I felt many of my emotional and therefore sexual needs were fulfilled through special relationships with Christian men. The boundaries we set meant no sex, but I did feel able to love and be loved. Many of the single people, especially women, in the Church were unable to experience the same fulfilment. Their emotional and sexual feelings were directed towards the opposite sex, but it was virtually impossible for them to experience any fulfilment of these desires outside marriage. They were unable to know the love and fulfilment with the opposite sex that I experienced with the same sex. Any attempt on their part to do this would usually be seen as a step towards marriage, rather than simply friendship. There were not enough single Christian men around. These women chose to deny themselves a sexual relationship simply because of their Christianity. My choice was for the same reason, but I felt in a 'more fulfilled place' than them, because I was able to love and be loved in a way that they were not. I am encouraged that the Statement does not try to define homosexual behaviour. The same boundaries are there for all unmarrieds. Some are clearly defined – for example, no genital stimulation and orgasm – others depend more on individual situations. However, our human tendency to compromise must be acknowledged before boundaries are set and choices made. I believe, as the Statement implies in part II of the Application, we all express our sexuality, with or without an orgasm. What do we mean by a homosexual relationship, apart from two people of the same sex having an orgasm together? There are other ways in which we express sexuality that are far less easy to define or judge as right or wrong for Christians. For those of us seeking to follow Christ, the calling is to chastity, whether one is married or not.

A Personal Issue for Many Christians

My early Christian experience of openness about my homosexuality is very unusual. In the current Church debate voices expressing a personal interest usually come from those seeking acceptance of their homosexual relationships. Of those disagreeing with this, some openly claim 'healing' from their homosexual struggles. The majority of Christians who do not believe their homosexual desires should be expressed in a sexual relationship are afraid to share this with others. They fear rejection by their brothers and sisters in Christ. This means their viewpoint is usually expressed in the Church debate by heterosexuals. *It may be that Christians with a homosexual orientation, seeking to be celibate for Christ are a silent majority.* This saddens me as a Christian man who felt safe to share his homosexual orientation with other Christians and experienced very little evidence of rejection. This has not been true for everyone. I know of fear and prejudice expressed to other Christians with homosexual feelings and I believe these anger our Lord Jesus and gravely dishonour his body. Having said that, I know many Anglicans (including leaders) with a homosexual orientation, but seeking celibacy, who have said privately they will feel betrayed if the Church of England changes its traditional viewpoint on homosexuality. Some say they already feel tempted to leave the Church of England. Maybe they will feel more able to say this publicly as a result of the discussion about the St Andrew's Day Statement?

Anger

Some Christians have struggled with homosexuality for many years, were attracted by offers of healing in terms of a change in orientation, but left angry and disillusioned when this did not happen. Sometimes they change their beliefs to a Christianity which accepts homosexual relationships, more often they reject

Christianity completely: 'It has not worked for me!' Accusations have been made against Christian counsellors who related inappropriately to those seeking help. In seeking to offer comfort and support they have either been dishonest with themselves about their feelings or been misinterpreted by those seeking their help. The boundaries have often been blurred. Responses to clients who say 'I don't want sex really, but just long to be loved – to be cuddled' have often been well intentioned but misguided.

A Church Confused?

Viewpoints differ considerably, but here are four perspectives.

1. Some say that Christians should not struggle with homosexuality if they are truly born again. In my opinion they misinterpret Paul's words in 1 Corinthians 6.11 'and that is what some of you were. But you were washed, you were sanctified, you were justified . . .'. They say this means homosexuals in the Corinthian church experienced a complete change in their sexual orientation and therefore so should all homosexuals when they become Christians. Paul's words refer to sinners saved by grace, including the greedy, slanderers and homosexual offenders (i.e. those involved in homosexual sex). He does not say whether or not they were still struggling with these sins. The impression can sometimes be given that idolatry, greed, pride and even adultery are 'normal' sins but homosexuality is an 'abnormal' one. Sometimes Christians struggling with homosexuality are disciplined and maybe even denied fellowship. This usually makes the problem much worse. Their already low self-image plummets and sexual desire attempts to dull the pain. The use of biblical discipline to convince of sin and prevent others from being misled has become grossly perverted. For example, take the case of a person addicted to casual sexual encounters, who sometimes fails to resist temptation and the resulting guilt keeps him in the addiction cycle. He is told by his church not to pray in public and consider moving out of the church and neighbourhood in case 'disgrace' is brought on the church by his problem. Is it surprising that so many gay people feel angry as a result of this kind of treatment? I have rarely come across a case of properly applied church discipline. It is usually a punishment for sin, rather than an expression of God's love and grace.

2. Some Christians campaign against the acceptance of homosexual relationships in their denomination, although they acknowledge the unacceptable level of fear and prejudice in the Church. They sometimes know Christians who have experienced some change in their sexual orientation and are now in a heterosexual marriage relationship. They acknowledge that for some this may not happen and therefore they should be celibate (see Jesus's words in Matt. 19:11, 12). In my opinion there is often an unhealthy tendency to see marriage as evidence of God's healing. There is a lack of positive teaching on singleness. As a result some Christians struggling with homosexuality are encouraged to marry, often by implication rather than directly. Marriage is wrongly seen as the only real answer to loneliness and sexual frustration. Many people, including children of course, are hurt. Often secular gay groups are left to pick up the pieces and respond angrily to Christianity for apparently causing this pain. The encouragement in the Statement to know more of true Christian community and friendship is very welcome.

3. Some Christians have believed that the Bible teaches homosexual relationships are incompatible with following Christ. However, in trying to follow this ideal they have constantly experienced a sense of failure and frustration. They now accept their homosexual relationships as compatible with Christianity. Some of their friends have to agree that the agony of failure and frustration appears to be over. The latter are in a dilemma. Can they really condemn this person to the loneliness they experienced before? Sometimes the homosexual concerned is involved in a costly ministry of caring for others that many evangelicals would avoid. So, whilst agreeing that the Bible condemns homosexual relationships, they feel reluctant to apply this to every situation they know. Perhaps it is seen as the 'lesser of two evils'. I find this frustrating. On the one hand I feel drawn to the compassion expressed towards the Christian with homosexual feelings, but find it difficult to understand the response of ultimately encouraging a relationship which is believed to be wrong. I assume the Statement's encouragement to be pastorally flexible is not saying this but recognising certain situations where a Church leader must sensitively and honestly encourage obedience to Christ, rather than demanding an immediate change in lifestyle. I can certainly identify with a reluctance to confront someone

else's wrong behaviour, but cannot agree with it. Surely loving one another should mean I feel safe enough to be honest? If Christ is central in my relationship I should be anxious to hear from another about aspects of my life which may dishonour God. This is not easy, but my goal.

4. Finally there are Christians who believe a homosexual relationship is compatible with Christianity. The definition of what is acceptable varies, as does the authority given to Scripture. Some regard themselves as conservative, others liberal in their theology. Many are admired for the quality of their lives and ministries. There have been many times when as a Christian with homosexual desires I wished I could believe homosexual relationships are pleasing to God, but I cannot – to do so would mean abandoning too much of what I have learnt about the nature and purposes of the Lord.

The St Andrew's Day Statement clearly wishes to promote discussion, whilst recognising the differing viewpoints already held, usually rigidly, by all involved.

There is More to Sexuality than Sex

As I said earlier, when first a Christian I was able to meet my same-sex (homosexual) needs through celibate same-sex relationships. I experienced some fulfilment and did not feel denied a lot without an orgasm, despite the fact that I had been very promiscuous as a non-Christian homosexual. This idea of meeting legitimate unmet same-sex needs through celibate special relationships was a major force in the teaching of True Freedom Trust (TfT) for the first ten years of our ministry. Whilst I still believe in the importance of special Christian relationships, I now realise they were overemphasised. Relationships with others were put first, even though they were supposedly based on Christ. I did not appreciate that I need to learn to be alone with myself and God before I can really begin to meet my emotional needs with others.

Loneliness is usually seen as the major driving force beneath sexual desire – the need for intimacy or closeness with another human being. It may also be a need to find oneself in another. In other words my level of self-worth is dependent on the other's love and affirmation. I believe this to be especially true of homosexual attraction. As I pursued the ideal of meeting same-sex needs in Christian relationships and encouraged others to do the same, I found what seemed to work for me not so helpful for others. For example, a close friend often said to me, 'I don't feel I belong! I am not being true to myself! I still feel lonely, even though I'm loved!' Whilst I could not identify with all these feelings, my so-called 'healthy' same-sex relationships brought to the surface in me insecurities and fears often expressed in jealousy, dependency and depression. Nevertheless, I was aware of God within all this and therefore never completely experienced the sense of 'non-being' expressed by others close to me. I realised that the presence of God that I had known, but not fully recognised, must have made the difference to me.

Are the Real Needs Sexual or Spiritual?

The deep-rooted feelings of loneliness which drive sexual desire are not simply needs for intimacy with another or even for God. The way towards wholeness (completeness) and away from loneliness must therefore involve *learning to be alone with myself and God*. Then I can relate to others without the same risk of the relationship becoming life-threatening. In other words, if the relationship fails, my sense of identity or self-value is not destroyed, because it is not the major part of my desire for another. This is because there is unity between my feelings, my lifestyle and God.

Accepting paradox is, I believe, a vital part of personal growth and spirituality. I learn to accept whatever is right or wrong in my life without necessarily condoning it. I live with paradox, rather than fighting against it. I accept my feelings, including my sexuality, and seek to make the right choices in terms of how I express them.

A Desire for Acceptance

Frequently, and this is especially true for homosexuality, the desire for a relationship with another is also a desire to find self-acceptance (finding myself). In other words, I may be searching for qualities in another which I believe I lack. This may seem perfectly 'normal' but it is unhealthy if my sense of worth is dependent on another. This search for identity is in my opinion one of the major driving forces in gay liberation. It is more than just a response to prejudice and fear of rejection. However it can easily become almost 'messianic' (i.e. idolatrous). My search for self means I 'worship the creature rather than the Creator'. I believe this is evident in aspects of the 'so-called gay theology'. For example, in some of the prayers used by gay Christians denying gayness is compared to denying Christ, 'coming out' is compared to God bringing us out of the wilderness into the promised land and, I think most offensively, wine and bread is used to symbolise people rather than the Creator. Admittedly, we may all be idolatrous in many subtle ways, but people on the receiving end of prejudice, like homosexuals and lesbians, are especially vulnerable.

This is why our focus should be on integrating our humanity and spirituality (incarnational reality). I must learn to accept myself. That does not mean a moral judgment, but simply an understanding of myself and my feelings. I must also work at understanding and accepting God's feelings (the truth). I will then begin to recognise the difference and can choose to accept and act on the truth, rather than simply my feelings. I can now begin to see my life as a unique story with myself and with God as a part of his story. Whatever happens to me has value in this story, whether it is in itself good or bad. God is sovereign and his ways are not our ways. How trite that can sound, but it is true. God allows things he hates, even sin and suffering. My logical mind cannot handle that seeming paradox. I therefore must just accept it.

Maybe healing is working at the baggage that makes accepting the 'paradox' difficult? For example, many of us with a low self-image problem have a tendency to be perfectionists and sometimes obsessive. The perfectionist will probably find Christian healing as often defined by the Church very appealing: a chance to be the perfect person I want to be. I may acknowledge it is not really that simple, but my feelings will go for it. Any sense of feeling a failure is devastating for the perfectionist and there may be a strong reaction against God or other Christians who seem to encourage this. Growth and healing therefore involves working at this perfectionism. I can most effectively do this by learning to accept the truth about myself and life from God (the 'Perfect One') and not my feelings.

A sexual feeling is a sexualised emotion. This means my sexual feelings can tell me something of what I feel about myself and others. They can then be compared with the truth from God. As I learn to approach God, others, myself and life with the truth from God, I am set free to become more whole. The truth which sets me free is actually saying that I will not have all the answers or know all the truth. I may simply know that God is good and is on my side, when circumstances may seem to say the opposite. In other words the real issues expressed in any type of sexual desires are similar for us all. They can be the catalyst to awareness of self and God – the truth of God's love which sets us free.

I am so pleased that the St Andrew's Day Statement suggests there is more to sexuality than a sexual act. It encourages us to think again about the often simplistic 'answers' to loneliness and sexual frustration which Christians on all sides of the Church debate often express. Finally, the Statement reminds us that our Lord Jesus calls his followers to be distinctly different in our lives and lifestyles. This must include our sexuality, whatever it may be. *If the teaching of the Church of England changes to accept sex outside of marriage, like homosexuality, then I believe it will be disobeying God.*

11

A Psychiatrist's Perspective

Tom M. Brown

IN ITS INTRODUCTION the authors emphasise that the St Andrew's Day Statement is not an exhaustive one, intended 'to cover every issue that must be considered'. My comments here should be seen in the light of my profession as a consultant psychiatrist. I emphasise this as it may be unwise to come to conclusions about the problems of homosexuals and homosexuality on the basis of experience of a group of individuals presenting with psychological and psychiatric problems. I should emphasise, however, that I also write as an ordinary Church member and an elder in the Church of Scotland, with experience of having everyday contact with people of homosexual orientation within and without the Church. I really make no comment about the credal principles affirmed in the first part of the statement. As someone with fairly orthodox and conservative Christian views, I accept these principles. I think they are concisely and clearly stated in the document and make the theological position of the authors eminently clear.

Application of Credal Principles

There is much in this section of the document which is welcome and needs to be emphasised. I would underline three things:

1. The comment near the beginning of the document 'that the issue should have become so highly dramatised calls for

repentance on the part of all members of the church' is well-founded and deserves to be highlighted. My experience (particularly of the conservative evangelical wing of the Church) is of a serious need for self-examination, as often our attitudes and behaviour reflect a considerable degree of bigotry and lack of charity.

2. The statement that 'our sexual affections can no more define who we are than can our class, race or nationality' is again an extremely important one. Indeed a patient recently expressed to me his great distress at being described as 'a homosexual' and made the important point that it would be highly unlikely for someone to describe me as 'a heterosexual'.

3. The emphasis in the Application on the fact that all human beings are summoned to 'various forms of self-denial' is good and helpful, as indeed is the emphasis that some of these struggles are 'not open to choice but are given to us as a situation in which we are to live faithfully'.

With regard to the comments in the document on the pastoral tasks of the Church, I think it would have been helpful to emphasise that all have departed from God's ideals in the arena of sexuality. Who for example has not had lustful thoughts? I think emphasising this would help those of homosexual orientation to realise that they are not 'beyond the pale' as far as the Church and certainly as far as Christ is concerned.

My experience of those of homosexual orientation who are within the Church is that for the large part they feel that their needs for warmth, understanding, friendship and fellowship are simply not being met. Those who are struggling to live chastely feel that many Christians of homosexual orientation simply 'give up' and opt for sexual relationships, as the quality of the relationships within the body of Christ is so poor. Whilst this of course does not exonerate them from responsibility for their own behaviour it certainly does seem to speak loudly about lack of support within the Church. Homosexual people perceive that heterosexuals in the Church understand the nature of their problems very poorly and in an overly simplistic way. This is reflected, for example, in efforts to pair them off – 'If only he could find the right woman' –

which although well-meaning are ill-founded. Those of homosexual orientation find this immensely distressing and frustrating.

The St Andrew's Day Statement exhorts the Church to give constant encouragement 'in following Christ' to those who are married and to those who are single (including those of homosexual orientation). I think it could have perhaps gone further in spelling out what this means in practical terms. People of homosexual orientation often find themselves treated as second-class citizens in the Church. Whilst most Christians, theoretically, accept the orthodox teaching, i.e. 'hate the sin and love the sinner', this has often not worked out in practice. I have already hinted at the isolation and lack of warmth and love which some of homosexual orientation find within the Church, and there is also often a problem with regard to their role. An anecdote helps to illustrate this. I recently asked some church elders (from various churches of conservative evangelical orientation) how they would feel about accepting into the eldership people of homosexual orientation, assuming they were living chaste lives. It was clear from the responses that there were considerable misgivings about this. How can this do anything other than give out the message that these people are regarded somehow as 'second rate'? The feeling I had was that individuals of homosexual orientation were regarded as somehow more 'perverted' than the rest of us and as being a 'high risk'. Indeed, more than one patient of homosexual orientation has commented to me that they feel excluded from Church activities involving children. This adds to the difficulties of homosexual people in two ways. First, there is the distress associated with being seen to pose a risk to children. Secondly, many homosexuals, even if they have no wish to form relationships with the opposite sex, would love to have children and enjoy being with them. For some, being with the children of friends, including those at church, is the only opportunity for such contact. To say this is not to ignore the fact that some men of homosexual orientation are attracted to young boys, but such problems also exist in a heterosexual context, for example when youth leaders have to work with adolescents of the opposite sex.

Section III of the Application part of the document is useful, particularly in highlighting the truth that people may be fulfilled without occasion to employ the power of sexual expression. These would be my main comments on the St Andrew's Day Statement.

A Review of Current Research

Most Christian psychiatrists writing in this area, e.g. John White and Gaius Davies,[1] have taken the orthodox Christian position of distinguishing homosexual orientation and preference from homosexual acts, and have highlighted the need to provide those of homosexual orientation with love and understanding, whilst at the same time affirming that homosexual acts are wrong in God's eyes. A slightly different slant comes from Elizabeth Moberly.[2] Moberly is a psychologist, who writes from a psychoanalytic, but also from a Christian position. She emphasises the need to understand the causes of homosexuality. Her hypothesis is that homosexuals have 'suffered from some deficit in relationship with the parents of the same sex and that there is a corresponding drive to make good this deficit – through the medium of same sex or homosexual relationships'. Moberly argues that homosexuals are in reality engaging in pre-adult relationships and that the reason homosexual acts are prohibited is 'not because they repudiate the man/woman relationship, but because sexual expression is not appropriate to pre-adult relationships'. She therefore adopts a traditional Christian position that homosexual acts are wrong, but for a completely different reason. Moberly wrote in the early 1980s, before the upsurge in biological research in homosexuality, and while her hypothesis bears scrutiny and respect it would seem to me slightly to over-simplify the causes of homosexuality, which are likely to be multifactorial and not the same for every individual.

Many authors have pointed out the difficulties in defining what is meant by homosexuality. Is everyone who has committed homosexual acts 'a homosexual'? Virtually everyone would answer this question in the negative. Kinsey, who was one of the great pioneers of scientific research into sexuality, felt that homosexuality and heterosexuality were at either ends of a continuum and while some people were exclusively homosexual and others exclusively heterosexual, many fell in between. Many Christian writers[3] have taken the same view. Bancroft[4] has made the interesting observation that exclusively homosexual behaviour is confined to human beings. It is nowhere seen in the animal kingdom. Further debate has centred on whether or not homosexuality is an illness, and whether or not it should be something which is treated by doctors. Traditional psychoanalytic writers certainly tended to see homosexuality as an illness and something worthy of treatment, but there has without doubt been a huge drift away from this within the psychotherapeutic community, and within psychiatry. Until 1974 homosexuality appeared as a disease in the major classification of psychiatric disorders in the USA. Its removal was almost certainly due to lobbying from gay activitists and not because the issue of whether or not homosexuality constituted an illness had been resolved on medical and scientific grounds. A number of Christian writers, whilst not explicitly answering the question of whether or not homosexuality is an illness, certainly see it as something which can be treated. Elizabeth Moberly is one such example, another such is Leanne Payne, who exercises a ministry in the deliverance of homosexuals and others with sexual problems.[5] Payne's work is based on the conviction that the key to healing the people of homosexual orientation is the forgiveness of sin. Her work embraces dealing with the psychological origins of homosexuality and uses a psychotherapeutic method, but also prayer for healing.

A recent and helpful addition to the literature is Jeffrey Satinover's book *Homosexuality and the Politics of Truth* (Baker, 1996). Satinover is an American psychiatrist with a psychoanalytic background. Satinover reviews the events which led the American Psychiatric Association to remove homosexuality from its classification of diseases, and concludes, as mentioned earlier, that this occurred for reasons of political correctness, rather than for scientific reasons. He reviews very rigorously much of the scientific evidence and the biology of homosexuality. He believes that both the secular psychological method and Christian healing, and particularly the latter, can change the orientation of homosexuals. The main weakness of Satinover's book is that he does not exercise the same scientific rigour in assessing the evidence for the efficacy of psychotherapeutic treatments as he does in dealing with biological research. This notwithstanding, Satinover's work is an important addition to the literature. Like others before him, he views homosexuality not as an 'all or nothing' phenomenon, but sees its origins as multifactorial and, despite his criticism of much biological research, acknowledges that biological as well as psychosocial factors contribute to sexual orientation. He affirms that homosexuals, like heterosexuals, are called to ethical demands to resist simple impulses. On the question of whether or not homosexuality is an illness Satinover states that homosexuality is not a true illness, though it may be thought an illness in the spiritual sense of 'soul sickness' innate to fallen human nature. Its treatment thus opens directly into the domain of the 'cure of souls'.[6] Whilst many Christians would agree with Satinover and Payne that healing can occur, it is not my experience that most Christian homosexuals do experience healing, at least in the form of changed sexual orientation. Satinover and Payne would doubtless argue that many may not have sought healing, thinking it not possible. Whilst there may be some truth in this, we have to be careful in this area, as in many others, not to suggest that, where healing does not occur, it is simply due to 'lack of faith'.

I think it is useful for Christians to debate this issue with some understanding of where current scientific research has got to with the understanding of homosexuality. As in many other areas of scientific endeavour, Christians seem to fall into two camps. The conservative, evangelical camp is generally unduly suspicious of scientific research, whilst those of more liberal views can be rather uncritical in their acceptance of it. For example, the report by the Board of Responsibility of the Church of Scotland on human sexuality in 1994 states that 'there are some who are convinced that in the light of scientific evidence, sociopsychological understanding, critical scholarship and personal testimony, the view that homosexual practice is necessarily sinful can no longer be held with integrity and sincerity'.[7] I suspect this view stems from an unduly simplistic notion of the nature of scientific evidence for the biological basis of homosexuality. This was very well reviewed by John Bancroft in 1994. He considers the search for a biological basis of homosexuality under four headings: (1) hormonal mechanisms, (2) brain structure, (3) neuropsychological function, (4) genetic factors.

Bancroft concludes that the idea that homosexuals are 'hormonally different' was abandoned some time ago. He reviews the evidence that hormones may influence sexual development and brain development *in utero* and likewise concludes that this is at the very least ambiguous and unclear. A number of studies have looked at brain structure in those of homosexual orientation. An example of this research is the work of Simon LeVay, who found that a small nucleus in the hypothalamus of the brain was smaller in homosexual than heterosexual man, a finding which was much publicised at the time.[8] Bancroft points out this finding has not been consistently replicated and also to methodological problems in the research, not the least of which is that a number of the subjects in the study had died of AIDS, a disease which itself may cause changes in brain structure. He concludes that 'it is unlikely that there is any direct relationship between the structure of a specific area of the brain and sexual orientation per se'. The third area of scientific research has looked at neuropsychological function in homosexuals. There is considerable interest in this area, but again no conclusive evidence for consistent differences between homosexuals and heterosexuals.

Finally Bancroft turns to the role of genetic factors. Here there is undoubtedly some evidence that genetic factors are of some significance in determining homosexual orientation, particularly in men. He cities the work of Hamer, who found a convincing correlation between homosexual orientation and the inheritance of a marker on the X chromosome.[9] Bancroft cautions, however, that 'this was not as the media chose to call it "a gay gene" but persuasive evidence of a genetic factor or factors, which in this section of the gay community at least, are sex linked ... It is unlikely to be a gene which determines sexual orientation per se'.[10] It may, for example, be a gene which is involved in pre-natal brain development. The scientific community acknowledges that, the genetic findings notwithstanding, there is still 'a lot of room for environmental influences'. There need be no particular problem for the Christian in accepting some biological and perhaps genetic basis for homosexuality. There are many aspects of our temperament which are to a degree heritable. To acknowledge this is not to concede to genetic determinism or genetic reductionism. Traits such as introversion, extroversion and many other aspects of our temperament are to some degree heritable, but few suggest that this abrogates us from responsibility for exercising some control over them. Bancroft concludes at the end of his article that 'it remains difficult on scientific grounds to avoid the conclusion that the uniquely human phenomenon of sexual orientation is a consequence of a multifactorial developmental process in which biological factors play a part, but in which psychosocial factors remain crucially important. If so the moral and political issues must be resolved on other grounds.' This conclusion is an important statement from a very eminent psychiatrist and scientist, who interestingly is writing in a purely secular context.

Conclusion

Scientific evidence thus far simply underlines the complexity of understanding the origins of homosexual orientation. The Church's task should be to make it plain that the Christian Gospel is relevant to all and that all of us need forgiveness, understanding, love and fellowship. The St Andrew's Day Statement clearly affirms this and it is to be welcomed. I hope it will fall into the hands of many in the Church and help us challenge preconceived assumptions and our attitudes to those of our fellow human beings struggling with problems related to homosexual orientation.

Notes

1. J. White, *Eros Defiled* (IVP, 1977) and G. Davies, *Stress: The Challenge to Christian Caring* (Kingsway Publications, 1988).
2. E. Y. Moberly, *Homosexuality: A New Christian Ethic* (James Clarke & Co, 1983).
3. e.g. White, *Eros Defiled*.
4. J. Bancroft, 'Homosexual Orientation: The Search for a Biological Basis', *British Journal of Psychiatry*, vol. 164, 1994, pp. 437–40.
5. L. Payne, *The Broken Image* (Crossway, 1981).
6. J. Satinover, *Homosexuality and the Politics of Truth* (Baker, 1996), p. 246.
7. Report on Human Sexuality by the Panel of Social Responsibility of the Church of Scotland to the General Assembly (1994), p. 595.
8. S. LeVay, 'A Difference in Hypothalamic Structure between Heterosexual and Homosexual Men', *Science*, vol. 258, 1991, pp. 1034–7.
9. D. H. Hamer, S. Hu, V. L. Magnuson *et al.*, 'A Linkage between DNA Markers on the X Chromosome and Male Sexual Orientation', *Science*, no. 261, 1993, pp. 321–7.
10. Bancroft, 'Homosexual Orientation', p. 440.

12

Can Hermeneutics Ease the Deadlock? Some Biblical Exegesis and Hermeneutical Models

Anthony C. Thiselton

1. Why Hermeneutics? Advances from Premodern Method to Modern and Postmodern Resources

All sides agree that even in Christian contexts current debates about gay rights and homosexuality tend to become polarised, and all too readily to talk past each other. The St Andrew's Day Statement rightly offers a warning about 'strong and conflicting passions' on different sides of the debate, in its very first lines. Often argument is replaced by a rhetoric which reflects a heavy investment of personal 'interests' on both sides.

By contrast the founder of modern hermeneutics as an interdisciplinary subject, Friedrich Schleiermacher, asserts: 'In interpretation it is essential that one be able to step out of one's own frame of mind into that of the author [or of the other]'.[1] The way was prepared for his hermeneutics, or theory of understanding, by his very early *Speeches* (1799). Reacting against a shallow scholastic rationalism, he spoke of a 'miserable love of system' which could obscure mutual understanding 'because some prior system which is 'mine' seduces us to reject what is strange, often without patient examination of its claims, because . . . the closed ranks would be destroyed'.[2] Hermeneutics has at its very heart the attempt to understand the 'otherness' of the other.[3] For this very same reason Hans-Georg Gadamer (usually regarded as the greatest hermeneutical theorist of this century) warns us of the limitations of imperialist 'method' or generalities of 'science' which seek to 'master' the other on *our* terms. Ricoeur notes similarly the limits of 'explanation' in contrast to understanding the otherness of the other in hermeneutics.[4]

In Gadamer's words, hermeneutics avoids establishing and imposing a prior 'method' onto our understanding of the other until we have come to respect 'the priority of the question' and indeed of the shape of the kind of question which we bring to what we seek to understand. In Gadamer's view, hermeneutics rests on, and instantiates, 'the primacy of dialogue and the structure of question and answer'.[5] Hence in his most recent retrospective reconsideration of his earlier work on Plato's Socratic dialogue, he shows how the 'open' stance of hermeneutics which respects the other *as* 'other' constitutes a key bulwark against rhetorical manipulation and propaganda.[6] Gadamer reiterates the importance of dialogue in his recent 'Afterword' to *Truth and Method*, concluding with the final sentence: 'It would be a poor hermeneuticist who thought he could have, or had to have, the last word.'[7] For in hermeneutics one never ceases to listen to 'the other', whether this 'other' happens to take the form of sacred texts, human person, corporate traditions, or social institutions.

Another major hermeneutical theorist of this century, Emilio Betti, regards hermeneutics as the most important discipline of the university, of ethics, of politics and of life. Hermeneutics facilitates and demands both open-mindedness (*Aufgeschlossenheit*) and receptivity to the 'other' (*Empfänglichkeit*). Hence it trains habits of mind which are characterised by patience, mutual understanding, and respect for the other, whether 'the other' be texts from different cultural worlds or value-systems, persons from different backgrounds who hold different beliefs, or social institutions with which the interpreter may be initially unfamiliar.[8]

Second only perhaps to Gadamer in importance stands the seminal work of Paul Ricoeur, who offers still more to theology and ethics than Gadamer's more theoretical approach. Ricoeur shares with Schleiermacher and Gadamer the rejection of purely rational 'explanatory' approach to texts which all too often merely seems to support some prior interpretation already reached. Alongside 'explanation' Ricoeur calls for 'understanding' in the sense of a creative process which fully respects the otherness of the other. However, he also recognizes, along with Freud and the biblical tradition, the capacity of the human heart to deceive itself in 'interpreting' data, including texts and persons. He draws constructively, for example, on Freud's account of how we 'scramble' experiences in dreams, sometimes to hide that from which the self seeks to protect itself, but also reflecting the tension of a simultaneous anxiety to come to terms with what should be known. This double principle applies, Ricoeur convincingly argues, to various kinds of interpretation. Hence the modern interdisciplinary study of processes of interpretation embodies the following axiom: 'Hermeneutics seems to me to be animated by this double motivation: willingness to suspect, willingness to listen; vow of rigor, vow of obedience.'[9]

Before we turn explicitly to the debate about gay rights and homosexuality, we should mention the fourth major thinker who has influenced the shape of hermeneutics in our own day, alongside Gadamer, Ricoeur, and Betti. Jürgen Habermas fully endorses Ricoeur's diagnosis of the self's capacity to be influenced by its own desires, whether conscious or unconscious, in interpretation and understanding. Where Ricoeur calls for 'a hermeneutic of suspicion' as well as openness, Habermas believes that only an approach which addresses fully the impact of 'human interests' (including the sense of vested interests) can lead to a hermeneutic that genuinely liberates understanding from the constraints which human selfhood places upon it.[10] Interpreters need to diagnose and to identify such interests and their effects on understanding texts and other persons.

It now begins to become clear why the debate about the ethics of gay rights and homosexuality has reached such deadlock in its handling of biblical material. For up until Schleiermacher hermeneutics tended to work with generalising 'method' and appeals to some 'hermeneutical principle' or supposed key. As we shall show, in this polarised debate both sides appeal to such 'hermeneutical principles' as 'the centrality of Christ', or 'Scripture as a whole', or 'the proper historical context', but usually with the effect of serving, in the end, to justify or to appear to validate the prior beliefs of each party to the debate. When this occurs each party may suspect the other of blindness, prejudice, or lack of moral integrity. Thereby a premodern hermeneutic generates circularity, frustration, anger, and a loss of confidence in Scripture to offer any relevant comment or verdict in the debate.

The very aim of Schleiermacher in formulating hermeneutics as a modern interdisciplinary area was to rescue the subject from being reduced into a service-discipline which merely offered manipulative tools to justify, or appear to justify, some prior position. For him it entailed an examination of the very processes of insight, reflection, judgment and understanding that characterise a first approach, and then successive subsequent approaches, to the texts or persons whom we seek to understand. It is the 'art' of thinking and understanding with the capacity for openness and imaginative rapport. His firm insistence that we are examining not a set of techniques concerning the interpretation of specific 'difficult' texts, but an interdisciplinary exploration of processes of understanding and their very basis in thought and life, helps to explain why none of the more transparent terms for 'hermeneutics', such as 'the theory of interpretation' or 'models of reading' can be coextensive with the broader, more technical discipline of hermeneutics. There is no way of avoiding this term, because it now addresses not only biblical studies, but also social science, literary theory, philosophies of understanding and even debates about postmodernity, and now approaches to understanding selfhood and agency in pastoral care.[11]

2. The Limitations of Traditional Methods for the Modern Biblical Debate

We may now note in a preliminary way the most relevant texts for the debate. It has become customary to follow D. S. Bailey in distinguishing between 'definite references' which bear on the debate, 'possible references', and spurious appeals to passages which are clearly proven to be irrelevant to the debate.[12] Bailey lists six 'definite references': Leviticus 18:22, 20:13; Romans 1:26, 27; 1 Corinthians 6:9, 10; and 1 Timothy 1:9, 10. All of these refer to some kind of same-gender sexual acts, in contexts of disapproval, divine judgment, impurity, or human fallenness. 'Possible' references include e.g. Revelation 21:8 and 22:15, for Bailey.

Each side in a frequently polarised debate tends to understand these six passages to convey radically different meanings, very often in the light of what premodern theory up to Schleiermacher's era termed 'a hermeneutical principle' or an interpretative key. If, for example, we cite Luther's Christocentric principle, this hermeneutical 'key' can be employed in diverse ways to validate either of two opposing conclusions.[13] On one side, for example, Victor Furnish points to the absence of any concern about homosexuality from the Jesus-traditions in the Gospels.[14] Adrian Thatcher begins his discussion of the debate with the observation: 'The Gospels are entirely silent about homosexuality.'[15] Michael Vasey appeals to the solidarity of Jesus Christ with 'the outsider'. Jesus calls the marginalised and victimised his brothers and sisters.[16]

Michael Vasey's comment (on the same page) that Jesus 'shares with them [other humans] the same flesh and blood' may be interpreted in a radically different direction from those arguments which affirm gay sexual intimacy. For as Schleiermacher and Barth insist in theology, and J. Murphy O'Connor argues with reference to Philippians 2:6 and elsewhere, Jesus Christ as bearer of the image of God is 'the criterion' of 'authentic' humanness.[17] Yet the narratives of the New Testament contain no suggestion that Jesus could not fully affirm and live out what it is to be human without experiencing sexual intimacy. It is nowhere suggested that celibacy hinders truly mature human development in the case of

Jesus. Indeed in Irenaeus and in Schleiermacher it is fallen humans who are perceived as examples of arrested development.[18] Hence the other side of the debate may appeal to the words of Karl Barth: 'Jesus is man as God willed and created him. What constitutes true human nature in us depends upon what it is in Him . . . The nature of the man Jesus is the key to the problem of the human. This man is *man*' (Barth's italics).[19] 'Nowhere but in this man' can we see 'man primarily and properly . . . revealed'.[20] All this bears very closely on the St Andrew's Day Statement about the nature of humanness, especially as an ideal.

Moreover, an appeal to 'Christ' suggests to Ulrich Mauser a *stricter* interpretation of Genesis and of Levitical purity than otherwise:

> The coming kingdom . . . in the work of Christ . . . intensifies the value of sexual life and heightens the demand expected in sexual behaviour . . . The radicality of perceiving homosexual practices as an outcome of idolatry stretches the Old Testament legislation into the arena of apocalyptic disaster . . . Homosexual practice cannot honour the creation of human life in the essential differentiation of male and female'.[21]

Appeals to 'Christ' as a hermeneutical key, then, may initially serve only to confirm each side in their different view, and escalate frustration.

It achieves only relatively little advance to note with Robert Morgan and John Barton that 'some disagreements about what the Bible means stem not from obscurities in the texts, but from the conflicting aims of interpreters'.[22] For, first, who is to rank these conflicting aims, and how are they to rank them? Second, Mark Bonnington and Bob Fyall concede that 'prior choices, often implicit, of what makes interpretation 'good' can decisively affect what we make of biblical material', and offer as the guide to exegesis in these passages 'the context of the whole of scripture, taking each text seriously . . . discovering the original meaning and keeping . . . Christ central'.[23] No one can fault their specific choice of 'controls'; the problem is that, rather, as we noted above about 'general methods', virtually everyone purports to use them, or at least has persuaded themselves that they use them, but with no apparent improvement in exegetical results. Thus, when D. S. Bailey argues that 1 Corinthians 6:9 cannot refer to 'homosexuals', this is not because he merely brushes this reference aside, but because he believes that allusions to homosexual *practices* especially outside the context of a loving relationship, tell us nothing about Paul's hypothetical attitude toward 'the homosexual *condition*', of which he believes that Paul was unaware.[24] Had Paul been about to distinguish between a condition of inversion and an act of perversion, as is common today, so Bailey believes, he might have written differently. Furnish expresses this no less strongly: 'The ancient world had no word for, or concept of, "homosexuality" '.[25]

It is impossible to unravel the tangles of the debate by any merely generalising hermeneutical criteria. They have all been tried, and most believe that they already observe them. Still less does one simply wash one's hands of patient exegesis and rational reflection in the name of some such banal slogan as 'It all depends on your presuppositions', as if these are incapable of adjustment in the light of Scripture, tradition, reason, common sense and human experience. The usefulness of speaking of an interpreter's working from within a pre-given 'horizon' is that horizons may be expanded, enlarged, and moved.[26] We must move from generalising 'methods' drawn from the era prior to Schleiermacher to explore specific models and nuances of a wider hermeneutic of understanding, which avoids laying down prior conditions for a supposed 'mastery' of the text. One does not 'master' a text by some *prior* generalising method determined in the abstract. As Gadamer urges in his ironic title *Truth and Method*, 'method' forces texts to fit prearranged categories of knowledge or argument. Instead, we should seek to *listen*, both with suspicion and with openness to the otherness of the other.

3. Three Provisional Models of More Sophisticated Hermeneutical Approaches

Before undertaking a more comprehensive and rigorous examination of the interpretation of the six 'definite' references, we may set the exploration going by tracing some two-way consequences which are suggested by certain models. To maintain a balanced debate, we shall initially select one model of hermeneutical enquiry which may seem to promote a 'pro-gay' reading of certain biblical texts; then one which is double-edged; and then a third which may seem to suggest a more rigorist ethical stance.

(a) The model of Reception Theory

Following his former teacher, Gadamer, Hans Robert Jauss has pioneered the approach known as Reception Theory or the history of the tradition of the transmission of textual effects (cf. the German, *Wirkungsgeschichte*, effective-history, or the history of effects). Jauss argues that each successive 'reading' of a text contributes to the shaping of a 'horizon of expectation' which subsequent readers bring to the text and thereby condition how it is understood.[27] The tradition of these successive readings reflects both continuities and disjunctions which should be taken into account when each new generation of interpreters engages with the text. 'The experience of the first reading becomes the horizon of the second one.'[28]

Although his book predates Jauss's work, D. S. Bailey's argument that the 'homosexual' interpretation of the sin of Sodom (Gen. 19: 4–11) carries no weight receives a measure of significant support from Reception Theory. Bailey argues that neither Genesis nor the rest of the canonical Old Testament nor the Apocrypha nor the Jewish Talmud explicitly identifies the 'abomination' (*to 'ebhâh*) of Sodom with homosexual acts, rather than with aggressive violence in breach of hospitality as a sacred trust. Bailey declares, 'Nowhere does it [the Genesis narrative] identify that sin explicitly with the practice of homosexuality.'[29] Lot simply tried to 'buy off' the aggressive violence of the Sodomite crowd by offering to the crowd the 'use' of his own daughters. Through a succession of readings a new meaning began to emerge by inter-textual allusion at a much later date. With the emergence of apocalyptic perspectives in the Book of Jubilees and in the Testaments of the Twelve Patriarchs (around the first century BC), the allusion to the demand of the Sodom crowd 'to know' (Heb. *yâdha'*) Lot's angelic visitors became identified with the allusion to sexual intercourse between 'the sons of God' (Hebrew text) or 'angels of God' (some Septuagint traditions, also 'watchers') and 'the daughters of men' (Gen. 6:2; cf. 6:4). Jubilees 7:20, 21, explicitly speaks of these 'Watchers' as having illicit sexual intercourse with women 'against the natural order'; and while Jubilees 13:17 simply repeats a general tradition about the sin of Sodom, Jubilees 16:4, 5 and 20:5, 6 ascribe Sodom's punishment of fire and brimstone to 'committing fornication in their flesh'. By the time we reach the Testament of Naphtali 3:4, 5 (dated by Bailey *c.* 109–106 BC) Sodom's sin has become 'changing the order of nature . . . like the Watchers whom the Lord cursed at the Flood'.[30]

Bailey points out, however, that this specific understanding of Genesis 19:4–11 (especially 19:5) nowhere appears in other Old Testament allusions to Sodom (Jer. 23:14; Ezek. 16:49–50); nor in the Apocryphal writings (Wis. Sol. 10:8; Ecclus 16:8); nor do New Testament allusions to homosexual acts allude to Sodom (Rom. 1:26–7; 1 Cor. 6:9, 10; 1 Tim. 1:10). Indeed the references in the Testament of Naphtali 4:1 and the Testament of Asher 7:1 remain unspecific, speaking only of 'Sodom which sinned against the angels of the Lord'. However, Philo in the first century AD understands the sin of Sodom in Genesis 19:5 to be pederasty (*Quaest. et Sol.* on Gen. 4:37) or more widely as 'males having intercourse with males without respect for sexual nature which the active partner shares with the passive' (*De Abrahamo*, 26, 135–6). Thus 'they threw off their respect for [*lit.* from their necks] the order of nature' (26, 134). Josephus places the emphasis on violence, but implies that of homosexual acts (*Antiquities*, book 1, ch. II, v. 1 [194–5] and 3 [200]).

A double tradition of reading, or horizons of expectation, has now become established. In the Talmud the sin of Sodom is understood as violence in breach of the rules of hospitality (Talmud Bab. Sanh. 109a). However, the Church Fathers explicitly attribute Sodom's judgment to 'shameless . . . insane love of boys' (Clement of Alexandria, *Paedagogos*, 3, 8); or 'a barren coitus' (Chrysostom, *Ad pop. Antioch*, homily 19, 7); or pederasty 'against nature' (Augustine, *Const.*, Apost 7, 2). By contrast, Bailey urges, Romans 1:26, 27, 1 Corinthians 6:10 and 1 Timothy 1:10 avoid linking homosexual acts with any allusion to Sodom.

In general, therefore, the Reception Theory model appears to lend support to Bailey's attempt to disengage the Sodom story of Genesis 19:4–11 from the homosexuality debate. It must be allowed, however, that the case for this remains far from conclusive. Indeed David F. Wright insists that Bailey's 'non-sexual interpretation . . . has had a far longer innings than it deserves, and is now rarely put in to bat'.[31] Wright argues that the steady explication of Genesis 19 emerges contextually 'only when Judaism encountered homosexuality in the Greek world, chiefly in the form of pederasty', when it became 'more than a marginal issue', and David Atkinson shares with Wright the more traditional interpretation.[32] He concedes that more was at issue in the sin of Sodom than homosexual acts, but that we cannot exclude this nuance as a component of it. Further, although an allusion in 2 Peter 2:4–8 retains some ambiguity, it appears that Jude 6 and 7 probably follows the apocalyptic interpretation of Genesis 19 as entailing sexual relations contrary to the natural order. J. N. D. Kelly interprets the Greek *heteras sarkos* in Jude 7 to denote the different status of humans from the angels or 'watchers', and as an issue of emphasis and of the effects of prior readings in shaping horizons of expectation, however, Bailey's arguments invite examination.[33]

(b) The model of socio-critical 'interest'

The second late twentieth-century model to be explored is that which is often associated partly with Paul Ricoeur's 'hermeneutic of suspicion', but more especially with the category of 'interest' in Jürgen Habermas. For the present writer the effects of exploring this model challenge all parties within this ethical debate, although considerable weight must be given to some very moving comments on the understanding of biblical passages put forward by Richard Hays.[34] Habermas argues that interpretations which often purport to convey truth may in practice function manipulatively to promote a social programme of 'interest'. *Every* interpreter needs to ask whether either homophobia or an over-rigid concern for dogmatic orthodoxy may dispose him or her toward regarding certain understandings of text as more plausible than others; or whether the desire to protect gay persons from pain, anguish, bitterness, or unnecessary confrontation may predispose him or her towards giving privilege to a different exegesis and understanding of certain texts.

The depth and complexity of the problem emerge when we appreciate the subtle arguments from theories of signs (semiotics) by Roland Barthes and by Jacques Derrida, or from within reader–response approaches to texts in literary theory in the work of Stanley Fish and others.[35] What seem to us to be merely 'natural' meanings, they argue, may seem to be *plain and natural meanings only because our own subculture* (whether of Christian orthodoxy or of gay rights) *has repeated them so often that they form habituated patterns of judgment which readily match our prior horizons of expectation*. Roland Barthes confesses to 'a feeling of impatience at the sight of the "naturalness" with which newspapers [or] art . . . constantly dress up reality . . . I resented seeing Nature and History [cultural habituation] confused at every turn'.[36] Thus, on one side of the present debate, Victor Furnish argues that only because we read the Bible armed with pre–given judgments about 'homosexuality' do we understand Paul to be referring to this phenomenon, as such, in Romans 1:26, 27 and 1 Corinthians 6:9, 10. What we may otherwise understand as the 'natural meaning' of these texts is obscured, he argues, by a prior unwillingness to allow that these passages may owe more to context–relative repetition of stereotypical Hellenistic-Jewish material than to a deliberate and explicit moral judgment by Paul which takes account of the distinction between inversion as an orientation and perverted sexual acts.[37]

On the other side, however, within the same volume of essays Richard Hays offers an entirely different view even more explicitly embodying a socio–critical hermeneutic of suspicion. Hays begins with the story of his best friend from student years at Yale, his friend Gary. Gary was Christian and gay. He read 'hopefully' through all the mass of gay literature on homosexuality and the Bible, including the writings of J. J. McNeill, J. B. McNelson and John Boswell, among others. Hays continues, 'in the end he came away disappointed, believing that these authors, despite their good intentions, had imposed a wishful interpretation on the biblical passages. However much he wanted to believe that the Bible did not condemn homosexuality, he would not violate his own stubborn intellectual integrity by pretending to find their arguments persuasive.'[38] In the example cited by Richard Hays, who is a specialist on the interpretation of the Old Testament in Paul, a hermeneutic of critical social 'interest' is perceived to unmask interpretations habituated within the gay Christian subculture which appear to owe more to habituated patterns of desired and interest than to disinterested exegesis.

At the same time, we must be alert to the possibility that ideological and social critique can be double-edged and applies to all parties in the debate. The Bible stresses the capacity of the human heart to deceive itself. Reinhold Niebuhr has offered a brilliant exposé of how corporate self-deception can be still more pervasive and destructive. What we do 'for the good of our family', or for our nation, or for our own social class, gender, peer-group or professional guild allows us to dress up evil as good. Ruthless ambition may be disguised as altruism 'for the family'; oppression of the two-thirds world or the use of 'defensive' weapons may be 'patriotic' for one's fellow-nationals. Niebuhr observes: 'Altruistic passion is sluiced into the reservoir of nationalism with great ease', but signals too often 'that self-deception [which] is an unvarying element in the moral life of all human beings'.[39] 'The dishonesty of nations becomes a political necessity.'[40]

Michel Foucault attacks 'establishment power' as defining 'norms' of social behaviour for the marginalised and oppressed, by means especially of the 'smiling face in the white coat' which masks the establishment professionals in hospitals, or otherwise in prisons, the army, or bureaucracy.[41] But, as Jean Baudrillard observes under the memorable title *Forget Foucault*, Foucault's own philosophy of suspicion in turn comes to constitute a new power-mechanism to promote the 'interests' of a counter-culture.[42] Self-deception is no respecter of persons, whether it be mainline 'establishment' groups, conservative theological traditions, peer-groups of socio-economic minorities, or some form of gay subculture. As soon as the marginalised become a power-group they may well become prey to the same motivations and interests as those which have seduced their oppressors. Hermeneutics by contrast attempts to explore how to *listen* with openness and respect for the other and seeks alternative strategies to the manipulation of texts and persons to serve the interests of the self or its group. Hence Habermas calls such critical hermeneutics 'emancipatory', in the fullest philosophical–theological sense.

(c) The model of pre-cognitive understanding, or surplus of meaning

We noted earlier that the decisive turning-point for the beginning of modern hermeneutics came with Schleiermacher's recognition of the limits of reason alone. He perceived a supra-rational 'feminine' quality (his word) of what he called 'divinatory' or intuitive understanding as an *inter-personal* process as fundamental for a creative openness towards texts, even if intellectual integrity and interpretative validity also equally demanded what he called the 'masculine' qualities of critical comparison in the light of rational rigorous, checking processes. He writes, 'Divinatory knowledge is the feminine strength of knowing people: comparative knowledge, the masculine.'[43] Gadamer and Jauss, in our own time, took Schleiermacher's insight further, reversing the traditional order of (i) exegesis, (ii) application. They insist 'scientific checking' follows each attempt to understand, and that 'application' forms an integral part of a never-ending to-and-fro.

As a Christian pietist and Romantic thinker contemporary with Wordsworth, Goethe, Byron and Chopin, Schleiermacher perceived that the rational or cognitive content of texts were often the product of a creative vision which had given birth to them. It was both a strength and a weakness of Romanticist hermeneutics to assume that the conscious thought-processes of the author were never entirely or exhaustively coextensive with this vision, and that interpreters could work back from the textual 'residue' of the vision to bring the vision back to life.[44] It was for this purpose, not for antiquarian interest, that Schleiermacher insisted on historical reconstruction and contributed to founding 'Introduction to the New Testament' as a study of those factors which helps the reader to reach 'behind' the text. We now reach a major conclusion: a later interpreter may obtain access by historical research into factors in the life and situation of the author which shaped the author's vision, but of which the author may not have been fully conscious.

Hence our aim should be 'to understand the text . . . as well as, and *then even better than, its author* . . . The task is infinite'.[45]

This at once addresses the most central and persistent argument of 'pro-gay' writers on the use of the Bible in this debate. Victor Furnish repeats the theme in several revisions of his essay on this subject. In perhaps the most recent to date, he asserts 'The word "homosexuality", as well as the very concept, is an anachronism when applied to the Bible, and to the ancient world . . . There were no such concepts [as "heterosexuality", "homosexuality"] in the ancient world . . . Thus there is no biblical text about "homosexuality" understood as a "condition" or "orientation" . . . "Homosexuals" [in 1 Cor. 6:9] is an anachronism'.[46] This argument is endlessly repeated. Robin Scroggs declares, 'Not only is the New Testament church uninterested in the topic . . . Biblical judgments . . . are not relevant to today's debate.'[47] D. S. Bailey insists that the biblical writers can have no concept of 'homosexuality' because they did not possess the conceptual or psychological tools to distinguish between *inversion*, in which same-sex acts naturally express intimacy, and *perversion*, in which same-sex acts are not true to the nature of the self.[48] If these arguments are valid, the implication may be that the St Andrew's Day Statement's allusion to 'the authority of apostolic testimony' (p. 8) would cease to remain relevant to the debate.

This argument, however, would place out of court, if it were valid, the kind of work found in Gerd Theissen's brilliant and incisive study *Psychological Aspects of Pauline Theology*.[49] For although Paul predates Freud's explorations of the unconscious and the subconscious, as Bultmann points out Paul is fully aware of the biblical tradition in which the heart (Heb. *lebh*; Gk. *kardia*) denotes a sphere of selfhood which can evade conscious reflection. The 'depths' of the heart can be hidden from conscious view, and embody hidden drives comparable to Freud's *libido*, (Heb. *yetser ha-ra'* and *yetser ha-tobh*, drive-to-evil and drive-to-good), without which, the rabbis observed, no one would marry, build houses, or engage in trade. Does this mean that Paul has no 'concept' of the preconscious or of subconscious drives powered by the libido? Bultmann declares 'The strivings (*boulai*) of hearts (1 Cor. 4:5) are purposes that need not be actualized in conscious will'.[50] What is the difference between this and what Freud would call a desire repressed back into the subconscious, probably with subsequent effects? In Romans 1:21–31, Robert Jewett argues, 'the darkened . . . heart . . . distort[s] and suppress[es] the truth about God'.[51] What else is this but an anticipation of a Freudian type of analysis of the preconscious conflict that leads to neurosis? Paul even suggests here that the fallen human copes with this neurotic conflict by projecting out idolatrous god-figures. Theissen spells this out further, associating negative aspects of 'the law' in Paul with the repressive role of the superego in Freudian traditions, release from which may sometimes given rise to a 'welling up' of the preconscious in glossolalia.[52] He insists, 'Three conceptual presuppositions of a conception of the "unconscious" are found within . . . 1 Cor. 4:1–5'.[53]

In more theological terms, does Paul have a 'concept' of the Holy Trinity? Many exegetes perceive his language in 1 Corinthians 12:4–8 and 2 Corinthians 13:13 as at very least 'a Trinitarian ground-plan'.[54] Recently in an excellent detailed study Neil Richardson has shown that the interaction in Paul between God-language, Spirit-language and cross-language within a theocentric frame presupposes a Trinitarian perspective in Paul, even if this is not yet explicit.[55]

What does this suggest about the claims of Furnish, Scroggs and Bailey about biblical 'concepts'? If they are right, Molière's gentle mockery of *Le Bourgeois Gentilhomme*, M. Jourdain, in Act 2, scene 4, falls flat on its face. M. Jourdain exclaims, 'Par ma foi! il y a plus de quarante ans que je dis de la prose sans j'en susse rien!' ('My goodness! For more than forty years I have been speaking prose without knowing it!') If M. Jourdain needs the *concept* of prose before it can be presupposed that he uses it, the laugh would be on M. Jourdain, not on Molière. But as James Barr demonstrated as long ago as 1961, simplistic language which confuses words and concepts, of a 'the Greeks had a word for it' ilk, has long passed into the folk-memory of the earlier volumes of Kittel and the less sophisticated writings of the 'biblical theology' school of the 1950s. Barr asks: 'Does the lexical stock correspond to the "concept" stock? . . . [Could authors] only stammer with such words and "concepts" as were available?'[56] Indeed, David Wright perceives much of the lexicographical research put forward by these writers as 'recalling . . . the pre-Barr era'.[57]

Is it imaginable that Paul was so blinkered in his own presuppositions that this man who travelled throughout Greece, Asia Minor, and Mediterranean world, never perceived genuine examples of loving same-sex relationships, or never discussed Jewish perceptions of the Hellenistic world in ways which sought, as far as theologically possible, 'to those outside the law [to] become as one outside the law . . . to the weak [to] become weak . . . [to] become all things to all persons' (1 Cor. 9:21–3)? Did Paul's understanding of the social realities which he witnessed break down at this one single point? Did he never reflect on the 'why' behind the phenomenon of transvestism (Deut. 22:5), as well as reflecting on the 'why' behind the Deuteronomic legislation which forbade it? We shall return in our exegetical section to examine the claims of two leading specialists on Paul's use of the Old Testament. Richard Hays and Brian Rosner are unwilling to view Paul either as governed solely by material from the Hellenistic world, or as merely repeating Old Testament language uncritically.[58]

We have begun to drift back, however, on to the ground marked out by Bailey, Furnish and Scroggs. We noted from Schleiermacher that a counter-argument need not rest on claims about Paul's *consciousness*. What is important is the stance that passages and text presuppose. Here Paul Ricoeur's notion of 'surplus of meaning' may serve to demonstrate that we need not depend on any merely Romanticist model of hermeneutics. For Ricoeur, a text may generate a 'surplus' of meaning as it interacts with other texts or with enlarged horizons, but without falsifying or bypassing a hermeneutic of suspicion which depends on 'rigour' as we approach the texts. In Ricoeur's view, hermeneutics includes the understanding of what a text sets going. Ancient authors, including Old Testament writers and Paul, may have wished to 'set going' more than their words alone may actually have said. Such devices as understatement, parable, riddle, and other forms of indirect communication prove the point. Most important among a variety of textual effects, for Ricoeur, is often the projection of a 'world' which draws the reader into new horizons of possibility.[59]

A number of writers who discuss the 'concept' of homosexuality in the light of modern clinical or social theory, express doubts about today's attempts at typification. Michael Ruse concedes that difficulty of definition still exists and David Cappon insists that to think of 'types of people' is unhelpful: 'there are no homosexuals – only people with a homosexual problem . . . They remain first and foremost a person'.[60] It is helpful to seek to clarify, with Scroggs, 'what is the model of homosexuality to which the biblical writings were opposed', but it is more problematic to accept John Boswell's conclusion that 'the New Testament takes no demonstrable position on homosexuals', even if it also speaks negatively of homosexual acts.[61] Boswell's initial argument that the Bible says nothing about homosexuality because 'none of these languages [i.e. Hebrew, Greek, Syriac and Aramaic] contains such a word', even if were true, breaks every modern consensus about lexicography, the grammar of concepts, and hermeneutics.[62] It ignores the work of Barr and others on the relation between words and concepts, and assumes a pre-Gadamerian, even pre-Schleiermachian, hermeneutic. Gadamer urges that the reality of what is presupposed may be determinative, even if it does not enter the boundaries of subjective consciousness. Thus prior horizons or 'pre-judgments' (*Vorurteile*) constitute 'the historical reality' of Paul or of another writer or of an interpreter as over against the contents of their conscious awareness.[63] The realities of same-sex intimacy of a variety of kinds in a variety of social and religious contexts would have fallen within the horizons of Paul's world.

4. The Situation at Corinth and the Interpretation of I Corinthians 5:9–11

Whatever theories may be advocated about the context of Leviticus 18:22 and 20:13 concerning only ritual purity or a contrast with Canaanite value-systems, and whether or not 'nature' in Romans 1:26, 27 has anything to do with later notions of 'a natural order', no amount of exegetical manipulation can disguise the ethical thrust of 1 Corinthians 6:9–11. Paul expounds the need for ethical transformation and a change of lifestyle on the part of those who claim to belong to the 'holy people' (1 Cor. 1:2, 3) to whom he is writing. As J. D. Hester argues, the word 'inherits' in these verses relates the present to the future in terms which identify continuities and discontinuities.[64] For those who will 'inherit' the kingdom of God, many specific earlier practices lie behind them as *habituated* practices. The NRSV 'This is what you used to be' is exactly right for conveying the continuous habituation of the imperfect *tauta tines ête*. The neuter plural signals Paul's sense of shock: 'this is the kind of thing that you were', bringing together an extended state of being or stance with habituated acts which instantiated it. The notion that the list of practices are somehow contradictory of the stance (as in the claims about contrasts between perversion and inversion) does not seem prima facie an obvious assumption behind the syntax and grammar, although the matter must be examined further.

It is axiomatic for all interpretation of this epistle from the mid-1960s (following J. C. Hurd and others) that the more tentative 'grey' areas of marriage, types of freedom, finance and the risk of patronage, and food offered to idols (largely 7:1–10:33) has a softer note of contextual give-and-take than the clear-cut language about the cross and spiritual triumphalism in 1:10–4:21 and the moral judgments of 5:1–6:20. In 7:1–10:22 Paul frequently observes that 'it all depends . . .' (e.g. especially 7:17–35; 8:7–9; 9:12–23; 10:27–33). But in 5:1–5 the man who has an incestuous relationship is to be expelled from the church until he changes his stance.[65] Christians must not 'dare' (*tolmâi*) to initiate civil actions against fellow Christians in the local magistrate's courts, since everyone knew that the verdict would depend largely on having influence through the patronage network by status or by money (6:1–8).[66] Similarly the misleading slogan 'I have the right to do anything' (*panta moi exestin*, usually translated 'All things are lawful for me', 6:12) introduces a clear-cut prohibition against intimacy with a prostitute, since this effectively tears the self, or the 'body' into two (6:13–19). Paul exclaims 'Don't even think about such a thing' – 'Perish the thought' (*mê genoito*, 6:15). The passage about same-sex intercourse falls between the abuse of freedom to use patronage for social oppression and the dismissal of involvement with a prostitute, and it introduces the slogan about 'having the right to do anything'.

We have seen, however, that the body of 'pro-gay' literature in such works as Boswell, Furnish, Bailey and Scroggs do not regard this passage as having any bearing on the modern debate.

How can this be the case? The general arguments, in addition to that already examined about the 'concept' of homosexuality, turn on the following: (*a*) that Paul is drawing on a merely standardised stereotypical 'catalogue of vices' drawn up in Hellenistic Judaism as characterising the pagan world; (*b*) that the stereotypical material may be found also among Stoic and Cynic lists of writers and vices, such as we find in Epictetus; (*c*) that the Greek terms often taken to refer to homosexuality denote pederasty or the use of paid call-or rent-boys; and (*d*) that no cash-meaning for today can avoid historical and sociotypical anachronism. We shall address these arguments in turn.

(a) Catalogues of writers and vices
These do indeed play a part in Paul, in Philo, in Epictetus, and in the homilies of the Hellenistic-Jewish synagogue. Paul lists twenty-one moral failures in Romans 1:29–31 (very tempting for an unkind examiner to set for a Greek unseen). Wisdom 14:22–6, itself a product of Hellenistic Judaism, lists twenty-seven 'vices' as springing from idolatry. In the history of New Testament research, however, after the extent of these 'catalogues' was noted by J. Weiss in 1910, B. S. Easton (1932) and A. Vögtle (1936) attributed them to a Stoic stereotypical expansion of Plato's 'virtues'.[67] Wibbing (1959) and Kamlah (1964) explored especially the settings of such 'catalogues'.[68] On this basis, not only Scroggs, Bailey, Furnish and Boswell, but also Lietzmann, Conzelmann and several others argue that the dispositions and acts listed in 1 Corinthians 6:9, 10, are not of specific individual contextual significance, but merely stereotypical traits to be understood *en bloc* as 'Gentile' characteristics. Conzelmann writes 'It is drawing on set tradition. The terms of expression . . . are not specifically Pauline.'[69] Scroggs also draws on this angle to urge that the Greek refers more narrowly to 'pederasty'; and Boswell, to male prostitution.[70] But we shall examine the lexicography shortly.

Several responses can be offered to these arguments. First, while those who refer the catalogues to the Gentile Graeco-Roman world (Conzelmann, Scroggs) face equally strong arguments for a setting in Philo, Wisdom and Hellenistic Judaism (Vögtle; although also in Seneca and Epictetus), A. Seeberg, C. H. Dodd, Philip Carrington and E. G. Selwyn attributed the existence of such lists no less plausibly to settings of common Christian catechesis in the pre-Pauline churches, even if they also overlap with those already found in Hellenistic Judaism.[71] Such catalogues perform a paranetic function, e.g. in 1 Thessalonians 4:1–9, 5:14–18, 1 Peter 1:13–22 and Hebrews 13:1–3. Second, Dodd shows that the settings of Christian catechetical instruction include precisely the distinctive emphasis which reflects Paul's concern: a new convert does *not* 'have the right to do anything' (6:12). Third, more recently this has received confirmation from two sides. Negatively, Sevenster shows that Seneca's concerns with 'lists of vices and virtues' operate differently, as virtually self-contained ethical value-systems.[72] In positive terms, S. Wibbing sees a closer parallel between Paul's 'lists' and the moral choices of 'the two ways' expounded in the writings of Qumran.[73] Recently O. L. Yarborough's work sheds further light in the Christian setting.[74] If, therefore, these 'lists' reflect examples of common ethical instruction prepared for recent Christian converts, it is unlikely that they were intended to be understood without reference to the specific moral detail which they embody.

(b) The Greek world, Hellenistic Judaism in Paul and the Old Testament?

It is also frequently claimed that this material is taken over from Hellenistic Judaism or from Cynic-Stoic writers in contrast to the Old Testament tradition. The decisive argument for the dependence of 1 Corinthians 6:9–11 on Old Testament material comes from Brian Rosner, among others, in *Paul, Scripture and Ethics: A Study of 1 Corinthians 5–7* (1994). Rosner explores 'the two ways' theme in Deuteronomy 27 and 30, which corroborates Wibbing's research on its relation to 'the two ways' in Qumran (1 QS 4:9–11).[75] Furthermore, he endorses the arguments of Berger and Dexinger that the influence of the Decalogue on this passage (Exod. 20:1–17; Deut. 5:6–21), especially in relation to Deuteronomy 27:15–26 and Ezekiel 18 and 22, 'would be difficult to overstate'.[76] Moreover every term in 1 Corinthians 6:9 (as well as in Rom. 1:26, 27) finds its place in Septuagint (the Greek translation of the Old Testament used in Hellenistic Judaism and usually in the early Church). Scrogg's note about a minor expansion remains of minimal significance, in relation to the whole.[77] Although I have set out the details elsewhere, a comparison with a Greek concordance of the Septuagint demonstrates the point.[78] Earle Ellis and other specialists on this issue agree in seeing Old Testament influence behind these verses.[79]

(c) Linguistic issues and context

The translation of the Greek words *malakoi* and *arsenokoitai* has become notoriously controversial. The four key factors include lexicography, textual context, the drift of an enormous weight of literature on these terms, and the specific relation of the terms to the situation at Corinth. Two incisive studies, one by P. Zaas and the other by Ken Bailey, cut the ground from under the analysis of Scroggs, Furnish and others who adopt Scroggs's view on the ground each item in the catalogue relates to specific moral issues at Corinth, not to some abstract ethical tradition.[80] Throughout 1 Corinthians 5 and 6, he urges, Paul draws a contrast between a desire for what is not one's due and the new lifestyle which shares with Christ the way of the cross and new creation. Thus 5:1 begins with an abrupt allusion to *porneia* as illicit sex, or more broadly 'immorality', in which the man who commits incest is determined to 'have' (*echein*) his father's wife. The ministering to the self is reflected in the 'inflated' self-importance (*pephusiômenoi*, 5:2) and complacency of the church as a whole. This self-sufficient self-centredness must be destroyed (*olethron tês sarkês* 5:5). In 5:1–13 Paul calls for boundary-markers as against the urge to 'autonomy' reflected in the triumphalism, realised eschatology, or 'prophets' of Corinth.[81]

In this light the largely parallel catalogues in 5:9, 10 and in 6:9, 10 are readily intelligible, and, as Rosner shows, reflect the stance of Deuteronomy 23:1–9, 27, 30 and the Decalogue, as relating to the lifestyle expected of the people of God. The first term in 5:9 and 6:9, *porneia*, denotes going beyond the proper boundaries in sexual relations of any kind, without narrower specification. 'Adultery' is a subcategory within *porneia* which is used in the Decalogue (Exod. 20:13; Deut. 5:17). The second word in 5:9 is technically what semantic specialists call 'transparent': *pleonektais* alludes to those who seek to grasp 'more' (*pleon*) than is their lawful due, and may well include manipulative grasping of property-rights (perhaps referring to 5:1–5 if the incest was to secure an inheritance from which the Church might benefit), or the exploitation of the socially vulnerable for sordid gain. In chapter 6 this word occurs in verse 10, rather than second in the list. Here a different word comes second: the association of immoral acts with idolatry (*eidôlolatrai*), which so often appears in such catalogues in Hellenistic Judaism. But the theological context of idolatry in the Old Testament offers a deeper explanation than the claims of such writers as Scroggs, Bailey, Furnish or Boswell about 'Jewish identity' as over against the Gentiles. This issue impinges on references to 'idolatry' in the St Andrew's Day Statement.

In the Old Testament an idol is 'empty', and also a symbol of self-indulgent unfaithfulness to the God of Israel. Hence, like sexual immorality which is illicit (*porneia*) and like grasping language for 'more' than is due, idolatry constitutes the human to desire to seek an illusory god-like construct for the self which the self can control and shape in its image, together with a turning away from whole-hearted faithfulness to give God his due, as part of this same stance of seeking some 'more' for the self than God has ordained. The discussion of idols in 1 Corinthians 8:1–13 again affirms that an idol is empty nothingness (*ouden*, 8:4). To be associated with it reflects a grasping regard for the self, in contrast to 'love' (*agapê*) which seeks the good of others in 8:1–13. It points forward to *pleonektai* in the next verse. But it also belongs closely with the third term *moichoi* (those who practise adultery). In the Decalogue (Exod. 20:13 and Deut. 5:18) from which this Greek term is drawn (*ou moicheuseis*) adultery entails taking for the self what is the due of another.

We may now review the context which leads up to and follows the critical words, providing our own considered translation:

> Stop being misled: neither those who practise immoral [illicit] sexual relations, nor those who pursue practices bound up with idolatry, nor people who practise adultery, nor *malakoi* [passive homosexual partners, those who practise pederasty, call-boys], nor *arsenokoitai* [men who habituate sexual intimacy with men],

nor *kleptai* [those who thieve what is not theirs], nor *pleonektai* [those who always grasp for more], nor *methusoi* [those who drink to excess, drunkards], nor *loidoroi* [those who speak beyond the bounds of courtesy, users of verbal abuse], nor *harpages* [those who exploit others for greed, those who grasp for gain] can [*according to logic*] inherit God's reign [*i.e. all of these practices logically pre-empt for the self that which God's own chosen ordaining as King has allotted as beyond the bounds of what is due, and hence his reign is usurped*]. And this is what some of you used to be! (*ête, [continuous, habituated imperfect]*). But you were washed clean, you were set apart as holy, you were put right in your own standing, in the name of the Lord Jesus Christ and by the Spirit of our God [*a series of aorist verbs to denote God's sovereign, redemptive act in which life was transformed*].

The first point to make about *malakoi* (outside a sexual context, usually 'soft', as in 'soft clothing', Matt 11:8) is that whether it means 'catamites' or 'passive partner in homosexual relations' (Barrett), 'pederasty' or 'call-boys' (Scroggs), 'paid male prostitutes' (Boswell), or 'unmanly', 'effeminate' (as in Dio Chrys 49–66 and Diogenes Laertius 7, 173 and some English versions), no amount of lexicographical manipulation over *malakoi* can avoid the clear meaning of *arsenokoitai* as the activity of males (*arsên*) who have sexual relations with, sleep with (*koitês*) other males. The adjective *arsenikos* is the adjectival form of the noun 'male' (*arsên*).[82] In the view of Scroggs the two terms together condemn an active male who 'uses' a passive 'call-boy' (*malakos*) like a mistress. W. Schrage gives careful consideration to the view that *together* the terms denote respectively 'the passive and active partners in acts of pederasty', but after discussion he concludes that 'pederasty' probably offers a narrower translation than can be defended. The words more probably reflect 'male with male' in Leviticus 18:22 and Romans 1:27.[83]

Second, the view that one or both Greek words refer only to pederasty or to male prostitution for payment, as advocated by Kenneth Dover, Robin Scroggs, and others, cannot withstand the battery of detailed linguistic arguments brought against it by a number of historical and linguistic specialists. Moreover, it positively violates the contextual theme which has emerged of a general grasping beyond ordained boundaries in the face of what God assigns as the self's due which characterises every other habituated act in the list, culminating in Paul's rejection of the Corinthian slogan within the church 'I have the right to do anything' or 'all things are lawful'. In the study offered by the Committee on Human Sexuality by the Anglican Church of Canada (1985) Geoffrey Parke-Taylor appears to fall precisely into the Corinthian trap: 'The New Testament . . . celebrates grace rather than [*his exclusive conjunctions*] law as the basis of the liberty whereby Christ makes us free'.[84] In a subsequent comment he adds 'this does not mean that the Law is abolished (an antinomian viewpoint)'; but how the two statements are related is not entirely clear.[85]

David F. Wright, among others, has offered several closely argued studies of the Greek terms. Wright takes up the argument about the Old Testament background, pressed home by Ken Bailey, Zaas, and most recently Brian Rosner, to point out that 'Now no-one claims that Leviticus had pederasty in mind'.[86] Although Scroggs argues that the Septuagint, from the vantage-point of the wider Greek world, gives a certain 'spin' to the Hebrew of Leviticus 18:22 and 20:13, linguistic arguments that the terms denote male acts of sexual intimacy with other males, not specified more narrowly as pederasty or as prostitution, are put forward by C. Wolff, Ken Bailey, de Young, Hays, Malick, Fitzmyer, Senft and several others.[87] Wright, for example, argues that references to 'boys' in many languages allude to persons who perform specific roles, not to age (cf. the usage in the South of the United States for black labourers or servants in the first half of the century). Indeed, rather than narrowing the scope of the term (with Boswell, Scroggs, and more surprisingly Fee and NIV, J. B. de Young argues that the common inter-textual tradition of Leviticus 20:13 and 1 Corinthians 6:9 includes more than one form of male sexual relation with male. Ken Bailey argues that the 'catalogue' concerns the use of the body in ways which go beyond boundaries, whether in greed in eating and drinking (cf. 11:17–34), or in sexual indiscipline (5:1–6:20). The principle, as I have already argued, is that 'idolatry' and everything associated with it breeds a *laissez-faire* attitude towards ethical boundaries. Here, Nietzsche was entirely correct: only when the Jewish-Christian God of theism is 'dead', can it be the case that 'anything goes'.[88] Nevertheless the St Andrew's Day Statement rightly suggests that dialogue between 'competing interpretations' can stimulate useful reflection.

(*d*) Relation to the modern era

The grammar and syntax refers to habituated acts, whether heterosexual immorality, adultery, an aggressive grasping of 'more' at the expense of the socially or economically vulnerable, habitual excess of alcohol or the habit of performing homosexual acts. First, the passage does not give special attention to homosexual practices as 'worse' than any of the other habituated acts cited in 1 Corinthians 6:9, 10. As *habits of action*, which this passage has in view, all in principle contradict a Christian lifestyle. Witherington urges in his recent study of Corinth, 'As with other sins in the list, Paul is talking about behaviour, not inclinations, orientations, or natures'.[89] However, he adds, 'such *were* . . .' (6:11) implies that the Christians at Corinth have been released from a compulsive bondage to serve the inclinations of the self.[90] In Freudian terms, every tendency to grasp 'for more' can be sublimated into the runner's passion to achieve the goal (in 1 Corinthians of serving others) even if this entails self-discipline (1 Cor. 9:25). If 'the prize' is the model of true humanness as revealed in Christ, as I have noted above this excludes the notion that every truly human person 'needs' either heterosexual or homosexual intimacy to 'fulfil' their human nature.

Second, in the most recent (to date) major commentary on 1 Corinthians Christian Wolff includes a careful 'Excursus' in which he reconsiders the background of Leviticus 18:22 and 20:13. He fully recognises the part played by considerations about Canaanite religion in these early passages, and the Stoic, Epicurean and Cynic background to Paul. As against the unconvincing claims of many 'pro-gay' writers that Paul knew only of pederasty or perversion in homosexual relationships, Wolff rightly cites a range of Greek literature which speaks of 'genuine love' between male partners: 'Die Knabenliebe ist unverfälschte Liebe' (e.g. Plutarch,

Moralia, 751A).[91] Yet there is *also* in the Greek world, no less, a counter-theme that homosexual acts are unnatural (*widernatürlich*, e.g. Musonius, *Rufus*, Fragment 12). Here Musonius uses the term *para physis* ('against nature'). With his cosmopolitan life-experience and education, Wolff rightly urges, Paul places a negative judgment over the active-living out of desire, but not homosexuality as an orientation or a disposition (*als Veranlagung*): this is 'not to be placed under a negative judgment'.[92] To be sure, Wolff does not exclude the possible distinction between perversion and inversion which Boswell and others press. Wolff believes that Paul's main emphasis of negative judgment falls on 'egoistic' or 'self-centred' gratification which amounts to giving actualised expression to an inwardly perverted desire, recognising that Paul hardly has the 'psycho-social' aspects in view. Nevertheless we must refer back to our comments in section 3 about pre-cognitive models and 'surplus of meaning' in hermeneutics. We cannot restrict the stance of the passage to the mental processes which passed through Paul's mind at the time. We have to ask whether a lack of modern clinical knowledge invalidates Paul's observations set against his biblical and cosmopolitan understanding of all kinds of persons in his day, especially since the phenomenon of cultural pluralism was the very stuff of the life of Corinth, most of all among the Pauline churches.

Third, even if she seriously overstates the case, A. C. Wire correctly diagnoses a serious conflict between appeals to the freedom of the Spirit by prophets at Corinth (in her view, especially women prophets) and Paul's view that the Holy Spirit witnesses to lifestyle of Christ's voluntary acceptance of constraints which led to the cross. Throughout the epistle Paul redefines 'spirituality'. To be 'of the Spirit' is precisely *not* to be autonomous (3:1–3, 'I could not address good as "spiritual"'); the Spirit is not immanent in fallen humanity but comes from the transcendent God (*ek tou theou*, 2:14). The notion that 'the spiritual person' cannot be judged (2:15) is qualified by defining 'of the Spirit' as 'having the mind of Christ' (2:16). Thus Schrage rightly insists that the central thrust of 1:18–2:5 (and 2:6–4:21) is that of 'the cross as criterion' of thought and life.[93] This immediately addresses the kind of claims put forward by A. C. Wire[94] that Paul 'sees the common good at Corinth served by people restricting their self-expression . . . They [especially the women prophets of Corinth] see the common good as served by celebrating their own empowerment'; and by Elizabeth Stuart[95] that male and female complementarity arises only from 'a reading into nature already held beliefs for the purposes of social control'.

Fourth, the very emphasis on order, distinction and complementarity, which A. C. Wire and Stuart reject in the name of a theology of freedom and humanness, characterises Paul's approach not only to ethics in chapters 5 and 6, but to marriage and physical union in chapter 7; to the administration of the Lord's Supper in 11:17–34; to the differentiation between spiritual gifts of grace in chapters 12 to 14; and to the resurrection 'in a proper order' (15:23) when God determines what *sôma* he will give 'to each kind' (15:36) and even Christ, into whose image Christians are being transformed (15:49), renounces power 'that God may be all in all' (15:28). Paul hints that this differentiation of boundaries is rooted in a dialectic between unity and relationality in terms of God, Christ and the Holy Spirit (1 Cor. 12:4–6, as the basis in differentiation of 'gifts').

E. Stuart, like A. C. Wire and Elizabeth Castelli, suggests that much turns on 'power' just as many did at Corinth: 'I have the right to do anything' (6:12).[96] Paul asks whether 'power', 'rights' and the self-initiated adjustment of God-ordained boundaries really points to Christ. Virtually an entire corpus of research literature on Corinth establishes this issue as *the* Corinthian problem beyond all question.[97] The Corinthians were 'status-hungry people'.[98] Recently I have tried to argue in detail how this concern to replace truth-questions by power-questions is a disease of postmodernity which the Gospel (including 1 Corinthians) profoundly addresses.[99] Meanwhile, in contrast to some of E. Stuart's comments, 1 Corinthians 5–7 accords special importance to physical life, and to the 'one flesh' of marriage. Whether or not Paul assimilated certain typologies from the ancient world, the whole notion or concept of body (*sôma*) is not only the public arena of discipleship, but also depends on 'differentiation' of roles as integral to what the body (whether of the individual or the church community) actually consists in and means. Dale Martin's incisive, suggestive and at times provocative book *The Corinthian Body* (1995) bears this out in full detail.[100]

Finally, we should note that among his pastoral advice Paul nowhere advocates a need for 'healing' persons of gay orientation, as if to imply that a gay person could not be fully 'human' without heterosexual intimacy. The way in which Christ bears the untarnished image of God remains for Paul the paradigm of true humanness, as Schleiermacher, Barth, and among more recent writers Murphy O'Connor emphasise (discussed above). It is a serious mistake to isolate this issue from Paul's perception that God's grace is experienced through a variety of 'limit-situations' which abounded at Corinth. The sexual freedom of slaves, of those trapped in patronage networks, of probably the majority of the Christian community at Corinth, was seriously restricted. If a slave-owner married off his slave to another slave for whom the partner felt no attraction, or if the slave were not permitted to have any intimacy, it was not simply 'gay Christians' who sublimated constraints into service to, and love for, a wider circle. The notion that persons cannot live without sex is a modern secular one, and devalues, for example, the lifestyles of many women who lost fiancés in the First World War and never married, or those whose standards for a Christian home are so high that they never found 'the right partner'. Here the St Andrew's Day Statement speaks of 'various forms of self-denial' (p. 5), and recognises that these relate to 'wealth or poverty . . . educational success or failure' and to numerous factors.

To be sure, Christians should not callously remain indifferent to those whose discipleship entails poverty, chastity or obedience. A more significant difference between ancient and modern culture lies not in speculations about a distinction between 'inversion' and 'perversion' (a distinction concerning which the Wolfenden Report observed 'We have not found this distinction very useful', para. 35), but in the care of the Church and of the household for 'extended' members, when to be outside a nuclear family is to experience a loneliness foreign to the ancient world. This does *not* mean that the nuclear family is merely 'modern': even slaves, for example, could live in nuclear families within a larger 'household' orbit.[101] But electronic media and modern transport have isolated the nuclear family in time and space or ways which the churches need to address, for those who do not have loving support.

5. Other Biblical Passages and the St Andrew's Day Statement

It has become customary to view Romans 1:26, 27 in the way instantiated in Richard Hays: 'the most crucial . . . text remains Romans 1, because this is the only passage in the New Testament that places the condemnation of homosexual behaviour on an explicitly theological context'.[102] Like the St Andrew's Day Statement it contextualises homosexual practice within a broader critique of idolatry.[103] Moreover the reference to 'nature' (*physis*), if this is what the Greek means in Romans 1, has implications for the nature of humanity and human personhood, to which the St Andrew's Day Statement also alludes.[104] I have already discussed the issue of whether 'humanness' should be defined in terms of the humanness of Jesus Christ, but Romans 1 does indeed expound issues about *fallen* humanity more explicitly than in many other passages. Nevertheless the St Andrew's Day Statement includes three further factors in the debate: (i) 'strong and conflicting passions' which the debate arouses; (ii) the stance of those who 'conscientiously dissent from the biblical teaching as the church understands it'; and (iii) 'special considerations [which] affect the behaviour of the clergy'.[105]

With regard to the last of these points, 1 Timothy 1:10 needs to be viewed in the broader context of whether more rigorous criteria for suitability to hold ecclesial office reflect a 'two-level morality' in the Pastoral Epistles, or merely a pragmatically stricter observance of the boundaries a single morality applicable to all Christians. We shall return to the view of ethics and ministry in the Pastoral Epistles. With reference to (i) and (ii), Romans 1, not to mention Leviticus 18:22; and 20:13, generates more passion and entails more controversy than Corinthians 6:9–11. For while many argue that Romans 1 merely offers an *ad hoc* argument about Gentile fallenness and its symptoms drawn from standard Jewish synagogue sermon material, it is far more difficult to avoid the clear context of Corinthians 6:9–11 as concerning Christian ethical lifestyle.

Only by quite unconvincing arguments that ignore backgrounds of catechetical instructions about 'two ways' from Qumran to the early Church against an Old Testament background, can the argument be sustained that the 'catalogue' in 1 Corinthians 6:9–11 has no particular reference to specified patterns of habituated conduct. Even those who still dissent from this virtually conclusive argument (set out in detail above) may share in the debate without undue heat and passion. It may therefore offer convincing and pastorally constructive material for debate.

Romans 1:26, 27, however, invites a storm of protest about 'missing the point' on both sides, for it appears to raise the stakes by linking the debate with perversion, idolatry, and coloured rhetoric on one side, and by what is perceived as wilful blindness to a corporate and Jewish context on the other. Hence, while we shall outline the issues, we suggest that these should not obscure the moral 'anchor' of 1 Corinthians 6:9–11.

(a) Romans 1:26, 27

At minimum, three or more issues must be addressed as major questions of interpretation. First, Boswell, D. S. Bailey, Scroggs, and Furnish all regard the argument from nature (Gk, *para physin*, 1:26) as misguided. It is 'a commonplace of Greco-Roman attack on pederasty [and] has nothing to do with any theories of natural law'.[106] Peter Coleman calls it 'standard Jewish propaganda', while Boswell injudiciously claims that 'natural law' did not become a working concept for Christian theology until 'more than a millennium after Paul's death'.[107] Second, these writers also interpret the 'catalogue' in these verses as a merely generalised description of the corporate 'reality of the human predicament' drawn *in toto* from Hellenistic Jewish homily material about the heathen.[108] Furnish comments, 'Paul is not enumerating specific "sins", but listing some representative consequences of sin', while Scroggs calls it 'Paul's real story of the universal fall'.[109] Third, Paul is indeed using standard Jewish synagogue sermon material to address the problem of sin in the Gentile world, the purpose of the passage must be understood within the context of some larger rhetorical strategy on the part of Paul. The purpose of the epistle is to show that both in terms of sin and in terms of grace, Jewish Christians and Gentile Christians, or Jews and Gentiles, stand on the same footing. Hence Paul first stands in solidarity with synagogue preachers in denouncing 'Gentile' sin (the Jewish readers cry 'Amen'); but then turns to his Jewish (or rather, Jewish-Christian) readers to exclaim: '*You no less* have no excuse, *you who pass judgment on others*' (Rom. 2:1). This sharpens Paul's point painfully and powerfully. Boswell, Scroggs, and others may legitimately press this point.

Nevertheless, we must not accept the first two of these three arguments too hastily, or overrate the significance of the third. As we argued in our discussion of the hermeneutics of Betti, patience and listening with respect to the other is required for interpretative integrity and truth.

1. The major commentaries agree that Paul explicitly describes lesbian (v. 26) and gay (v. 27) intimacy in parallel terms. Charles Cranfield translates: 'Their females have exchanged natural intercourse for that which is contrary to nature (*para physin*) and likewise also the males, having abandoned natural intercourse with the female, have burned in their lust for one another, males with males perpetrating shamelessness . . .'.[110] J. D. G. Dunn comments, 'Paul's attitude to homosexual practice is unambiguous', and interprets 'contrary to nature' not in a Stoic or Greek sense, nor in the sense of 'convention', which arguably occurs in 1 Corinthians 11:14, but as part of the cosmic distortion which results from idolatry.[111] He explains how a process of 'internal' judgment comes to operate here. If people substitute the empty, barren, hollow constructs of deity in place of the creative Creator-God, even human creativity stands under threat. It results in 'a perversion of *the creature's share in creating*'.[112] This interpretation sufficiently explains the coherence of Paul's argument to invite respect.

The fact that *para physin* occurs in Stoic texts should not mislead us. Word-occurence is not to be confused with word-use, i.e. which words are used is a different issue from how words are used, and for what purpose. By way of example, Samuel Laeuchli readily shows that gnostic texts take up many major items of Pauline vocabulary; but they use these words in utterly un-Pauline ways.[113] I have urged this principle of semantics and of philosophy of language elsewhere repeatedly.[114] To be sure, 'contrary to nature' has a corporate dimension; the individual is an instantiation of a broader principle. But Dunn does not exclude an *added* Stoic nuance: Paul uses the word 'unnatural' with full awareness of the resonances which his readers will perceive from their currency in the many writings and discourses in the Graeco-Roman world. Joseph Fitzmyer adopts a similar exegetical standpoint. Paul stresses that homosexual acts are 'unnatural', in the same sense as that in which Paul will employ *physis* in Romans 11 when he speaks about olive branches which grow 'naturally' (*kata physin*) in contrast to those which are 'grafted' by human interference in the course of nature (*para physin*). Fitzmyer interprets the Greek here in Romans 1 to mean 'the natural order of things'.[115]

It is only by a misuse of what James Barr has called 'illegitimate totality transfer' that counter-arguments about the use of *physis* in Corinthians 11:14 could carry any weight.[116] Any serious exegete or lexicographer knows that the same Greek word may denote one of several distinct but related meanings which depend on the context of discourse. Thus whether *physis* in 1 Corinthians 11:14 means 'nature', 'convention', or 'habituated patterns determining what is expected' has little or no bearing in Paul's use of the word in Romans 1.[117] It is not entirely relevant to assert with Boswell, even if it were true, that only with Thomas Aquinas did Stoic concepts of 'natural law' enter Christian theology. For while Paul relativises such natural capacities as 'conscience', which is a functional mechanism and not 'the voice God', he nevertheless accords conscience and *physis* a significant role. The themes of 'order' and 'boundaries' are Pauline ones, as we have argued with reference to 'autonomy' and 'disorder' at Corinth. The careful exegesis of Cranfield, Dunn, Fitzmyer and others shows that to draw the inference that Paul is merely repeating stereotypical Stoic polemic against pederasty is too sweeping an account of these verses which invites correction in the light of more painstaking exegesis.

Richard Hays has provided an explicit rebuttal of Boswell's arguments in his careful research article 'Relations Natural and Unnatural: A Response to John Boswell's Exegesis of Romans 1'.[118] The central point in Romans 1:18–28, Hays argues, is that 'idolatry finally debases both the worshipper and the idol'.[119] The irony of sin and fallenness 'plays itself out'; the creature's original impulse towards self-glorification ends in self-destruction. The result is 'distortion': animal-forms become distorted objects of worship: God's gifts for creativity and life likewise become turned in on themselves and debased. Hence Paul uses the word 'exchanged' to set in contrast what results from what was purposed.[120] The contrast between 'natural' (*kata physin*) and 'unnatural' (*para physin*) is central and deliberate; not a mere spin-off from Stoic or Hellenistic-Jewish discourse.

2. The 'catalogue', then, is more than a generalised rhetorical block: it offers a series of concrete, specific, instantiations of the issue under discussion by Paul, all the more powerful for its concrete, cumulative, logic. It is not merely a matter of cashing in on general Jewish 'indignation' at Gentile conduct, but part of a carefully constructed logical argument about the place of God in people's lives and the respective series of consequences which flow from divine judgment and divine grace.[121] Hays asserts:

> Boswell is able to defend [his] assertion only by disregarding completely the argumentative context of Rom 1: 26, 27 . . . The reference to homosexual behaviour functions as prima facie evidence of the moral confusion and blindness which has come upon the human race as a result of its refusal to acknowledge God as the creator . . . The association of *physis* in Rom 1:26, 27 with some notion of ideal, universal, norms, cannot be dismissed.[122]

Hays specifically appeals to hermeneutics here. Boswell, he points out, makes his case too easy by asking whether Paul is *either* addressing homosexuality as a condition of a group of individuals *or* using general Hellenistic rhetoric. Hermeneutical reflection suggests that neither option hears what Paul is saying. Paul is defining an ideal and a distortion; but he is not singling out specific groups for ethical rebuke or instruction. There is no hint that some 'group' is 'constitutionally "gay"' but there is a general inference to be drawn that gay intimacy is not the kind of sexual intimacy which God ordained for humanity.[123] Hays concludes his article with a refutation of Boswell's argument that early Christians were tolerant of 'gay' sexuality.[124] He has more respect for Scroggs's more careful presentation of arguments (Scroggs and Hays are biblical specialists; Boswell is not); but observes 'in the end I am not persuaded by Scroggs' argument' on exegetical grounds. The restriction of the issue to pederasty is not only speculative; it also ignores the force of Paul's broader logic in this chapter.

A very recent work definitively endorses Hays' approach and his critique of Boswell and Scroggs. Mark D. Smith discusses these issues in Romans 1:26, 27 in a research article of thirty pages, during which he observes, 'Most recent scholars agree that Boswell's interpretation of Rom 1: 26, 27 is untenable.'[125]

3. I have already considered the claim, in the course of my other argument, that Romans 1:26, 27 forms only part of a rhetorical device to permit Jewish or Jewish-Christian readers to find common ground with Paul's expression of stereotypical 'indignation' against Gentile sin, only to find themselves on the same general footing. This is part of Paul's rhetorical strategy, but a far deeper theology of fallenness is at issue. The 'barren emptiness' and lack of covenant faithfulness which follows abandoning exclusive loyalty to God as Creator and source of grace constitutes part of the larger concern of Romans. Hence Romans 1:26, 27 does indeed bear on the current debate. But great care and sensitivity is demanded in ascertaining the precise hermeneutic, interpretation, and exegesis which does full justice to the complexities of these verses. The St Andrew's Day Statement speaks of 'disordered desires' in a general, corporate, sense (p. 7).

(b) 1 Timothy 1:10: Double standards or practical stringencies?

It is generally agreed that this verse alludes to homosexual practices (Gk. *arsenokoitais*). But it does not isolate homosexual acts from other acts which express 'lawless' attitudes. Here these include acts of general heterosexual immorality (*pornois*), those who unlawfully deprive people of their freedom probably to sell them into slavery (*andrapodistais*) perhaps simply 'slave-dealer', possibly procurer', and those who go in for perjury (*pseustais epiorkois*), presumably for unlawful gain or advantage. All this stands in contrast to 'healthy teaching' and 'healthy' living, which is expected of every Christian. As in 1 Corinthians 6:9–11, the issue is primarily that of an ethics which observes God-ordained boundaries, and the mistaken view that a Christian is 'autonomous': 'I have the right to do anything' (1 Cor. 6:12). Barrett rightly notes the appeal to *nomos* as a constraint on 'autonomy' to promote healthy lifestyle.[126] A. T. Hanson links the context with 'wholesome' ethics for new converts, as we identified for the background of 1 Corinthians 6:9–10.[127]

It is instructive to compare the 'virtues and vices' listed in 1 Timothy 1:10 with those mentioned in 1 Corinthians. Clear parallels can be traced between habituated acts which are regarded as 'off-limits' for Christians in 1 Corinthians and in the Pastoral Epistles. But the Pastorals use 'stricter' criteria when the issue becomes one of suitability for the work of office-holders in the Church, without the slightest hint of promoting any 'two-level morality'. Thus, while 1 Corinthians 6:9 views 'drunkenness' (*methusoi*) as a practice of habituated action to be off-limits for Christians in general, 1 Timothy 3:8 insists that deacons (Gk. *diakonoi*) should go one step further, and should 'not indulge excessively in wine' (*me oinô pollô*). We cannot read too much into the terminology alone, since bishops or elders (*episkopoi*) also are expected to be sober and to avoid 'addiction to drink' (*mê paroinon*, 3:3). Yet the general sense is that of self-control for all believers, while those especially in the public eye as officials or functionaries of the Church should be still more careful to maintain 'a good reputation with outsiders' and to avoid public disgrace (3:7).

In the context of the current debate in the contemporary churches, the Pastoral Epistles seem to suggest that while as a general principle habituated practice of gay intimacy is off-limits for all Christian believers, to propose more rigorous application of general ethical criteria to clergy need not imply a two-level moral standard, but a pragmatic concern that a Christian witness which may be undermined by a less-than-ideal lifestyle constitutes an even more serious obstacle to credibility for clergy or officers than in other cases. For while 1 Timothy rejects such conduct for all Christians, given that Christians also fail and fall, a more consistently transparent lifestyle is expected of leaders or office-holders. This is necessary for practical reasons of public witness and credibility, not because it suggests two levels of ethics. Once again, homosexual practice must not be isolated from parallel issues. The morality of speech (lying, verbal abuse or courtesy and honest speech) for example, like the issue of excessive drink, concerns all Christians. But anyone who has written references for ordinands or for Church appointments knows that a 'stricter' application of what is required for all must be observed when considering ordination and appointments. The ruling of the Church of England's House of Bishops of 1991 may not be the ideal but, given a fierce lack of consensus in the Church, it cannot be accused of a lack of consistency or moral integrity.

(c) Leviticus 18:22 and 20:13

Just as in my view 1 Corinthians 6:9–11 and perhaps 1 Timothy 1:10 offer more transparent and less controversial sources for present discussion than Rom 1:26, 27, even though on closer inspection Rom 1:26, 27 proves to add weight to the issues, so Leviticus 18 and 20 can add fuel to the heat of the debate without adding initially to the New Testament witness. Each party all too readily finds point-scoring material to hand, and this can add bitterness to the debate.

Within the traditional conservative horizon of reading, Leviticus 18:22 urges that 'to lie with a man as with a woman' is abomination (Heb. *tô'êbhâh*) which is categorized alongside bestiality ('having sexual relations with an animal', 18:23), with child-sacrifice (18:21) and various forms of 'perversion' and 'defilement'. Martin Noth comments, 'Verses 19–23 give a general veto on all non-permissable and especially unnatural sex relationships (*allem widernatürliche Geschlechtsbeziehungen*)'.[128] The magisterial and detailed German commentary by Karl Elliger of Tübingen heads the material of 18:1–30 'Sexual Intercourse' (*Geschlechticher Umgang*).[129] Hence, the argument runs, there can be no suggestion that 18:22 addresses the present debate only as a 'proof-text' torn from a different context. Elliger points out that the Hebrew translated 'abomination' demonstrates its nature as 'the unthinkable horror' by equally denoting what it is to blaspheme the name of God, as 'absolutely forbidden' without reference to some socio-ethical viewpoint.[130] Further, it will be argued that in Leviticus 20:13 homosexual practice 'with a male as with a woman' is an abomination (*tô'ēbhôh*) to be punished by *death* for both parties.[131] What could demonstrate the seriousness of the prohibition more conclusively?

From the other side of the debate, however, it is frequently urged that the Levitical Holiness Code (Lev. 17–26) is concerned with purity laws designed to mark off Israel's distinctiveness as over against her Canaanite neighbours. Canaanite practices are 'abominations', and so whatever coincides with them, from homosexual practices to child-sacrifice, comes within this category. Thus 'death' becomes the penalty for consulting departed spirits (Lev. 20:6:8), for children who 'curse' (i.e. habitually dishonour) their parents (Lev. 20:9; cf. Exod. 21:17), for child-sacrifice and involvement in the cult of Molech (Lev. 20:2–5, death by stoning), and for adultery as well as homosexual acts and incest, or sexual relations with animals (Lev. 20: 10–16). Nevertheless, so the argument runs, today we do not in fact execute adulterers, mediums or sexual perverts, let alone children who 'curse' their parents. The concern of the Holiness Code (Lev. 17–26), it is argued, is to protect *ritual purity* not morality, and it conceives of purity in terms of unmixed types and tokens of identity. To be 'pure', Furnish declares, is 'to be an unblemished specimen [token] of one's kind [type] unmixed with any other kind . . . This is why the Holiness Code prohibits such things as . . . wearing a garment that is "made of two different materials" ' (Lev 19:19).[132] But today we do not hesitate to wear mixtures of wool and cotton, or of nylon and polyester, or whatever. The 'sexual prohibitions', Furnish concludes, have more to do with ritual purity as over against Canaanite and Egyptian identity than with morality, or with love for the other.

This response to the more traditional view cannot simply be brushed aside. It is a matter of hermeneutical integrity to compare the impact of a variety of prohibitions in the Holiness Code on modern life, and on life within the Christian Church. Thus Choon-Leong Seow compares qualification for the levitical priesthood in Leviticus 21 with criteria for Church office-holders today, in the light of such prohibitions as that which forbids 'shaving off the edges of their beards' (Lev. 21:5), or a veto on the physically handicapped (Lev. 21: 17–20) as imperfect models of the human species. Seow concludes: 'Yet this is rarely discussed. It hardly needs to be said that all the notions of purity and holiness as set forth in the Levitical Code are culturally conditioned'.[133] In historical and theological terms, D. N. Fewell and my former colleague at Sheffield University, David M. Gunn have argued in detail that 'man's seed' represents the central theme of Leviticus 18, but probably in the context of patrilineal inheritance of 'the land' which God has promised and given, in contradistinction to the people and practices of the Canaanites.[134]

On the other side, however, verdicts concerning the role of the Holiness Code remain diverse, not least because of possible sources and perhaps multiple editing. K. H. Graf first argued for the special compositional integrity of Leviticus 18–26 in 1866, and A. Klostermann coined the term 'Holiness Code' for it in 1877. More recently J. Milgrom, perhaps the major authority (with Elliger) on Leviticus, does not wish to isolate the Holiness Code from its broader Levitical context so sharply. To date, unfortunately, his commentary reaches only to Leviticus 16. Milgrom shows in a succession of books and articles how 'purity' and ethics are closely interrelated, even if the history of the interpretation of the Holiness Code addresses a succession of differing cultural situations.[135] As our discussion of hermeneutics revealed, *prior* judgments of *generalising method* (e.g. whether this Levitical material is 'theology' or 'ethics'or as contextually conditioned ritual) prejudice the agenda before discussion and dialogue has begun, and generate more heat than light. In his detailed commentary on Leviticus, Gordon Wenham, for example, does not ignore issues of social context, but perceives a trans-contextual theme as running through various contexts of reading, namely 'exclusive allegiance to God'.[136] This theme provides coherence and integrity to Leviticus 17–26, and reflects the background of the Decalogue. As Milgrom perceives it, the core concern is 'Be holy, as I the Lord am holy'.

Part of what is entailed in exclusive allegiance to God 'is that a man will seek a partner among his own people' and will respect the ordained boundaries of appropriate sexual relationships.[137] The nature of the relationship with Canaanite, Ugaritic, Mesopotamian and Egyptian practices is not only controversial. But as against what Bonnington and Fyall call a 'Marcionite' view of the Old Testament, expose the distinctiveness of a covenant relationship with God which excludes both marital unfaithfulness (e.g. heterosexual adultery) and 'autonomy' (e.g. freedom for children to dishonour parents; freedom to practise sexual relations with animals; and freedom to choose any pattern of sexual intimacy which is self-chosen rather than ordained by God within the terms of the covenant).[138] In Old Testament theology W. Eichrodt and in modern theology Barth, Pannenberg, and Jüngel, all urge as central the theme of a sovereign God who freely in sovereignty chooses to limit his own sovereign freedom through covenant promise for the good of the whole created order so that security and trust become possible, and people 'know where they stand' with God.[139] On the human side, this brings us back to 1 Corinthians 6:9–11 and its relation to 6:12: does a Christian 'have the right to do anything'? (1 Cor. 6:12). Or are there, as the Holiness Code and Paul enjoin, 'boundaries' which transpose 'freedom' into self-destruction?

In the view of Martin Noth, followed in the New Testament context of interpretation by Brian Rosner, these 'boundaries' point back to the Decalogue.[140] For example, prohibitions against children who 'curse' their parents arise because this violates 'Honour your father and mother' (Exod. 20:12). Many of the sexual boundaries are extensions of the commitment to marital faithfulness. 'Thou shalt not commit adultery' (Exod. 20:14). The so-called ethical commandments, however, flow from the first four: exclusive commitment to God as husband, father, and source of true humanness finds expression in contented faithfulness to what God has ordained, in contrast to the striving for 'more' (the tenth commandment and 1 Cor. 6:9–11) which distracts persons from that exclusive worship of God. Rosner declares 'The significance of the Decalogue (Exod. 20:1–12; Deut. 5:6–21) . . . would be difficult to overstate. Other collections of laws, such as Lev. 19, Deut. 27:15–26 . . . have been compared to the Decalogue.'[141]

Nevertheless, we have said that we cannot simply brush aside issues about our different attitudes to the scope of the death penalty and the wearing of mixed fabrics today. We must conclude, therefore, with a brief return to hermeneutics.

6. Hermeneutics Again: Speculations on Shifting Horizons of the Present

I have endeavoured to rank and evaluate the biblical passages which usually play a major role in the debate in such a way as to combine the least possible polarisation and confrontation with exegetical and hermeneutical integrity. Had space allowed, I should have also addressed broader questions about biblical material. I have showed that both Reception Theory and a hermeneutic of suspicion of interests can be double-edged; but neither can they be avoided. A hermeneutic which takes full account of preconscious stance and 'surplus of meaning' placed a question mark against the view that the biblical writers could have known nothing of same-gender attraction without sexual intimacy, or of same-gender intimacy which was neither violent, commercial, nor pederastic. Although I have allowed for dialogue concerning a variety of understandings of Leviticus 18 and 20 and of Romans 1, 1 Corinthians 6:9–11 and 1 Timothy 1:10 seem to raise only illusory problems concerning their relevance, since they occur in contexts of ethical lifestyle for all Christians.

Nevertheless, a valid hermeneutical approach should take more account than we have so far achieved of the horizons of experience today which all sides bring to the text. Clinical accounts of homosexual orientations remain relevant; but we need to note that no clear consensus about these issues yet exists among professional researchers.[142] We noted that a number of clinicians doubt whether the distinction between 'inversion' and 'perversion' assists the debate at all. Yet in the light of what consensus there is, a hermeneutic of selfhood suggests that it is *intellectually distorting and morally questionable to encourage people who are in process of reflecting on their own sexuality to categorise or 'label' themselves prematurely*, or to box in their humanness by such generalising labels as 'straight' or 'gay', not least since most clinicians tend to speak of a spectrum or sliding-scale of orientation. This coheres exactly with what Gadamer, Ricoeur, Habermas and Betti insist upon in hermeneutics; they warn against laying down criteria and labels in advance of a long, patient, journey of corrigible attempts to understand the self or texts, or truth. Ricoeur's hermeneutics of selfhood bears on this and I discuss his approach and my own hermeneutic of selfhood elsewhere.[143]

To understand 'present experience' may enhance rather than necessarily obscure the relevance and force of the biblical witness. I conclude with a speculative anecdotal example. It is often argued, as we have seen, that since we wear mixed fabrics and genetically manipulate the production of crops and even the breeds of animals without special alarm, we can hardly take seriously claims that the Levitical Holiness Code addresses ethical value-systems today. Yet my own horizon of interpretation is partially coloured by my appointment by the Ministry of Health to the Human Fertilisation and Embryology Authority. Our task is to monitor and to inspect clinical practices of fertility treatment which entail *in vitro* fertilisation, and related applications for research licenses in the field. Codes of Practice and clinical protocols must match the intention of parliamentary legislation which treats 'mixing and boundaries' in human embryology as of a qualitatively different order from genetic mutations or mixing in vegetable matter or even in certain specified species of animals. Even in the case of animals, however, not all share the same status in the field of genetics and embryology.

Clinics would be eager in some cases merely to use criteria of 'success' and 'autonomy', i.e. free choice by a mother in consultation with her clinician. But the UK Government rightly charges us with evaluating a network of related ethical issues, including the welfare of the future child. Under the heading of the welfare of the child, for example, the Human Fertilisation and Embryology Act 1990 includes within 'licence conditions for *in vitro* fertilisation': 'A *woman* shall not be provided with treatment services unless account has been taken of the welfare of any child who may be born as a result of the treatment (including the need *of that child for a father*)' (my italics, chapter 37, section 13, subsection (5) [HMSO, 1990, 7]). The work of inspecting clinics and of granting licences for clinical practice and for scientific research entails a constant rigorous scrutiny of 'boundaries'. Some researchers and some women's groups would perhaps value a stronger emphasis on the slogan used at Corinth, 'I have the right to do anything', just as some would question the relevance of 'boundaries', distinctions and order which Leviticus (however we recontextualise the legislative practice) perceives as a legal principle of order for the welfare of creation or of national life as a *principle*. In these terms Leviticus speaks to us.

The issue raised by such works as those of Elizabeth Stuart and Michael Vasey concerns the status of traditional 'boundaries' in sexual or gender relations. Stuart argues, against the Congregation for the Doctrine of the Faith, in a letter to the Roman Catholic Bishops about homosexuality, that the complementarity of sex is not 'divinely ordered'; it is a social construct derived from contextual and cultural variables.[144]

Here we must return to hermeneutics of biblical material and the hermeneutics of human selfhood. First, I referred in passing, in connection with the Boswell–Hays controversy about Romans 1:26, 27, to what I regard as a definitive discussion by Mark Smith of this passage in this context in a substantial research article of 1996.[145] We also noted his evidence that far from being aware of same-sex intimacy only in terms of narrow socially constructed 'models' of the Old Testament and Hellenistic Judaism (as Scroggs claimed) 'the kaleidoscopic picture that emerges from the ancient evidence sounds strangely familiar [in the light of] American sexual behaviour [today]'.[146] With evidence and wisdom Smith dissociates *sexual 'models'* (concerning which a wide distance stretches from the ancient world to today) from *sexual phenomena* about which Paul observed included the spectrum of variety which we see today.[147] It is therefore misleading, Smith concludes, to appeal to theories of social construction to disengage Romans 1 from today on the grounds of 'hermeneutics'. Smith, however, also reminds us that Paul sees homosexual intimacy as *one among many* symptoms of human fallenness, along with greed, materialism, self-assertion, and other qualities which fall short of the ideal, in contrast to today's obsessiveness with this particular phenomenon.

If we apply Smith's research to our own agenda in the Church, two consequences follow. First, while gay or lesbian sexual acts fall short of the ideal along with, for example, materialism or self-indulgence, we require a more rigorous standard in *all* these ethical matters from our church officers than from others. The gay lobby would be right to regard as discrimination the ignoring of a record of greed, laziness and self-indulgence on the part of one ordinand if gay practice is seized upon as decisive in the case of another.

Second, we cannot shelter behind the mistaken assumption, drawn from M. Foucault, that 'homosexuality' is a nineteenth-century social construct which could not have entered Paul's horizons. I have discussed the claims of Barthes, Foucault and Derrida elsewhere.[148] Foucault offers overlapping accounts of the concept of 'madness' in his *Folie et déraison: Histoire de la folie à l'age classique* (1961, 2nd edn 1976; abridged version in English as *Madness and Civilization*, 1965) and the concept of 'sexuality' in *The History of Sexuality* (3 vols, Pantheon, 1978, 1985, 1986). What *counts as* 'madness' depends on such context-variables as the ambivalence in pre-modern times between '*non-rational*' or 'inspired' and '*non-rational*' or animal-like and therefore to be confined. But in the nineteenth century madness came to be perceived as *illness* to be treated by people in white coats in so-called asylums of safety or hospitals for the insane with locked doors. Nowadays 'treatment' within communities is possible, and attitudes vary.

Foucault blames Christianity for viewing madness as 'a scandal against reason'. He views sexuality also in terms of variable perceptions and social practices, but fundamentally in terms of power-play. The supposed 'binary' complementarity dissolves when we perceive that powerful and powerless are no longer two self-contained categories, corresponding to sovereignty-obedience, domination-subjection.[149] The concept of homosexuality suffers similar pejorative developments as 'madness', Foucault argues. Just as madness changed currency, so homosexuality acquired the status of threat to protect 'the bourgeois family' and become the object of 'policing'.[150] But anyone who knows the works of Foucault knows that his entire philosophical agenda is to attack all notions of 'norms' and 'normality' as social constructs of institutional guilds, especially medical professionals, police officers, the higher ranks of the army, clergy and especially bishops, bureaucrats and politicians.

Here hermeneutics emerges again. For a hermeneutics of suspicion and of 'interest' will reveal two difficulties. First, Foucault's own truth-claims offer a disguised *politics*. They are a left-wing politics of *power* themselves, just as J. Baudrillard perceives in his incisive *Forget Foucault* (see above). Second, postmodern writers notoriously confuse *extra-linguistic reference* (madness or sexual conduct as *a phenomenon* in the public domain) and *intra-linguistic sign-systems* (by what *language* are these identified as what we perceive them to be?) As Hays and Mark Smith so clearly observe about Romans 1:26, 27, Paul speaks of *phenomena*, under whatever linguistic guise signals aspects of social construction. I have even heard it suggested that because the *word* 'homosexuality' did not belong to first-century vocabulary stocks, the *concept* could not have existed. This is tantamount to suggesting that because Eskimos have a language-stock for different degrees of whiteness in snow, English-speaking people can neither observe them nor draw inferences from them.[151]

If we had space, we could elaborate a broader hermeneutics of humanity and human selfhood, developing further the themes which I have tried to develop in *Interpreting God and the Postmodern Self*, especially in the light of the biblical themes well-expounded by J. Murphy O'Connor in *Becoming Human Together* (cited above) and by Udo Schnelle in *The Human Condition*. Schnelle sees freedom not as 'autonomy' or 'self-fulfilment' but in terms of God's giving himself in 'the one human being, Jesus, [who] lived not from himself . . .'[152] Likewise the Church of England Doctrine Commission Report, *The Mystery of Salvation*, insists that 'fulfilment is the more appropriate term for non-religious aspirations'.[153]

In a very subtle discussion of Paul's interpretation of gender-identity in 1 Corinthians 11:2–16, Judith Gundry-Volf has recently (1997) proposed that Paul superimposes the three 'maps' of culture, eschatology and creation on to the subject to offer a distinctive angle of view. Culture re-enforces gender-differences, which Paul utilises, especially in view of the perceptions of the Church by outsiders. Eschatology subverts gender-hierarchy. But, she concludes, 'creation serves Paul as a theological locus for reflection on gender. *Creation supplies the fundamental ground for the distinction between male and female that Paul wants to uphold by re-enforcing its cultural expression.*'[154] But creation avoids hierarchy, since the mother-son model complements traditional understandings of the husband-wife model. All are fundamental.

The St Andrew's Day Statement seeks to defuse 'conflicting passions' not least by re-exploring 'competing interpretations' of Scripture and of humanness. We have attempted to consider a hermeneutic of humanness and more fully of certain Scripture passages. Apart from careful exegesis of 1 Corinthians 6:9–11 and 1 Timothy 1:10, which otherwise appear in straightforward ethical contexts about Christian lifestyle, the other more complex biblical allusions invite a more sophisticated hermeneutic than that which has usually marked this debate. The aim of this essay has been to provide, here, at least in part such a contribution as that which the St Andrew's Day Statement invites.

Notes

1. F. Schleiermacher, *Hermeneutics: The Handwritten Manuscripts* (Engl. from Germ. edn by H. Kimmerle, Scholars Press, 1977), p. 42.
2. F. Schleiermacher, *On Religion: Speeches to its Cultured Despisers* (Engl. Kegan Paul, Trench, 1893), p. 55.
3. Rightly identified as the aim of hermeneutics, e.g. by David E. Klemm, *Hermeneutical Inquiry* (2 vols., Scholars Press, 1986), vol. 1, p. 3.
4. Hans-Georg Gadamer, *Truth and Method* (2nd Engl. edn from 8th Germ. edn., Sheed & Ward, 1993), p. 363; cf. 362–79.
5. Gadamer, *Truth and Method*, p. 369.
6. H.-G. Gadamer, *Gesammelte Werke* (10 vols., Mohr, 1986–94), vol. 10, *Nachträge und Verzeichisse* (1994); cf vol. 7, *Griechische Philosophie III: Plato im Dialog* (1990). See further his article in the *Frankfurter Allegemeine* (Oct. 1989) repr. in H. J. Silverman (ed.) *Gadamer and Hermeneutics* (Routledge, 1991), pp. 13–19.
7. Gadamer, *Truth and Method*, p. 579.
8. E. Betti, *Allgemeine Auslegungslehre als Methodik der Geisteswissenschaften* (Mohr, 1967), p. 21.
9. P. Ricoeur, *Freud and Philosophy: An Essay in Interpretation* (Yale University Press, 1970), p. 27.
10. J. Habermas, *Knowledge and Human Interests* (Engl. 2nd edn, Heinemann, 1978); cf more recently *Zur Logik der Sozialwissenschaften* (5th edn, Suhrkamp, 1982) and *The Theory of Communicative Action* (Engl. 2 vols., Polity Press, 1984 and 1987).
11. e.g. Zygmunt Bauman, *Hermeneutics and Social Science: Approaches to Understanding* (Hutchinson, 1978); Charles V. Gerkin, *The Living Human Document: Re-visioning Pastoral Counselling in a Hermeneutical Mode* (Abingdon, 1984 and 1991); and Donald Capps, *Pastoral Care and Hermeneutics* (Fortress, 1984).
12. D. S. Bailey, *Homosexuality and the Western Christian Tradition* (Longmans Green, 1955), pp. 29–41; as against 'possible references', pp. 41–5.

13. Luther, *On the Bondage to the Will* (Clark, 1957): 'Take Christ from the scriptures, and what more will you find there?' (71). Luther's key was '*was Christum treibt*'; Scripture points 'to Christ alone' (Luther, *Works* vol. 35, Muhlinberg, 1960, p. 132).

14. V. P. Furnish, 'The Bible and Homosexuality', in J. S. Siker (ed.), *Homosexuality in the Church: Both Sides of the Debate* (Westminster and Knox, 1994), p. 23.

15. A. Thatcher, *Liberating Sex A Christian Sexual Theology* (SPCK, 1993), p. 18.

16. M. Vasey, *Strangers and Friends. A New Exploration of Homosexuality and the Bible* (Hodder & Stoughton, 1995), pp. 249–50.

17. J. Murphy O'Connor, *Becoming Human Together* (Glazier, 1982), pp. 33–57.

18. F. Schleiermacher, *The Christian Faith* (Engl. T. & T. Clark, rept. 1989 from 2nd Germ. edn), pp. 282–314 (ss. 70–3)

19. K. Barth, *Church Dogmatics*, vol. 3, part 2 (Engl. T. & T. Clark, 1960), p. 50 (s. 43).

20. Barth, *Church Dogmatics*, vol. 3, part 2, p. 43 (s. 43).

21. U. W. Mauser, 'Creation and Human Sexuality in the New Testament', in R. L. Brawley (ed), *Biblical Ethics and Homosexuality: Listening to Scripture* (Westminster and Knox, 1996), pp. 3–15, 13.

22. R. Morgan with J. Barton, *Biblical Interpretation* (OUP, 1988), p. 8.

23. M. Bonnington and R. Fyall, *Homosexuality and the Bible* (Grove Books, 1996), p. 5.

24. Bailey, *Homosexuality*, p. 39.

25. Furnish, 'The Bible and Homosexuality', p. 18; cf. pp. 19–35.

26. Hence the deliberate title, A. C. Thiselton, *New Horizons in Hermeneutics: The Theory and Practice of Transforming Biblical Reading* (HarperCollins, 1992; rept. Paternoster, 1995) and *The Two Horizons* (Paternoster, 1980).

27. H. R. Jauss, *Toward an Aesthetic of Reception* (Engl. University of Minnesota Press, 1982), p. 142 and throughout.

28. Jauss, *Aesthetic of Reception*, p. 145.

29. Bailey, *Homosexuality*, p. 9.

30. Bailey, *Homosexuality*, p. 13.

31. D. F. Wright, 'Homosexuality: The Relevance of the Bible', *Evangelical Quarterly*, vol. 61, 1989, p. 292; cf. pp. 291–300.

32. Ibid. and D. J. Atkinson, *Homosexuals in the Christian Fellowship* (Latimer House, 1979), pp. 80–2.

33. See further Bailey, *Homosexuality*, pp. 1–28, and R. C. Holub, *Reception Theory* (Methuen, 1984) and J. N. D. Kelly, *The Epistles of Peter and of Jude* (Black, 1969), p. 258.

34. R. B. Hays, 'Awaiting the Redemption of Our Bodies: The Witness of Scripture concerning Homosexuality' in J. S. Siker (ed.), *Homosexuality in the Church*, pp. 3–77.

35. R. Barthes, *Mythologies* (Engl. Jonathan Cape, 1972); J. Derrida, 'White Mythology', in his *Margins of Philosophy* (Engl. Harvester, 1982) and S. Fish, *Doing What Comes Naturally: Change, Rhetoric and the Practice of Theory in Literary and Legal Studies* (Clarendon Press, 1989).

36. Barthes, *Mythologies*, p. 54.

37. Furnish, 'The Bible and Homosexuality', pp. 24–33.

38. R. B. Hays, 'Awaiting Redemption' p. 4; cf. pp. 3–17.

39. R. Niebuhr, *Moral Man and Immoral Society* (SCM, 1963), pp. 91 and 95, cf. pp. 89–90 (on trade with poor nations) and pp. 142–51 (on class-interest).

40. Niebuhr, *Moral Man*, p. 95.

41. M. Foucault, *Madness and Civilization* (Engl. Pantheon, 1965), *The Order of Things* (Engl. Random House, 1970), eg. pp. 324–54; *Discipline and Punish* (Engl. Pantheon, 1977), p. 190 (on medical regimes) and pp. 176–7 (on 'anonymous' bureaucratic power); and *The History of Sexuality* (Engl. 3 vols., Pantheon, 1978–86).

42. J. Baudrillard, *Forget Foucault* (Engl. Columbia University, 1987).

43. Schleiermacher, *Hermeneutics*, p. 150.

44. Ibid., esp. pp. 97–113, 168, 205–7 and 211.

45. Ibid., p. 241 (my italics).

46. V. P. Furnish, 'Homosexual Practices in Biblical Perspective', in J. J. Carey (ed.) *The Sexuality Debate in North American Churches 1988–1995* (Mellen Press, 1995), pp. 253, 254 and 266; cf. pp. 253–81.

47. Robin Scroggs, *The New Testament and Homosexuality* (Fortress, 1983), pp. 101 and 127.

48. Bailey, *Homosexuality*, p. xi.

49. T. & T. Clark, 1987.

50. R. Bultmann, *Theology of the New Testament* (Engl. 2 vols., SCM; vol. 1, 1952), vol. 1, p. 224.

51. R. Jewett, *Paul's Anthropological Terms* (Brill, 1971), p. 332.

52. G. Theissen, *Psychological Aspects of Pauline Theology*, pp. 17–39, 59–80, and 267–341.

53. Ibid., p. 59.

54. D. E. H. Whitely, *The Theology of St Paul* (Blackwell, 2nd edn, 1974) 129.

55. N. Richardson, *Paul's Language about God* (JSNT Suppl. no. 99; 1994), esp. pp. 240–315.

56. J. Barr, *The Semantics of Biblical Language* (OUP, 1961), pp. 209 and 244.

57. Wright, 'Homosexuality', p. 298.

58. R. B. Hays, *Echoes of Scripture in the Letters of Paul* (Yale University Press, 1989) and esp. B. S. Rosner, *Paul, Scripture and Ethics* (Brill, 1994), pp. 94–122 and throughout for an excellent study of this subject, including 1 Cor. 6:9, 10.

59. Paul Ricoeur, *Time and Narrative* (Engl. 3 vols. Chicago University Press, 1984–8) and *Interpretation Theory* (Engl. Texas Christian University Press, 1976).

60. M. Ruse, *Homosexuality: A Philosophical Inquiry* (Blackwell, 1988), e.g. pp. 265–7; and D. Cappon, *Toward an Understanding of Homosexuality* (Prentice Hall, 1965), p. vii.

61. Scroggs, *New Testament and Homosexuality*, p. vii; and J. Boswell, *Christianity, Social Tolerance and Homosexuality* (University of Chicago Press, 1980), p. 117; cf. pp. 91–118 on the Bible.

62. Boswell, *Christianity, Social Tolerance*, p. 92.

63. Gadamer, *Truth and Method*, p. 245 (German, p. 255).

64. J. D. Hester, *Paul's Concepts of Inheritance* (Oliver & Boyd, 1968).

65. For this interpretation see A. C. Thiselton, 'The Meaning of *Sarx* in 1 Cor 5:15', *Scottish Journal of Theology*, vol. 26, 1973, pp. 204–28.

66. J. K. Chow, *Patronage and Power: A Study of Social Networks in Corinth* (Sheffield Academic Press, JSNT Suppl. no. 75, 1992), pp. 123–41; A. D. Clarke, *Secular and Christian Leadership in Corinth* (Brill, 1993), pp. 59–72; and Bruce W. Winter, 'Civil Litigation in Secular Corinth and the Church: The Forensic Background to 1 Cor. 6:1–8', *New Testament Studies*, vol. 37, 1991, pp. 559–72.

67. J. Weiss, *Der erste Korintherbrief* (Vandenhoeck & Ruprecht, 1910), pp. 140–5 and 152–6; J. S. Easton, 'New Testament Ethical Lists', *Journal of Biblical Literature*, vol. 51, 1932, pp. 1–12; A. Vogtle, *Die Tugend und Lasterkataloge im Newen Testament* (Aschendorff, 1936).

68. E. Kamlah, *Die Form der Katalogischen Paränese im Neuen Testament* Mohr, WUNT, no. 7, 1964), esp. pp. 11–14 and 27–31.

69. H. Conzelmann, *1 Corinthians* (Engl. Fortress, Hermeneia, 1975), p. 106; cf. pp. 100–2.

70. Scroggs, *New Testament and Homosexuality*, pp. 85–97; and Boswell, *Christianity, Social Tolerance*, pp. 111–14.

71. C. H. Dodd, *Gospel and Law* (CUP, 1951), pp. 10–17; P. Carrington, *The Primitive Christian Catechism* (CUP, 1940); A. Seeberg, *Der Katechismus der Urchristenheit* (Bohme, 1903).

72. J. N. Sevenster, *Paul and Seneca* (Brill, 1961), pp. 52, 78 and 154–66.

73. S. Wibbing, *Die Tugend- und Lasterkataloge im Neuen Testament* (Topelmann, BZNW, no. 25, 1959), pp. 14–16.

74. O. L. Yarborough, *Not Like the Gentiles: Marriage Rules in the Letters of Paul* (Scholars Press, 1985), pp. 8–26.

75. Rosner, *Paul*, pp. 51–5 and 164–6; cf. pp. 46–7.

76. Rosner, *Paul*, p. 210.

77. With Scroggs, 'New Testament and Homosexuality', in Sider, p. 103, cf J. A. Kirk, 'En torno al concepto del reino en Pablo', *Revistista biblica*, vol. 41, 1979, pp. 97–108 (publ. in Rome).

78. E. Hatch and H. A. Redpath, *A Concordance to the Septuagint* (2 vols., Beneficial Publ., 1977), e.g. vol. 2, pp. 1125–8, 1142 and 1194–5; and A. C. Thiselton, *A Commentary on the Greek Text of 1 Corinthians* (forthcoming from Eerdmans and Paternoster, not yet complete).

79. E. E. Ellis, 'Traditions in 1 Corinthians', *New Testament Studies*, vol. 32, 1986, p. 483; cf. pp. 481–502.

80. P. Zaas, 'Catalogues and Context: 1 Cor. 5 and 6', *New Testament Studies*, vol. 34, 1988, pp. 624 and 622–9; and Ken E. Bailey, 'Paul's Theological Foundation for Human Sexuality: 1 Cor. 6:9–20 in the Light of Rhetorical Criticism', *Near East School of Theology Theological Review*, vol. 3, 1980, pp. 27–41. See also P. Zaas, '1 Corinthians 6:9–11: Was Homosexuality condoned in the Corinthian Church?' *Society of Biblical Literature Seminar Papers*, vol. 2, no. 17 (Scholars Press/SBL, 1979), pp. 205–12.

81. The general difference of stance between Corinthian 'freedom' and Pauline 'discipline and order' is generally agreed, but specialists differ in their explanations of it. I followed Barrett and Käsemann in attributing much (not all) to 'over-realised' eschatology in A. C. Thiselton, 'Realized Eschatology at Corinth', *New Testament Studies*, vol. 24, 1978, pp. 510–26; Antoinette C. Wire regards the cry for 'freedom' as a valid cry by the women prophets against Paul's power-leadership, cf. *The Corinthian Women Prophets* (Fortress, 1990). The best exegetical account can be found in W. Schrage, *Der erste Brief an die Korinther* (2 vols. to date, Benziger and Neukirchen-Vluyn: Neukirchen Verlag, 1991 and 1995).

82. C. K. Barrett, *A Commentary on the First Epistle to the Corinthians* (2nd edn, Black, 1971); Scroggs, 'New Testament and Homosexuality', 106; Boswell, *Christianity, Social Tolerance*, pp. 107 and 341–4; and Scrage, *Der erste Brief an die Korinther*, vol. 1, p. 431.

83. Schrage, *Der erste Brief an die Korinther*, vol. 1, p. 432.

84. G. Parke-Taylor, 'The Bible, Tradition and Sexuality', in James Reed (ed.), *A Study Resource on Human Sexuality* ([Council of the Anglican Church of Canada], Anglican Book Centre, 1986), p. 30.

85. Parke-Taylor, 'The Bible, Tradition and Sexuality', p. 40.

86. Wright, 'Homosexuality' p. 296; cf. pp. 291–300. See further D. F. Wright, 'Homosexuals or Prostitutes? The Meaning of *arsenokoitai* (1 Cor. 6:9, 1 Tim. 1:10)', *Vigiliae Christianae*, vol. 38, 1984, pp. 125–53; and 'Translating *arsenokoitai*: 1 Cor. 6:9, 1 Tim. 1:10', *Vig. Christ*, vol. 41, 1987, pp. 396–98; also D. F. Wright, 'Early Christian Attitudes to Homosexuality', *Studia Patristica*, vol. 18, 1989, pp. 329–34. See further R. Wengst, 'Paulus und die Homosexualität', *Zeitschrift für Evangelische Ethik*, vol. 31, 1987, pp. 72–80.

87. C. Wolff, *Der erste Brief des Paulus an die Korinther* (Evangelische Verlagsanstalt 1996), pp. 119–20; D. E. Malick, 'The Condemnation of Homosexuality in 1 Cor. 6:9', *Biblica Sacra*, vol. 150, 1993, pp. 479–92; R. B. Hays, 'Relations Natural and Unnatural', *Journal of Religious Ethics*, vol. 4, 1986, pp. 184–215; C. Senft, *La Première Épître de S Paul au Corinthiens* (2nd edn, Labor et Fides, 1990), p. 80, 'L'homosexualité (*malakoi*, passive; *arsenokoitai*, active) était considerée comme un des vices les plus abominables . . .'; J. A. Fitzmyer, *Romans* (Doubleday, 1993), pp. 287–8 (on 1 Cor. 6:9); J. B. de Young, 'The Source and New Testament Meaning of arsenokoitai with Implications for Christian Ethics and Ministry', *Master's Seminary Journal*, vol. 3 1992, pp. 191–215;

and Ken Bailey, 'Paul's Theological Foundation for Sexuality', *Near East Theological Seminary Theological Review*, vol. 3, 1980, pp. 22–9 and 31–40. Against all this, it is surprising that G. Fee, *First Epistle to the Corinthians* (Eerdmans, 1987), pp. 243–4, inclines towards 'male prostitute' with NIV.

88. Friedrich Nietzsche, *The Complete Works* (18 vols., Engl. Allen & Unwin, 1909–13), vol. 10, no. 3, p. 108.

89. Ben Witherington, *Conflict and Community in Corinth: A Socio-Rhetorical Commentary on 1 and 2 Corinthians* (Eerdmans and Paternoster, 1995), p. 166.

90. Witherington, *Conflict*, 166–7. He notes that homophobia is equally non-compulsive and to be renounced, 166 n. 21.

91. Wolff, *Der erste Brief* p. 119.

92. Ibid., p. 120.

93. Schrage, *Der erste Brief an die Korinther*, pp. 165–238; cf. pp. 239–367. The cross is the 'basis and criterion' (*Grund und Kriterium*) which makes the community a Christian community (pp. 165–92).

94. A. C. Wire, *The Corinthian Women Prophets* (Fortress Press, 1990), p. 19; cf. pp. 73–9, 90–7, 136–144 and 181–96.

95. E. Stuart, *Just Good Friends: Towards a Lesbian and Gay Theology of Relationships* (Mowbray, 1995), pp. 75–6, cf. pp. 73–7 (on complementarity) and 3–5, 197–202 on social control.

96. Further, E. Castelli, *Imitating Paul: A Discourse of Power* (Knox and Westminster, 1991), pp. 35–58, 97–117; Stuart, *Just Good Friends*, pp. 197–202; Wire, *The Corinthian Women Prophets*, pp. 63–7.

97. Among the most notable, Andrew D. Clarke, *Secular and Christian Leadership in Corinth* and T. B. Savage, *Power through Weakness* (CUP, SNTS Mon. Ser., no. 86, 1996), pp. 35–102 and throughout; and S. M. Pogoloff, *Logos and Sophia: The Rhetorical Situation of 1 Corinthians* (Scholars Press, 1992).

98. Witherington, *Conflict*, p. 24.

99. A. C. Thiselton, *Interpreting God and the Postmodern Self: On Meaning, Manipulation and Promise* (T. & T. Clark, 1995).

100. D. Martin, *The Corinthian Body* (Yale University Press, 1995).

101. The evidence is too complex to summarise here. But the chief source is first-century to fourth-century tomb inscriptions which often mention husband and wife, or husband, wife and child or children. Cf T. Wiederman, *Greek and Roman Slavery* (Croom Helm, 1981); A. Watson, *Roman Slave Law* (Johns Hopkins, 1987); D. B. Martin, *Slavery as Salvation* (Yale University Press, 1990).

102. Hays, 'Awaiting Redemption', p. 7.

103. St Andrew's Day Statement, p. 6.

104. Ibid., p. 5.

105. Ibid., pp. 3 and 7.

106. Scroggs, *New Testament and Homosexuality*, p. 114. See also Boswell, *Christianity, Social Tolerance*, pp. 109–13; Bailey, *Homosexuality*, pp. 40–1; and Furnish, 'The Bible and Homosexuality', pp. 30–1.

107. P. Coleman, *Christian Attitudes to Homosexuality* (SPCK, 1980), p. 91; Boswell, *Christianity, Social Tolerance*; p. 110. Thomas Aquinas formally expounded 'law' as of four categories: divine, 'natural', state and civil. But the concepts go back to Aristotle and the Stoics (see below).

108. Furnish, 'The Bible and Homosexuality', 28; cf Boswell, *Christianity, Social Tolerance*, pp. 111–16; Bailey, *Homosexuality*, p. 40; Scroggs, *New Testament and Homosexuality*, pp. 110–12.

109. Scroggs, *New Testament and Homosexuality*, p. 110 (cf. Furnish, 'The Bible and Homosexuality').

110. C. E. B. Cranfield, *The Epistle to the Romans* (2 vols., T. & T. Clark, vol. 1, 1975), p. 105; cf. pp. 126–7.

111. J. D. G. Dunn, *Romans* (2 vols., Word Books, vol. 1, 1988), p. 74.

112. Ibid., vol. 1, p. 74 (my italics).

113. S. Laeuchli, *The Language of Faith* (Epworth Press, 1965).

114. e.g. A. C. Thiselton, *New Horizons in Hermeneutics*, pp. 152–3; and *The Two Horizons*, pp. 124–33.

115. J. A. Fitzmyer, *Romans* (Doubleday, 1992), pp. 285–6.

116. Barr, *Semantics*, pp. 217–19; Thiselton, *Two Horizons*, pp. 127–9.

117. Schrage, *Der erste Brief an die Korinther*, vol. 2, 1995, p. 521.

118. *Journal of Religious Ethics*, vol. 4, 1986.

119. Ibid., p. 190.

120. Ibid., p. 192.

121. Ibid., p. 195.

122. Ibid., pp. 195–6.

123. Cf. ibid., pp. 200–2; I have paraphrased rather than quoted Hays, except for the first part of the sentence.

124. Ibid., pp. 202–11.

125. M. D. Smith, 'Ancient Bisexuality and the Interpretation of Romans 1:26, 27', *Journal of the American Academy of Religion*, 64, 1996, pp. 223–54.

126. C. K. Barrett, *The Pastoral Epistles* (Clarendon Press, 1963), pp. 42–3. This analysis remains valid whether or not Dibelius and Conzelmann are right in speaking of Hellenistic forms or functions of Jewish ethics by way of origin or other settings (M. Dibelius and H. Conzelmann, *The Pastoral Epistles*, Engl. Fortress, 1972).

127. A. T. Hanson, *The Pastoral Letters* (CUP, 1966), p. 25.

128. M. Noth, *Leviticus: A Commentary* (Engl., SCM, 1965), p. 138; Germ., *Das dritte Buch Mose Leviticus* (Vandenhoeck & Ruprecht, 1962), p. 117.

129. K. Elliger, *Leviticus* (Mohr, 1966), p. 229.

130. Ibid., p. 232.

131. On *tôʿêbhah*, see the new edn of Brown-Driver-Briggs, *Hebrew and English Lexicon* (Associated Publishers, 1980), 1072–3, as denoting that which is ritually and/or ethically abhorrent.

132. Furnish, 'The Bible and Homosexuality', p. 20.

133. Choon-Leong Seow, 'Textual Orientation', in R. L. Brawley (ed.), *Biblical Ethics and Homosexuality: Listening to Scripture* (Westminster Knox, 1996), pp. 18 and 17–34.

134. D. N. Fewell and D. M. Gunn, *Gender, Power and Promise* (Abingdon, 1993). See further M. Noth, *Leviticus*, p. 136, and N. H. Snaith, *Leviticus and Numbers* (Nelson, 1967), p. 126.

135. J. Milgrom, *Cult and Conscience* (Brill, 1976); 'The Biblical Diet Laws as an Ethical System', *Interpretation*, vol. 17, 1963, pp. 288–301, and 'Leviticus', in *Interpreter's Dictionary of the Bible Supplementary Volume* (Abingdon, 1976), pp. 541–5. See further Elliger, *Leviticus*, 'Geschechtlicher Umgang', pp. 229–33 and throughout.

136. G. J. Wenham, *The Book of Leviticus* (Eerdmans, 1979), p. 246.

137. Wenham, *Leviticus*, p. 253; cf. Noth, *Leviticus*, pp. 138–9.

138. Bonnington and Fyall, *Homosexuality and the Bible*, pp. 12–13.

139. The language comes from W. Eichrodt, *Theology of the Old Testament* (2 vols. Engl. SCM, 1961 and 1967), vol. 1, p. 38. See K. Barth, *Church Dogmatics*, vol. 2, part 1, ss. 25–30; vol. 2, part 2, s. 33; vol. 3, part 1, s. 62 (explicitly on covenant with creation); vol. 3, part 3, especially 301–41 on evil as 'chaos' and reconciliation as 'order'; E. Jüngel, *God as the Mystery of the World* (Engl. T. & T. Clark, 1983), pp. 199–232.

140. Noth, *Leviticus*, p. 139; Rosner, *Paul*, pp. 47–50 and throughout.

141. Rosner, *Paul*, p. 42.

142. Cf. Ruse, *Homosexuality*, and Cappon, *Toward an Understanding of Homosexuality*.

143. Thiselton, *Interpreting God*, pp. 47–80. Ricoeur's masterpiece is *Oneself as Another* (Engl. Chicago University Press, 1992). On Ricoeur's hermeneutics of the will and of texts, cf. Thiselton, *New Horizons in Hermeneutics*, pp. 344–78.

144. Stuart, *Just Good Friends*, p. 75, cf. pp. 66–85.

145. M. D. Smith, 'Ancient Bisexuality and the Interpretation of Romans 1: 26, 27', *Journal of the American Academy of Religion*, 64, 1996, pp. 223–54.

146. Smith, 'Ancient Bisexuality', p. 248.

147. Smith, 'Ancient Bisexuality', p. 249.

148. A. C. Thiselton, *Interpreting God and the Postmodern Self* (T. & T. Clark, Edinburgh 1995), pp. 12–16, 19–22, 41–2 passim; and *New Horizons in Hermeneutics* (HarperCollins, repr. Paternoster, 1992), pp. 80–141, 393–405, 529–57.

149. M. Foucault, *The History of Sexuality*, vol. 1 (Pantheon, 1978), p. 94.

150. M. Foucault, *Histoire de la folie à l'age classique* (Gallimard, 2nd edn, 1972) p. 104.

151. Discussed in more detail in A. C. Thiselton, *The Two Horizons: New Testament Hermeneutics and Philosophical Description* (Paternoster, 1980), pp. 133–43.

152. U. Schnelle, *The Human Condition* (T. & T. Clark, 1996), p. 149.

153. *The Mystery of Salvation* (Church House Publishing, 1995), p. 32.

154. J. M. Gundry-Volf, 'Gender and Creation in 1 Cor. 11: 2–16. A Study of Paul's Theological Method' in J. Adna, S. J. Hafemann and O. Hofins (eds.) *Evangelium, Schriftauslegung Kirche: Festschrift für Peter Stuhlmacher* (Vandenhoeck & Ruprecht, 1997). p. 170; cf pp. 151–71.

13

Beyond Stereotypes: Towards Truth and Faithfulness

The Chairman of St Andrew's Day Group

THE PROCESS OF inviting comment has proved successful not only in eliciting essays which are inherently interesting, but in helping those who wrote the St Andrew's Day Statement to test and appraise their work by engaging with the range of opinion expressed. The responsive essays have offered eloquent criticism and affirmation of several aspects of the Statement, and have suggested ways of developing its thinking and its method.

Principles

The core trinitarian principles, designed to embrace all those who affirm orthodox Christianity, attracted little disagreement. Comment has been made on the Christocentric start given to these, with God the Father being linked with the goal of creation. Hence the doctrine of creation, which is presupposed, may need explanation; this point lies behind the criticism that marriage is not defined fully enough in the Statement. This important point aside, the principles seem agreeable to all contributors: it is their application that gives rise to the real disagreements.

Application I

Identity and Sexual Affections

The Christological way into the credal Principles is also the way into the Application. We know who and what we are in Christ, the one Word of God. Christ is the defining reality for us as human beings, he is true humanity. This claim raised questions about the human race in general outside Christ, and questions about fallen human nature. We are created and fallen, knowing the deepest truth of who we are only when we have been incorporated into the death and resurrection of Jesus. In Jesus we know our origin, our failure to be what we are destined to be. There is no quarrel with the contention that we are created and fallen people, nor that we need to hear and obey the will of God, as did Jesus. Creation, fall and redemption are all assumed in the grand Christian narrative and are here assumed under the person and work of Christ.

This sharp focus on the second Adam concerns both our knowing and our being, both the way into thinking theologically about who we are, and the reality of humanity in the ultimate sense. In this, the Statement follows the instincts of the very early theologian Irenaeus, who refused to allow creation to be interpreted apart from the fulfilment of creation, the human Jesus. There can be no general description of creation, how things are, simply drawn from the current cultural mores and then linked to the figure of Jesus. Jesus brings with him his Hebraic inheritance of the Lord of the universe and his good creation. The whole Old Testament tradition of ethics and worship is summed up in Jesus.

This caution about gaining an interpretation of reality from some generally available cultural stock of ideas also applies to our self-understanding, where natural theologies must be carefully scrutinised. Our very identities must be understood with reference to Christ. The example of the 1930s has been given to illustrate the disaster of a cultural interpretation of society and race without serious critical rooting in the person of Jesus. We need to apply just such critical testing to our self-interpretations.

The Statement insists on applying this principle. We can all misunderstand who we most truly are, we can all elevate some attribute of ours into a defining characteristic, which becomes a priority and into which we seek to integrate Christ, rather than vice versa: academics, athletes, and business executives; white and black, Jew and Greek. Our innermost feelings and drives too can gain an absolute priority in our self-understanding, as can our nationality or personality type. Today some churches encourage people to spend time at workshops discovering their particular character type – shy or outgoing, rational or intuitive, and so forth – so as to be able to categorise themselves and feel safe in knowing who they are. Such a process risks over-simplification by locating ourselves on one of two poles, ignoring the fact of our complex mixture of characteristics. It can place blinkers on us by suggesting a single personality type as a helpful guide to understanding how we 'should' respond to people and situations.

'Sexuality' today has become a key marker of identity, so that people are encouraged to work out whether they are 'straight or gay',[1] two modern categories or 'orientations', presented to us as a fork in the road of life, one path of which we must take. We are urged to follow our inner desires in this process of self-understanding, and then own an identity which will control our place in society and the conduct of our relationships. 'Sexuality' is a noun, formed from the adjective 'sexual' which describes our 'erotic' and also 'glandular' personal feelings of attraction towards others, which might result in genital physical contact and intercourse. We are moreover probably, in a sense, all 'bisexuals' in that, in some circumstances, we might be attracted by either sex.[2]

Perhaps the major flaw the group found in the Bishops' Statement[3] was its advice to any who were confused because their 'sexual orientation is ambiguous' that they should seek counselling 'to discover the truth of their personality and to achieve a degree of inner healing'. This advice flies in the face of the complex nature of sexual affections and desires, reducing them unrealistically. (The Bishops cannot be faulted, of course, for seeking to channel people who do not feel called to celibate life, towards marriage as the given form or vocation within which sexual intercourse is to be conducted.[4]) The St Andrew's Day Statement strongly affirms the complex, multifaceted nature of our affections and desires. It also raises questions as to the wisdom of accepting contemporary advice to delve into the ocean of our feelings, in the course of the development of our life, and, at one given moment, isolate one affection so to fix on a prescribed sexual 'orientation' and identity. We must refer back to Christ and our being in him as created and redeemed. This is so for the interpretation of our knowing, feeling and being. 'At the deepest ontological level' we are simply human beings, male and female, broken and on the way to repair in Christ, the pattern for our salvation.

Whether we are English or Chinese is not the main point of who we are, indeed we can change nationality.[5] Whether we are introvert or extrovert, likewise, although we can be mistaken about such attributes, and indeed can undertake 'assertiveness training' to press ourselves into a different self-image and relationship to the world. 'Sexuality' has become a major category thrust at us from primary school onwards. We read it in terms of two models set out in modern culture, and work out, directly or indirectly, which of the two sexual signals controls us. If we are not 'successful' in relating to the opposite sex, we must have the signal for the same sex, and that is an ultimate factor in our identity.

Furthermore, the signal, or 'orientation', now developed into a definite and exclusive reality within, goes beyond attraction to persons and desire for deep relationships, but must involve physical sex; not simply 'Eros' but 'Venus', using the distinction drawn by C. S. Lewis.[6] Lewis takes for granted that sexual experience can occur without Eros, that is without 'being in love', and that Eros includes other things besides carnal sexual activity, Venus. Eros is *person*-centred: 'A man in this state really hasn't the leisure to think of sex. He is too busy thinking of a person. The fact that she is a woman is far less important than the fact that she is herself. He is full of desire, but the desire may not be sexually toned.'[7] Our ultra-modern culture has collapsed Eros into Venus, removing the expectation or desirability of emotionally deep but non-genital relationships. This is a loss to the modern world, and the culture of Church life has done very little to offer a counter-model. Society shepherds us into its narrowed sexual identity pens, which we own as we incarnate these social constructs for ourselves. This may be an aspect of what liberation theologians have called sinful structures, which grip and trap us, with the result that we collude with them and so reinforce their power on us and others.

The Statement raises the issue of mistake. We may be mistaken about our affections for all sorts of reasons, the quixotic phases of adolescence or the effects of depressive illness, for example. It also raises the question about the social constructs through which we interpret our feelings. Our affections need to be rightly understood in Christ, not simply in the light of a particular culture which may be confused and misleading in the roles it commends. The Statement also wishes to play down the ultimacy of sexual self-understanding as a kind of constitutor of people groups. Are there really 'heterosexuals' and 'homosexuals' as there are blacks and whites? Is there a fixed 'orientation' or are we rather far more complex, and indeed in the midst of phases of affection at different stages of life?

Our feelings towards males and females will fluctuate and vary.[8] In the Western cultural context we will confuse Eros and Venus, and will find it hard to establish the former as distinct from the latter. Church culture has given the impression that deep, fulfilling relationships can only be had in marriage, and criticism of this disastrous pastoral error must be taken with utmost seriousness. The single life, chosen or involuntary, can therefore be so lonely as to almost encourage some single people into the gay culture through neglect. In such ways the Church's failure to address our Western culture's relational barrenness can be said to foster misunderstandings of the self by abandoning people to new solidarities that purport to clarify identities.

At the deepest level of being we are indeed men and women with needs and complex potentialities which can flourish and can degenerate. We all have multifaceted sexual capacities and desires, but whether these define our identity, underwriting an associated pattern of behaviour, seems to be very questionable.[9] It may be more accurate and insightful to say that we all have 'homosexual' and 'heterosexual' affections, deep feelings towards both sexes, which could potentially be channelled into genital sex. The claim that individuals are created in the image of God must also be complemented by the claim that the human race has a destiny as a whole. The unity of the race knows one basic distinction, male and female, the created context for sex and procreation.

The Path of Discipleship

Having highlighted the issue of the complexity of our sexual affections and emotions, cautioned against some current assumptions about fixed 'orientation', and asked for the recovery of the distinction of Eros from Venus, we give thought to the path of discipleship, still under the heading of the life and work of Jesus Christ, the one Word of God. Here the shoe has been felt to pinch somewhat for a range of our respondents who asked that creation be made less invisible and more fully articulated. Does creation have an ordered character, including an order for human sexual relations, or are we to fix on the history of the life of Jesus alone for any guidance on this? The Principles speak of 'a life of obedience' lived by Jesus, which indicates not only moment by moment obedience to divine intutions, but obedience to the whole way of the Torah, which he sums up. The obedience of Jesus presumes the order woven into creation.

The fact of human disordering of creation is clear in the Statement's insistence on the judgment on our sin borne by Jesus, his renewal of humanity, his promise and call. The disciple, baptised in the death of the Lord, enters security and the challenge of the right ordering of life. Christians, by virtue of their baptism, have put off unregenerate modes of life, and this calls for self-denial. Disordered desires or misdirected innocent desires are found in all our lives. The struggle must be joined in obedience to the risen Lord, who took human flesh to judgment and renewal.

The Statement clearly recognises that our situation is not simply of our own making or choosing. Conversion to Christ, however, reveals to us, individually and corporately, the truth of our energies and springs of behaviour in relation to the divine order of creation. This point of the Statement attracted much important and interesting comment. What is the nature of the self which must deny itself? Is this some sliver of will detached from, and yet availing itself of, the body: the body which is somehow 'value free', part of the realm of scientific reason, divorced from inherent meaning and moral significance? The Statement intends to speak of the disciple as a redeemed person not in the sense of escaping from the body and affections, but as on the way to transformed, created personhood.

The term 'dissonance' was introduced into the discussion by one contributor to speak of the alienation of the individual from the created order. The analogies of race and class were helpfully explored, and of disability: given and not chosen, posing the problem of how to cope with it under God. Here disagreements become clear. Some argue that singular desire for the same sex can be managed creatively, indeed is a benefit to the Church. It is the traditional line of moral teaching that has erred in stigmatising the homosexual or gay mode of life, that has therefore suppressed the truth (Rom. 1). If homosexual affections are as complex as has been urged above, far from being monochrome and fixed for ever in a person, how should these affections be judged? Race cannot be changed, nationality can, so can class and even attitudes learned and lost (as some students passing through higher education will testify). Overstrong desires for the opposite sex, and as 'sex objects', need resisting and bringing into the order and structure of the Gospel way of being, rooted in the path of the cross. Such desires will also change and modify, although they can be indulged and cultivated into hedonist delicacies, as seduced victims can be inducted into sexual habits otherwise not opened up to their imaginations.

How do we discern a disordered desire, or the misdirection of an innocent desire, say for warmth, love and expression of admiration? In an adolescent, a 'crush' on a person of the same sex may be intense and passionate, and take the form of a yearning for closeness. This may be a wholly different kind of affection to that known by the practising homosexual later in life, although interpreted as the early emergence of a gay identity. In fact it will probably pass, was probably innocent and hardly even misdirected, very likely part of the process of growing into maturity. One needs even to press the question as to the definition of 'the' homosexual desire as opposed to a wide range of feelings.

One essay insists with the Statement that there are misdirections of desires which should be properly and fruitfully directed into honest and intense emotionally charged relationships. The Church urgently needs to undertake most serious self-examination to allow such relationships to flourish, to create a context in which people can relate deeply, in ways appropriate to the people of God. Do these ways include active, structured sex as a pattern of life between members of the same sex? One essay asks whether such a lifestyle can be part of the way a disciple honours Christ, since it accords with his or her individual nature, which is dissonant with bodily shaping. Choosing to go along with this structuring because of the pull of desire, or of the sheer attractiveness of a beautiful and vibrant person,[10] contradicts the wisdom of the law and the prophets, and of the apostolic testimony, prima facie. Eros in its proper full sense of real emotional attraction, without Venus, is the Church's one way of structuring the homosexual desires into a pattern for discipleship; indeed such an integration could only strengthen the community of the people of God.

If the suggestion, that in the conflict some 'prophetic' message can be discerned from the gay community, is to have plausibility, it is likely to be this, that single people also need community, warmth, depth of honesty and support in their relationships in the body of Christ: a message highlighting forgotten truth,[11] rather than spinning a novel and apparently contradictory revelation from culturally new phenomena. Such a message urges reclamation of Eros and passes judgment on the Church for 'family-olatry', a message to build up the whole Church, improving its implementation of the existing given order in creation. Such a challenge carries with it struggle for all in the Church, a radical review of openness and honesty and mutual care.

Interestingly, this summons to attend to the communal life of the Church, this warning against an exclusivist family-olatry, may be directed to the Church in the West, while 'Third World' Christians may be far ahead spiritually and relationally. Western churches in particular need to examine the bargains they have made with secularist culture, and work for deeper love and fellowship. In such a way could the affections felt by those tempted, often in pain, frustration and loneliness, to label themselves according to a pattern of behaviour, be channelled to the upbuilding of all, and so prove to be a way of living out life in Christ, and in the dying and rising of Christ according to the baptismal pattern.

Application II

The second section of the Principles spells out the person and place of the Holy Spirit and the parallel Application deals with the task of interpreting and understanding the phenomena of homosexuality in modern culture. It could be argued that even to agree to engage in this task initiates a process of recognising patterns of conduct clearly outside traditional Christian ethics, a kind of collusion akin to governments agreeing bomb-warning codes with terrorists. But there is surely a case, going beyond the purely pragmatic need for some more careful work to be done in the face of the polemics and even invasive violence in the present campaign, for suggesting that faith can seek deeper understanding. The heremeneutical challenge cannot simply be ignored: serious questions have been put to the tradition. The Church of England, responsible to the Scriptures and the Patristic tradition, can do no other than be led back to the texts and contexts and engage in this 'task'.

Discerning the Spirit

The guidance of the Spirit has been an important theme in several responses. The difficulty of being open to modern empirical observation while governed by the authority of the apostolic word is indeed acknowledged as part of the hermeneutical challenge. Confusion of well-meaning Church bureaucrats is all too possible in the light of competing 'empirical' observations which never come free of interpretative theory, itself shifting and developing. Hasty innovations, given these variables and the contested claims, will no doubt be wisely avoided by the overseers of the flock. No contributor seemed to contest the warning against the dangers of initiating a wide-ranging programme of discussions of an open-ended nature with little in the way of theological, as opposed to socio-psychological, guidance on hand.

The uncritical assumption of a 'theory' of homosexuality, which more than one contributor has claimed to be a modern phenomenon, seems to have become unfortunately common. As with many less than convincing sermons, the 'present horizon' is taken for granted and all the attention given to the 'then'. Theories which fail to understand human nature in the light of the Gospel are said by the Statement to imprison the imagination, and so to close options and even hope. Theories will attempt to categorise what are disparate phenomena across, for example, age ranges. The logic of the wife of the man coming home inebriated may be used: on hearing that on successive nights he drank gin and soda, whisky and soda and brandy and soda, she concluded that the soda must the uniting factor behind his loss of faculties.[12] A deep affection for the same sex, at several stages of life, in response to different individuals, in different social contexts, etc., do not spell 'homosexuality' as commonly defined. Likewise a powerful desire to engage in physical exploratory union with another human being, or simply for closeness and warmth, if experienced after several years in prison, for example, may be a manifestation of our general potential for homosexual activity under severely deprived circumstances, not a fated identity.

Similarly the phenomena of same-sex desires, attractions, bondings, may be quite different in the male and the female.[13] The feminist movement opens up the *intellectual* route to commitment to exclusively lesbian intimacy, for example, as a form of protest against 'patriarchy'. Such a woman may even be making a great sacrifice in denying her felt glandular desire for male sexual congress in the sisterly cause. This reverses what is often claimed by gay Christian apologists who testify to sexual 'affections' which are only subsequently rationalised and 'set forth in speech'.[14] There appear to be a wide variety of group identities, all uneasily covered by the category 'gay and lesbian', some of which are contradictory in tone and lifestyle (as illustrated by the rejection of the term 'gay' by some 'homosexual' men who wish to distance themselves from the 'gay bar' scene of vigorous social life).[15]

This variety of 'dances in the Spirit' (borrowing the vivid revisionist phrase from an essay) some critical of others, makes it difficult to locate any possible single prophetic message emerging from the lesbian and gay movement, or a possible 'development' of doctrine.[16] Each strand of homosexual opinion and feeling nestling under the lesbian and gay umbrella will have positive aspects, and it will therefore be hard to develop a 'best case' version to integrate into the orthodox Christian mode of being. Liberating release from legalistic modes of morality, the slave-mentality of collusion with a repressive way of life, might be claimed as a major gay benefit, for example. This experience of 'dancing in the Spirit' identifies sins in the structures of the old-fashioned moral system. Moral order in the new covenant, it is claimed, breaks the narrow banks of regimentation, associated also with patriarchy.

Such freedom in the Spirit sounds eschatological and joyous, a best-case scenario, a heavenly self-actualising. Likewise the aesthetic soul, whose inner self relates to the serene beauty of the arts and is repelled by domesticity and family life, may represent another type of homosexual feeling, and indeed such a figure may well feel drawn to the priestly role, with its mixture of dramatic liturgical beauty and close pastoral relationship.

The figure of Jesus and his disciples is appealed to for justification of the new way of appreciating the created potentialities given to us, since Jesus cast doubt on marriage and the family and developed an eschatological community which broke down barriers and proclaimed the presence of the Spirit. When the Principles speak of Jesus as the one Word of God, therefore, such revisionism can claim its support in his breaking of conventional moulds. His treatment of women must be classed as a new mode of relationship in his context. The message to be gained is that Jesus did bring renewal in relationships, and this needs attention. The further claim that the historical figure of Jesus can be used to underwrite homosexual activity as a pattern of life, ventures on an analogy that begs all the other questions. It can be sustained only if the case for the compatibility of such a pattern of life with his has already been made.

Interpreting the Times

The Statement speaks of the need to interpret the times, to listen to the testimony of people and groups and their claim to insight about the activity of God. Freedom in the Spirit, however, cannot be absolute; freedom requires form to be creative. The debate boils down to the nature of the form, or order, given by God for the conduct of sexual relationships. Freedom lived out by Jesus accorded to the form of his Father's will, and that included the law and the prophets. Attempts at new forms of lifestyle, challenging for example 'family-olatry' and selfishness, will need to ensure they avoid elements incompatible with the tradition and theology of Jesus.

While many analogies for such integration of new sexual patterns have been essayed, to be true to the Gospel successful analogies must include the note of transformation as well as of acceptance. Otherwise such suggestions risk being ultimately unloving to the wild olive shoots grafted into the Hebraic cultivated olive tree (Rome. 9–11). Those who advocate 'dancing with the Spirit' rightly, on the other hand, reject legalistic Mosaism and fundamentalism, but assume that this rejection sweeps away not only ancient ritual law but also the old moral tradition. Paul, after all, faced down Peter over imposing Jewish conditions on Gentile believers. The person and work of Christ absorbs the ritual sacrificial priesthood and fulfils the law. But the apostolic message does not deconstruct patterns of sexual order as if these were merely part of the old preparatory ritual law. The new way of love runs through the patterns, but does not destroy them; spiritual freedom respects created form.

Indeed the counter question must be put as to whether reconstruction of sexual patterns amounts to collusion with what has been called 'affective fundamentalism'.[17] Just as fundamentalists of the right are thought to elevate the direct, uninterpreted words of holy writ to unquestioned divine status, so with the affections for the fundamentalists of the left. Direct application of such feelings, entrusting onself to them, seems equally idolatrous. This is no wilful or rapacious idolatry, rather more like the unquestioning, and apparently harmless, consumerism of the well-meaning, and alms-giving, average Western wage-earner. It just feels right.

We are all afflicted by our darkened understanding and will; we repress the truth, we turn the Nelsonian eye to the unwanted reality. The Statement speaks of this state, and of sexual patternings as not free from its effects. The fact of the cultural popularity of some sexual repatternings is no surety of the Spirit at work, and the secret identification of God with human aspiration is a real danger. Affections need interpreting, conditioning, sanctifying in the path of baptismal discipleship. This is for the good of individuals, the Church and the destiny of the race. 'If we are easy with what we are', says the secularist Matthew Parris in response to Andrew Sullivan the Roman Catholic gay apologist,

> why is it important to us that 'we couldn't help it'? . . . 'We can't help it' is a demeaning argument intended to foil the finger waggers. But it doesn't anyway. We can help our actions, if not our inclinations . . . Sullivan half acknowledges this argument, but seems to suggest that sexuality so completely defines us that to stigmatise its expression must destroy the inner man. I don't agree.[18]

Parris feels easy with his homosexuality and regards it as a moral equivalent to heterosexuality; Sullivan does not, pleading instead *force majeure*.

Parris is aware of reconstructing moral patterns. Paul in Romans 1 regards such a process as a product of worshipping the creature instead of the creator. Sullivan would also make that criticism, but not of himself because of his 'affective fundamentalism', his uncritical interpretation of his desires. Parris begins the article, 'I knew Andrew Sullivan before he was a homosexual', indicating a process retroactively validated, almost as in false memory syndrome.[19] The impulse reigns and gives moral validity to newly adopted behaviour structures, a refashioned use of the body.

The Church will be neither honest nor loving to accept such a definition of our being, and cannot lovingly graft into its own pattern of life different bodily deployments as commendable behaviour patterns, bodily deployments which for the whole Judaeo-Christian tradition, indeed the whole Abrahamic tradition if one wishes to include Islam, has ruled out as harmful and rooted in self-referential schemes of life – what Paul calls idolatry – however well-meaning and non-violent they may feel. The Church recognises two vocations, marriage and singleness, by which it means monogamous marriage between male and female, and celibate singleness, as fitting in with God's creative intention, an intention which is given in the order of creation, rather than one in process and development. The Church, mindful of individual and generic destiny, cannot commend the gay path of sexual patterning either to individuals or to the race. Indeed, if it acceded to revisionist claims, the Church would, thereby, become the central agency for commending and expanding the new structure of sexual conduct as a possibility open to all.

The Church's love here can be expressed only in transformative acceptance of those who perceive themselves 'homosexual'. Justification and sanctification are inseparable facets of the saving reality of the risen Christ. Our acceptance comes with the baptismal message to become what we are through dying and rising with Christ. Our past attitudes pass through the waters of baptism, we enter the struggle of sanctification for which the Spirit is given. The Church has the ministry of constantly encouraging us to integrate the Gospel into our patterns of life, since we are adopted into the family of God. The Gospel calls for transformation, openness and willingness to break with old patterns of life: this applies to all Christians, and to the quality of their fellowship and mutual support.

Gay Marriage?

The plea for same-sex 'marriage' has been powerfully and movingly made among the foregoing essays: two partners committed to each other for life, forsaking all others till death do them part, sensitively bonding genitally, infertile as are many marriages. This plea regards friendship as an inadequate model for same-sex unions, since friendship is not the appropriate context for full sexual bonding. Interestingly this view finds support from traditionalist essayists who agree that friendship is not the covenant context for genital sex, and finds criticism from some more experimental opinion which thinks that friendship is the proper context for same-sex genital union, marriage being by definition between males and females only.

Marriage cannot, according to the Statement, be defined simply in terms of functions observed, be they external or internal, physical or emotional; nor by a consequentialist argument from spiritual or psychological fruitfulness for the individuals concerned. Generically the race has one fundamental distinction, that between male and female,[20] and marriage needs to be seen in the light of that corporate reality as well as in the light of individual self-actualisation and fruitfulness. The fundamental otherness of the sexes is so obvious a given fact, that it can be overlooked; it is surely one of the bases for the biblical analogy for God and his covenant people, Christ and his Church: there is an otherness – which has been astonishingly bridged.

Gender, maleness and femaleness, is the first-order category of differentiation, no peripheral attribute but fundamental to our personhood and its development: each gender is a mystery to the other and to the inner sexual imagination of the other.[21] While this does not give a functional answer to the plea for same-sex 'marriage', it helps to unfold the phenomenon of marriage as marriage, inherently between a male and a female. Accordingly gay 'marriage', as some revisionist and conservative essayists maintain, is an impossible model to entertain; marriage is between men and women. The Church's principled pastoral care recognises two forms or vocations in which life can be lived, marriage and singleness, and there is no place for the Church to confer legitimacy upon alternatives to these, formally or informally.

Elusive Analogies

The analogy of 'second' marriages between divorcees presents an example of the ideal having broken down, but the ideal remains as the clear basic pattern, behind the failure to live up to it. This is not an analogy, therefore, of a new form of life to be enthusiastically commended, but very much of an unfortunate second best, and a structure which the Church should be keen to limit and to see fading out. The same is true of the analogy of polygamy, which in the case of new converts the Church often treats permissively, to avoid cruelty to several wives, but as a phenomenon to be phased out.

The use of analogies to suggest developments in this tradition can provide interesting and sincere attempts to reach across the definite boundary dividing the various revisionist arguments from orthodox Christian ethics. Such analogies can often prove to be double-edged and contested. That of the persecuted minority language group as illustrating an unjustly oppressed, or grudgingly tolerated, gay community implies a monochrome homosexual identity. It forecloses discussion of the desirability of openness to change and may even suggests the desirability of fostering the language, inducting children into it, and avoiding the language of the larger 'big brother' nation. Such features would mark the vocation to speak, spread and confirm the minority language.

Again the analogy of slavery can be used to defend contrary positions, analogies being illustrative of prior positions. The analogy can be deployed in terms of an economic structure of sin in which the slave-owner is caught up, with which he is colluding, and from which he needs delivering. Conversion to Christ hardly sits easily with continuing in cruel slave practice. Those arguing in favour of homosexual practice may see this as analogous to the abolition of prejudice against gays; those arguing otherwise may see patterns of homosexual lifestyle as analogous to a damaging economic structure. Accordingly, the apostolic message of Philemon constitutes an encouragement to live out the Gospel message in such a way as would eventually, when generalised, fade out the former practice, washed away by the waters of baptism. Slavery as a sinful pattern of life needs to be affected by the Gospel, giving it an interim shelf-life, rather than being allocated space within it to continue its existence permanently.

Attempts to construct novel forms of life or vocation need much care. To regard a vocation as constituted by recognising the situation in which one finds oneself and *ipso facto* finding that to be something through which witness must be shaped, begs many questions. It runs the risk of coordinating the situational pattern with God's creative intention. Not all situations in which we find ourselves are compatible with integration into the will of God, as is clear from baptism. Prima facie, homosexual desire for continuing sexual intercourse with the same sex is precisely such a situation.

There is, of course, in this area as in any other area involving 'difficult' moral decisions, a casuistry to unfold, and it is important to give it its space. Here is a case, it is suggested, in which someone judges it right to prolong a homosexual friendship to avoid hurting a partner. We may recall Graham Greene's *The End of the Affair*, where the leading character is a woman who, on her conversion, gives up her lover to save his life. Is that the only possible answer? The point of posing such cases is that they should be pondered, not met with quick decisions. Yet precisely for this reason they tend to be unhelpful for moral policy. Yes, there might have been a case for prolonging the relationship, there might have been a case for breaking it off as the more loving way. Such cases attune us to the need for an attentive and undoctrinaire approach to particular crises of decision. But in settling what *course* we shall set for our lives, and for those who seek our guidance, they bring us no further forward.

Alternative Scripts

Gifts or charisms making an individual fitted for marriage or singleness is an idea to be found in the New Testament, and so may possibly be indirectly linked with the notion of vocation in a weak sense. But extrapolating from this to envisage a gift making one suited for what the New Testament regards as sinful seems to be floating an idea with too much inner contradiction, and indeed a reading of Scripture which ignores the obvious (Rom. 1 for example) to make room for the highly speculative. The concept of gifting by God in preparation for gay 'para–marriages' carries personal vocation back into the will of God, as also indeed the asserted matching social 'scripts', reordering God's creative intention away from what has been revealed, or supposing a nominalist view of divine intentions as regards both objective and subjective dimensions of act and pattern of act.

Such a theological enterprise of suggesting possible life 'scripts' and matching these with selected aspects of our multifaceted emotional make-up, could equally lead to other surprising justifications. The phenomenon of the mistress, in a lifelong faithful relationship, might be said, for example, to link up with our emotional need for playfulness and space away from the conventional grind of family *ennui*. It is a fact of life in many nations, accepted as a custom 'which will not go away' and harmless; indeed it is said to have saved many marriages and to have provided otherwise lonely women with a happy form of communion. It has led to spiritual joy and release, to social cohesion, thus fulfilling the criteria specified by Bishop Baker in his lecture.[22]

It is a quasi-institution, a vocation of a kind, and often a suffering one because forced into secrecy, and fulfils that part of our created being which cries out in exhilaration in the created order. It is a para-marriage, quasi-marital, similar to a marriage of divorcees although without the formalities and concurrent rather than consecutive, with all the facets of faithful marriage saving that of the domestic arrangements, although even this is not absolute if the mistress has her own home to which her lover is always welcome.

This given fact of the mistress, quasi-wife or special kind of friend, it might be argued, has been with us since the dawn of time and may need integrating into the Christian way, somehow, given its harmlessness and benefit, testified to in confidentiality so as to avoid public scandal. If sinful at all it can only be so in a light way, a question of merely venial sin. To select some other pieces from Scripture in justification of this pattern, one could argue that it merely extends the apostolic advice against 'burning' by regularising an arrangement to avoid promiscuity. It enables one to function in a society into which one is thrown, in which one finds oneself, and to make something of it responsibly. In an emotionally dead marriage, taking a willing mistress could be argued to be the most adult and responsible course. The analogy of polygamy[23] is there to add credibility to the vocation and its implementation as neutral or mildly regrettable, a script for some, given in the glorious diversity of creativity. Whether this should be a permanent vocation, into which one would wish to induct perhaps initially reluctant recruits but quick learners, is another matter.

Talk of the 'inclusion' of those fully incarnating gay scripts needs very careful attention, since it tends *ipso facto* to marginalise those ordering their homosexual affections according to the traditional way, living out the baptismal pattern.[24] The new patterns of gay order, para-marital or tribal, would mean the most serious questioning, even alienating and excluding, of the orthodox Christian who feels strong same-sex affections and is seeking to live within the vocations of marriage or chaste singleness. Indeed revision would mean the advertising of the gay script for all who wish for it, or wish to try it, for whatever reason, as the normal way of responding to and conducting homosexual feelings.

The Friendship Model

Friendship is suggested by some essayists as another model of making something out of 'a' homosexual identity and vocation, the latter concept being questioned as too rigid, permanent and fated by the St Andrew's Day Statement. Presumably this model need not be mutually exclusive with respect to the para-marriage model if indeed there are varieties of gifts fitting us for varieties of scripts, and the homosexuality into which we find ourselves thrown might take a variety of forms, all harmless and all bestowing benefits personally and socially.[25]

The friendship model sometimes claims the example of the medieval monastic movement, a different way of being with the capacity for erotic emotional life, which may in an unstructured way go beyond Eros into Venus for the sake of intimacy and love. The vision is of a group whose tribal consciousness is gay, who have a kind of indulgence for indulgence – in the sense of a well-meaning occasional overflow of sexual energies. Such people will typically be aesthetic, with a keen consciousness of suffering because of their dissonance with creation and feeling no vocation to celibacy as the resolution of that dissonance. This is another way of harmonising the bodily duality of the human race as men and women, with its complex, multifaceted emotional potential. Acceptance of, indeed recovery of, intense emotional feeling between members of the same sex as friends, Eros, is common ground for all; whether this should stray into the various forms of gay genital intimacy, Venus, is the point of disagreement.

This friendship model claims that sex itself should not be exaggerated in importance, but should be regarded as a second-order issue, belonging to the category of matters 'adiaphora', the term used by the Reformers[26] to indicate questions on which disagreement was legitimate and concession could be made. The Church, it is therefore urged, should ease its position towards a more tolerant attitude of gay practice, which is merely edging from Eros into Venus. On the other hand, it is also urged, gay practice should no longer be kept private to individual friends, but opened out into a recognised public category. This seems something of a contradiction, in that a minor matter which requires no great attention should most appropriately remain in the realm of private conscience, whereas the matter in reality is considered to be of such vital import as to require a new public form of life in which it can be conducted and advertised. Can same-sex conduct in fact be 'adiaphoron' if it requires the creation of a third form or vocation of life?

The St Andrew's Day Statement prefers to emphasise the two given vocations of marriage and celibate singleness as the forms within which we conduct our sexual affections. In upholding this, the Statement resists accepting 'a' gay identity and then turning that into a vocation, reconstituting and diversifying the two vocations into several possible ones. For the St Andrew's Day Statement, baptismal openness to future transformation must not be bracketed off in favour of a fixed, packaged, consciousness, which could well be commended to others, including even adolescents going through all the complex phases of maturation.

The friendship model also has the inherent problem that it would gradually stereotype all same-sex friendships as probably involving genital sex. The common phenomenon of celibate friends sharing a house now, in the light of the media campaign, may carry a message totally unwanted and unfair. Friendship itself may become a casualty of this revisionist vision of sexual indifferentism or adiaphorism.[27] Revision could, that is, work *against* the recovery of deep emotional relationships between members of the same sex, by labelling all such friendships inevitably gay.

Conscientious Dissent: Clergy and Laity
The conduct of those who conscientiously dissent from the Church's teaching represents a 'problem area' for the Church. They are not to be excommunicated from the Church, but accepted as people of faith who are prepared to allow the Gospel to touch their lives on the journey through life. This does not mean that the Church is not sure of her ethical teaching, but that those who 'conscientiously' dissent,[28] are seriously intending discipleship and are willing to enter the struggle of coping with their dissonant feelings. The unmarried cohabiting man and woman who come to church are not cast out, but under the teaching ministry and love of the fellowship it is hoped they will, and often do, undertake the covenanted lifelong vows of the vocation of

marriage. The tax evader, the prostitute, the plutocrat, all those who conscientiously dissent (or indeed who may be confused and puzzled from their experience of the world), are not thrown out but welcomed creatively, in the prayerful hope that horizons will be widened and the Gospel increasingly implemented in their lives. Such is the constant encouragement in the Gospel.

The claim that there is a gay vocation as a prophetic word of God to the Church[29] raises deep questions, and not only because of the ambivalence of any such message. Can the gay advocate rise above sectional self-interest to speak to the *whole* Church of its calling? Also, to what extent could such a message criticise the prevailing culture, as its advocates intend, and to what extent does it actually endorse the deepest orientations of liberal culture and erode the distinctiveness of the Church? Can such a message be of benefit to the human race in its cosmic destiny? The claim and the debate, as has been indicated, may have grains of truth in addressing a challenge to Church culture, but a message of judgment, to the effect that the Western churches have been freezing single people out of warm relationships, and that this has fostered the confusion now evident in the gay consciousness and in the fragmentation of that consciousness into competing identities and vocations.

The Church must heed the Word of the Lord, and it must not contradict the apostolic word. Therefore it cannot go around, for example, the first chapter of Romans, a text in which a theological rationale is given for interpreting homosexual patterns. Women exchanging natural relations (Rom. 1:26) exemplify, for Paul, the results of idolatry, hence not in the first place violent male patterns of homosexual vice. The message must concern a culture which is idolatrous, and perhaps similarly a Church, left to the consequences of its anthropocentric orientation, its secret identification of God with human cultural aspiration. The gay movement, and even conscientious dissent, may be best seen as a symptom of this *confusion*, in which case it should be looked after with care and love pending a repentance by the Church and a fostering of a context for right relationships.

This reading fits with the apostolic testimony far better than one which turns Scripture on its head, interpreting the homosexual movement as the saving and forgotten suffering servant figure, neglect of which is idolatrous.[30] The case for the traditional reading has not been refuted. We are all under judgment, confusion washes at our houses, we need to attend to the state of our Church, to principled pastoral practice, to fostering care and love. It may be also that the churches of the West need to hear the voices of their 'third world' brothers and sisters about lifestyle, family, the aged, marriage and wider forms of family life. The Western drive towards the idolisation of the autonomous self may have reached the point of self-destruction.[31]

The clergy are bound to be distinct from the laity in any Church which has an ordained ministry. The clergy are pastors and teachers of the faith, with a confessionally defining significance. If a clergyman begins to teach the non-existence of God, that is significant in a wholly different way than if a member of the congregation comes to believe in the non-existence of God. Clerical teaching becomes integrated into the fabric and definition of the contemporary Church. The same applies to clergy lifestyle: a problem area may be allowed for laity in a way which it is simply contradictory of the Church's responsibility to the tradition and Scripture to allow to clergy. Pastoral flexibility has its place, but knowingly to ordain practising gay clergy constitutes serious ecclesial irresponsibility, a breach of Church discipline, and amounts to a cruelty to the minister and to future congregations.[32] There is a *de facto* ecumenical consensus on this pastoral *modus operandi*, of a stricter regime for the clergy than for the laity across all the denominations, none of which excommunicate lay people for homosexual practice although none endorses it, leaving it a 'grey area'. 'The Form of Ordaining or Consecrating an Archbishop or a Bishop' in *The Book of Common Prayer* might usefully be recalled, especially the questions put to the candidate during the service by the Archbishop.

Application III

The Individual Summons

Testimony to individual emotional experience of both faith in Christ and homo-erotic affection is important, part of the multifaceted make-up of all human beings, for there is a sense in which we all have the potential for sexual relations with either sex. As individuals we all have a destiny to fulfil, and we all struggle to become more Christlike, to walk in the Spirit of holiness, to incarnate the baptismal pattern of life.

The St Andrew's Day Statement, however, also points to the other, and even more important, destiny, that of the whole race and even of the cosmos of which we are part. The debate about sexual affections, acts, and patterns of action relates to this wider destiny. Humanity is created male and female, in the image of God. The two vocations of marriage and singleness relate to the generic destiny and to our individual being. Marriage is the vocation in which male and female relate in exclusive faithfulness as one flesh; singleness is the vocation of chastity and greater freedom, archetypally lived out by Jesus. This given order patterns our psychological and socio-cultural conditionings in the path of discipleship. Our feelings, in all their complexity and sometimes confusion, must be expressed through these two vocations.

We all need to look to the future for our transformation as individuals, and the Holy Spirit deals with each uniquely in summoning us to choose life against death, to cut against the grain of the sinful structures of culture and society. This is the truth emphasised by the existential Christian tradition. Our own historicity is a matter for me and the Holy Spirit enabling me to make the choice which only I, in the whole universe, can make and which no one can make for me.[33] Choices must be made in discipleship, and cannot be a matter simply of legalistic rule-obedience, but rather according to the pattern of life and vocation found in Jesus and the Hebrew tradition he embodies and brings with him, as the Church learned from Irenaeus. There will be exceptions to rules, and it is on this very individual basis that pastoral flexibility can alone be considered, rather than as a matter of reconstituting structures of creation and so affecting the generic destiny and responsibility of humanity.

Individual choice in the Spirit as we face the raw material of life, including the subjective stuff of our make-up, our past, our culture, hopes and fears, cannot simply give itself up to the tide of current thought and tendencies. There is no 'transparent and necessary progress of thought working itself out in history, with which [the Church] has only somehow to keep abreast'; Hegel was wrong and Kierkegaard right here. It is therefore disappointing to read accounts of the problem of the homosexual consciousness in terms of God envisaging every phenomenon which arises as potentially good and to be synthesised into the divine project of the world. The question 'how do we use homosexuality to good and godly purpose?'[34] seems to be of this nature, assuming that the abstraction, homosexuality, must be patient of good and godly synthesis into the pattern of the whole process of history, ignoring the question as to what specifically may be good or bad in homosexuality.

In fact we meet not 'homosexuality' but men and women with their emotional make-up; we meet specific individuals in their concrete communities, not a set of humanity in the abstract. The Holy Spirit meets us in particular specific occasions, and we steer though the very concrete paths of life as individuals, making our own decisions about sex in the light of the guidance of the Church under the Word, with the support and encouragement of the community of faith. This latter point is more than rhetoric, or should become more than words; the community, if it is to be an encouragement, must encourage frankness and honesty, adult truthfulness and the bearing of pain between friends.[35] As individuals we have our unique problems and common problems, and need to develop honest openness to enable us to face these together. This is the common ground, painful to both sides of the argument, that must be claimed together and possessed.

It may be that essayists advocating change along the line of the friendship model are closest to the traditionalists at this point and might be asking for deep friendships between people of the same sex to be encouraged, with no assumptions made as to any acts of intimacy which may or may not be happening, asking for no structuring of sex at all but an individual approach to the matter, asking that the Church judges not nor draws any conclusions. The label 'homosexual' might thereby fade into redundancy.

The important spiritual question as to how we can serve God with our own personality and character, including our own unique sexual emotions,[36] demands attention, but this question must be correlated with the simultaneous counter-question as to how God will change us in the process. The Spirit will use us, but in so doing we will be taken more deeply into the baptismal life. There is a future, and what seems inevitable and fated must be open to the God of the open future.

Distinguishing Eros, Venus and Christ

This bears on the mystical approach to the debate over sexual emotions as it asks about the 'Christ in the homosexual', and what we can learn from this Christ within.[37] The Church knows no Christ of 'the homosexual' which can be any different to the Christ of 'the heterosexual', any more than of a man or of a woman: such a dualism risks the unity and universality of Christ. It also offends the multifaceted character of our affective life and runs into the mists of affective fundamentalism, which will inevitably produce a characterisation of the particular Christ looked for in terms of a set of stereotypical psycho-social phenomena. Here lies the path to the secret domestication of God, far from the historical Jesus and his theological context.

The St Andrew's Day Statement opens up the question of fixed 'orientation' for anthropological discussion, querying the objectivity of both the abstractions called 'heterosexuality' and 'homosexuality'. We are all male or female human beings, with emotional lives largely shaped by our social context and experience, given two forms of life in which to order our sexual feelings. The Statement's axiom that there is one Word of God finds the concept of 'Christs within' defined according to fixed sexualities particularly difficult and unconvincing. Only so far as it is possible to objectify an orientation or a sexuality and confirm it in lifestyle, will it be possible to attempt such a move in terms of Christology. Christ is surely an objective reality independent of, while related to, our emotional selves; the Holy Spirit within sanctifies and leads us in the baptismal way of dying and rising with Christ.

How God can use the raw material of my 'sexuality' remains therefore a contested way of putting the issue; better is how can God use me, in my particularity and uniqueness of personality and network of relations in this time and culture. How will I, created as male or female, thereby, be open to change and open to help others in their journey with the one risen Christ in the created order? Faced with the question of affective emotional drives, it is a diversion to concentrate on the issue of ecclesiastical permission. The question has to be about moral health and the creative intention of God.

Bishop Baker requests debate over his arguments[38] for justifying such permission, and his request must be not be ignored. Gay people have much moral achievement to their credit and, as all of us, much debit. Gay sex no doubt gives much release, causes much loving bonding, conveys deep feelings from one to another at the time and has after effects; partners living together do live in a neighbourhood and do provide role models for all ages around them. Close and tender relationships do exist, and partners dying of AIDS are nursed with great compassion and love. Bishop Baker is arguing that gay sex implies these goods in and of itself, just as marriage implies certain goods (such as covenant love, physical sex, and children), and that these goods are intrinsically dependent on gay sex, as the goods of marriage are dependent on marriage. To argue that 'the fruit of the Spirit has grown in that soil' of same-sex physical intimacy suggests that life patterned on gay sex is itself inherently grace-bearing.[39]

To associate gay sex with the fruits of the Spirit is to argue selectively. Are we to credit homosexual practice with all the blessings that belong to simple humanity or with the graces that belong to the Spirit, while denying it responsibility for its disruptive and disturbing aspects? If we are seriously to weigh genital homosexual lifestyle in the scale of good and evil, then we must be prepared to look at the whole phenomenon and not select only worthy elements.

There are many communities and interest groups focused on particular activities which result in close personal bonding. Such caring, loyal and loving bonding, however, has no bearing on the moral rightness of the shared communal activity or interest which provides the wider context (or soil, to use Bishop Baker's analogy) for the group. Bishop Baker assumes that if gay practice were wrong then gays would not display all these virtues. On what ground could Bishop Baker have supposed that deep feelings, care for the sick, the fruit of the Spirit of every kind are somehow dependent on physical homosexual relations? Has he never observed such fruit of the Spirit in evidence in the lives of the celibate people who conduct their same-sex feelings along different lines, without genital expression? Or does he imagine that God would deny such a high degree of creativity and virtue to those who fell short in some measure of chastity in accepting their vocation to singleness?

Theologically we may also ask whether the Bishop inverts the apostolic teaching, for which marriage is the form or vocation in which the gift of sexual intercourse is to happen. Sexual intercourse is not inherently a way of reaching *towards* God, not the soil of spirituality, but is a gift *from God* to be used in the properly ordered way. Rather than acknowledging the two forms or vocations of human life, marriage and singleness, as the way for conducting sex, the Bishop seems to begin with gay sex and then look for virtues in the lives of particular practitioners, which in turn validate new generic patterns of sexual bonding. The argument would seem capable of legitimating other forms of sexual cohabitation as evolving under the hand of God.

Attention does need to be given to the horizon of current experience, which tends to be dealt with as if it is clearly and fully comprehended, the only problems being with the past horizons of the text of Scripture. Eros, which can be reduced to Venus, is indeed a powerful surging emotion, binding people together. World literature is full of meditations on the diverse nature of romance, love, and sex. C. S. Lewis' discussion provides a valuable and accessible example.

It is in the grandeur of Eros that the seeds of danger are concealed. He has spoken like a god. His total commitment, his reckless disregard of happiness, his transcendence of self-regard, sound like a message from the eternal world. . . . We must not give unconditional obedience to the voice of Eros when he speaks most like a god. Neither must we ignore or attempt to deny the god-like quality. This love is really and truly like Love Himself. In it there is a real nearness to God (by Resemblance); but not, therefore and necessarily a nearness of Approach. . . . Our conditional honour to Eros will vary with our circumstances. Of some a total renunciation is required. Others, with Eros as their fuel and also as their model, can embark on the married life. Within which Eros, of himself, will never be enough – will indeed survive only insofar as he is continually chastened and corroborated by higher principles.[40]

Lewis articulates the nature of Eros, and discusses its deployment in our lives, its all-commanding character, calling for total and reckless commitment and sacrifice. The 'soil of physical sexual intimacy' can be a *result* of Eros, but hardly the cause or seedbed of spiritual good works, according to Lewis's analysis. At the very least this signals the need for profound reflection, rather than hasty assumptions, at this point. Dogmatic statements asserting *the* 'homosexual' or 'heterosexual' consciousness as a monochrome, simple, brute fact, which we know with total clarity, close off analysis of the current horizon of meaning. What must it mean for Eros, felt between two people of the same sex, to be 'continually chastened and corroborated by higher principles' than the soil of physical intimacy? *Should* the intimacy of Venus be a part of genuinely Christian same-sex, emotionally deep commitment?

Lewis points out that the voice of Eros feels compelling and without that pang of guilt felt by other compelling urges.

When lovers say of some act that we might blame, 'Love made us do it,' notice the tone. A man saying, 'I did it because I was frightened,' or 'I did it because I was angry,' speaks quite differently. He is putting forward an excuse for what he feels to require excusing. But lovers are seldom doing quite that. Notice how tremulously, almost how devoutly, they say the word *love*, not so much pleading 'an extenuating circumstance' as appealing to an authority. The confession can be almost a boast. There can be a shade of defiance in it. They 'feel like martyrs.' . . . Where a true Eros is present resistance to his commands feels like apostasy, and what are really (by Christian standards) temptations speak with the voice of duties – quasi religious duties, acts of pious zeal to love.[41]

Some such analysis, prompting clear distinctions, must be heard in the interpretative debate about the phenomena of same-sex desire. Both orthodox and revisionist 'homosexual' Christians call for intense and deep relationships, sharing something of what Lewis calls Eros. They disagree about acceding to any imperious demand of Eros to culminate in patterns of behaviour which accommodate genital sex.

One simple point must emerge from listening to the historian of literature and culture, that 'Eros' is not simply to be equated with 'Christ within'. The two can look similar, especially at moments of crisis and the hour of death of a gay lover. But such arguments can be very double-edged because based on selective evidence, even when insisting on 'best case' gay unions. Gay intimacy, even when accompanied by gay passion, can no doubt go sour, lead to addictive sex, to domination and seduction of insecure people. Eros can end up with mutual obsession, as well as, and perhaps interwoven with, mutual sacrifice. Alone it is no criterion by which behaviour patterns can be established or judged; indeed it needs to live within prior given patterns. The generic fulfilment of human destiny, moreover, fails to gain treatment in any such apologetic, raising the suspicion that such advocacy is in the end deeply individualistic.

Ultimately it would be unloving for the Church to open a third form of life as a context for same-sex practice, for individuals and for the race. It would be unloving because untruthful, and so inevitably an empty gesture. The Church is not capable of opening any kind of life, only of recognising and bearing witness to the forms of life which God has opened to us.

God can use many things, and God can make the best of many bad situations which we create, collude with, and find ourselves involved in. That does not mean that systems or patterns are to be constructed from such common grace which brings light out of darkness. God provides the fig leaf for his fallen creatures, as in confusion they scrabble about in the dust after losing their place of confident well-being. If God provides for his confused and dissonant creatures, how much more must the people of God give up severe and unforgiving attitudes and seek to reach out friendly hands of love, acceptance and yet Gospel hope, seeking to make ecclesial life more real, adult and frank.

Notes

1. This call issues forth from the national media strongly, e.g. the programme targeted at the youth audience, *Out This Week*, broadcast by the BBC's Radio 5 Live.

2. Matthew Parris disagrees with Andrew Sullivan 'that sexual orientation is fixed early', preferring a more socially constructionist view. 'For my part I believe that we are all placed somewhere on a scale between other-sex and same-sex attraction; and that it is human conditioning which "herds" us towards the most accessible pole.' *The Times*, 19 October 1995, review of Sullivan's *Virtually Normal*. Here he approaches the analysis of the St Andrew's Day Statement, although it would prefer a portrait of multifaceted complexity, rather than Parris's linear scale, and it would not rule out 'herding', a socialising process, as a continuing possibility for change.

3. *Issues in Human Sexuality* (Church House Publishing London, 1991), para. 5.7; cf. Peter Tatchell's letter to *The Times*, 20 February 1997 in which he questions whether 'heterosexuality and homosexuality are, indeed, mutually exclusive', and affirms that 'most studies indicate that genetic influences are of secondary significance compared to social mores and expectations . . . both the incidence and expressions of same-sex desire vary vastly between different societies'.

4. The multifaceted nature of our sexual affections and proper pastoral care can be illustrated from Lord Runcie's biography. 'Yet there are one or two quite outstanding clergy, now happily married, who were homosexual when training for ordination. One of them was seriously at risk with the police for going out to hunt for partners. And yet, with treatment, and with the right sort of girl determined to marry them, they're happily married and have children.' Humphrey Carpenter, *Robert Runcie: The Reluctant Archbishop* (Hodder & Stoughton, 1996).

5. The declaration by the American golfer Tiger Woods rejecting the label 'black' or 'Asian' is an interesting analogy: 'I'm just who I am – whoever you see in front of you. Growing up, I came up with this name Cablinasian [a compound word for Caucasian, black, Indian and Asian].' *Guardian*, 24 April 1997. Just so are we all sexually complex and do well to reject absolute imprisoning labels.

6. *The Four Loves* (Geoffrey Bles, 1960), pp. 106 ff. (see also n. 37 below).

7. Ibid., p. 108.

8. Matthew Parris says 'Dancing with women, I have sometimes noticed an involuntary arousal: is something being suppressed? In intimate physical contact with other men, men who think they are completely heterosexual often experience the same. Is something being suppressed?' *The Times*, 19 October 1995.

9. '"There are lots of girls", she [Caroline Meagher] says, who gravitate towards the army for the same reasons she did – it offers an escape from "feeling other", and rewards them for being tomboys, and allows

them to spend their time "driving tanks instead of having 2.5 children." It's only later that some discover they are lesbians . . . .' It was her job to hunt down lesbians in the Army. Then one day she saw herself out there.' Maureen Freely, in *The Observer Review*, 27 April 1997, p. 9. The reader's attention is drawn to the term 'discover': was she shaped into lesbian consciousness in an all-female community, and after intimate interviewing women about sexual practice, or was she always 'a' homosexual in a way hidden from herself?

10. American actress Ann Heche testifies to her lesbian relationship with celebrity Ellen DeGeneres, 'I was not gay before I met her. It wasn't immediately a sexual attraction.' (Nando.net, 30 April 1997).

11. Prophecy 'is not free and exploratory innovation, but is always predicated upon careful attention to the testimony of Israel's prophets and apostles to the Christ event'. Oliver O'Donovan, *The Desire of the Nations* (OUP, 1996), p. 188. The notion of a community which is inherently prophetic seems theologically difficult: the prophetic word is always through a single lone figure, marked out from the community, not a community itself.

12. Ronald Knox, *Some Loose Stones* (Longmans, Green & Co, 1914), p. 49.

13. Roger Scruton, *Sexual Desire* (Phoenix, 1986), pp. 307–8.

14. To adjust, or narrow, F. D. E. Schleiermacher, *The Christian Faith*, tr. H. R. Mackintosh and J. S. Stewart (T. & T. Clark, 1928), p. 76.

15. John Lyttle, a homosexual writer, appears to distinguish between a 'biological' or 'essential' identity called 'homosexual', and a socially formed 'gay' identity, from which he distances himself. Simon Edge, on the other hand, writing a parallel article, proclaims himself 'glad to be gay', and this in turn 'has become a lifestyle', an identity, a liberation of the repressed self. *The Independent*, 13 December 1996.

16. George Tyrrell commenting on Newman's doctrine of development says: 'Others may not share his religious experiences, or, if they do, may seek their explanation in psychology rather than in divinity; and for these his method is indeed a two-edged sword.' *Christianity at the Cross Roads* (Longmans, Green & Co; 1909), p. 34.

17. Dave Leal, *Debating Homosexuality* (Grove Books, 1996), p. 20.

18. Matthew Parris, *The Times*, 19 October 1995.

19. Parris (ibid.) rejects Sullivan's retroactive self-interpretation, even self-construction: 'Gay men, he [Sullivan] implies, have some kind of window into the history of their own sexuality. And we remember that we could never have been anything but gay.' One is on the verge of a Platonic doctrine of anamnesis, memory of the *real* self, and perhaps the suggestion that there may be a family resemblance between such gay doctrine and gnostic anthropology might contain some truth.

20. 'When making love I am consciously being a man, and this enterprise involves my whole nature, and strives to realise itself in the motions of the act itself . . .' They are intending to "make love", that is, to unite as sexual beings, in an experience guided by the concept of gender. It is "man uniting with woman" rather than "penis entering vagina" which focusses their attention.

The latter episode is perceived simply as a "moment" in the former, which provides its indispensable context.' Scruton, *Sexual Desire*, p. 227.

21. According to Scruton 'the homosexual has a peculiar inward familiarity with what his partner feels. His discovery of his partner's sexual nature is the discovery of what he knows.' He goes on to ask, 'Are there moral consequences to be drawn from this dissimilarity between homosexual and heterosexual desire?' *Sexual Desire*, p. 283.

22. John Austin Baker, *Homosexuality and Christian Ethics: A New Way Forward Together*, given at St Martin-in-the-Fields Church, London, 21 April 1997, p. 8.

23. Also found in Bishop Baker's lecture.

24. The connection of the notion of 'inclusivity' with baptismal vows and eucharistic sharing takes the issue to the deepest possible level of the Church's official life. The Report of the Open Synod Group dislikes 'professions of faith or rigid doctrinal formulae . . . Protestantism sees a basis in a common Confession of Faith, which inevitably means excluding people. Catholicism expresses its basis in a Sacramental Union, which can embrace people with very different views.' *By What Authority: The Open Synod Group Report on Authority in the Church of England*, ed. R. Jeffrey (Mowbray, 1987). Similarly the ECUSA Justice, Peace and Integrity of Creation Committee of Executive Council convened a summit meeting in Cincinatti on 27 March 1997, at which renewal of baptismal vows included 'full inclusion of gays and lesbians in the life of the church'.

25. See Bishop Baker's lecture, p. 11.

26. The notion of matters adiaphora itself is difficult: how can we tell what is and is not a first-order issue? Some Lutherans held such practices as veneration of the saints adiaphora; some pietists held dancing to be sinful, their opponents held them adiaphora. Today some people leave the Church of England to espouse a polity of 'believers' baptism', others regard the matter as indifferent or adiaphoron.

27. The modern culture of sex is deeply paradoxical: it is everything, while nothing at all; this seems to be reflected in this version of the gay demand to the Church for liberalisation.

28. The notion of 'non-conscientious' dissent may need some attention.

29. One notes the absoluteness with which AIDS is excluded from this purported message. 'In the 1980's,' says a gay and lesbian report, 'media hostility [to homosexuals] was commonly countered with the assertion that everyone is at equal risk from HIV and AIDS – that AIDS is not a gay disease. Such a response was understandable and well intentioned, but had the effect of denying the reality that gay men are at high risk of HIV infection relative to other community groups.' Tony Green, Brenda Harrison, Jeremy Innes, *Not For Turning* (published by the authors, 1996), p. 19.

30. Detailed exegesis of the text and context has been forced on the Church by radical revisionist readings; only careful painstaking scholarship even on single words has prevented wish-fulfilment glossing the core ethical treatise in the New Testament.

31. cf. Thomas C. Oden, *Agenda for Theology: After Modernity What?* (Zondervan, 1990) for an accessible account of the analysis that ultra-modernism has left Western society gripped by autonomous individualism, narcissistic hedonism, scientific reductionism and moral relativism.
32. Bishop Baker's lecture (see n. 22) acknowledges that few congregations will accept the ministry of open homosexuals. The *consensus fidelium*, an ARCIC criterion, seems to be considered insignificant in much debate, where the rights of the clergy are taken as paramount.
33. Bishop Stephen Neill, *Christian Holiness* (Lutterworth Press, 1960), p. 94.
34. Bishop Baker lecture (see n. 22) p. 8.
35. A 'central principle of the holiness of the Church', taught Bishop Stephen Neill, 'is what the New Testament calls *parrhesia*, which is often and rightly translated "courage", but which means literally "speaking out", saying everything that needs to be said. Where love rules a community, it is possible for people to be genuinely open with one another in the generosity of mutual confidence. Is not this perhaps the very thing which our modern churches are most lacking? We are lost in the anonymity of the large modern Church. We are afraid of one another and so remain closed to one another. Countless Christians are fighting their battles in solitude, discouraged by defeat, unaware of the resources that are available to help them if the Church can really learn to be the Church. This is one of the fields in which it ought to be true that perfect love casts out fear (1 John 4.18) and fear is evidently the greatest enemy of a robust and vigorous Christian holiness.' *Christian Holiness*, p. 72.
36. Bishop Baker lecture (see n. 22), p. 8.
37. This approach was advocated by the chaplain designate to the 1998 Lambeth Conference on BBC Radio 4's *The Sunday Programme*, 27 April 1997.
38. Bishop Baker attempts such a justification on pp. 8–9 of his lecture.
39. Which is what Bishop Baker does argue, ibid.
40. Lewis, *Four Loves*, pp. 126–7.
41. Ibid, p. 129. Lewis's discussion of Luke 7:47 bears meditation, p. 128.

Further Reading

Homosexuality, the Bible and Interpretation

Countryman, L. William, *Dirt, Greed and Sex: Sexual Ethics in the New Testament and their Implications for Today*. London: SCM, 1989.

Fowl, Stephen E., *Engaging Scripture: A Model for Theological Interpretation*. Oxford: Blackwell, 1998.

France, R. T., *A Slippery Slope? The Ordination of Women and Homosexual Practice: A Case Study in Biblical Interpretation*. Cambridge: Grove Books, 2000.

Gagnon, Robert A. J., *The Bible and Homosexual Practice: Texts and Hermeneutics*. Nashville: Abingdon Press, 2001.

Gagnon, Robert A. J., 'The Bible and Homosexual Practice: Theology, Analogies, and Genes', *Theology Matters*, 2001, 7 (6, Nov/Dec): 1–13. Available electronically at http://theologymatters.com/BackIssues.html

Goddard, Andrew, *God; Gentiles and Gay Christians: Acts 15 and Change in the Church*. Cambridge: Grove Books, 2001.

Hays, Richard B., 'Relations Natural and Unnatural: A Response to John Boswell's Exegesis of Romans 1', *Journal of Religious Ethics*, 1986, 14: 184–215.

—— 'Awaiting the Redemption of Our Bodies: The Witness of Scripture Concerning Homosexuality', *Sojourners*, 1991, 20: 17–21.

—— *The Moral Vision of the New Testament: A Contemporary Introduction to New Testament Ethics*, Edinburgh: T. & T. Clark, 1997.

Johnson, Luke T., *Scripture and Discernment: Decision Making in the Church*. Nashville: Abingdon Press, 1996.

Larson, John David, *Holy Scripture and Homosexual Activity: God, Church and Mission*, 2001.

Moberly, Walter, 'The Use of Scripture in Contemporary Debate about Homosexuality', *Theology*, 2000, 103 (July/August): 251–8.

Sanders, E. P., *Paul*. Oxford: Oxford University Press, 1991.

Scroggs, Robin, *The New Testament and Homosexuality: Contextual Background for Contemporary Debate*. Philadelphia: Fortress Press, 1983.

Seitz, Christopher, 'Sexuality and Scripture's Plain Sense: The Christian Community and the Law of God', pp. 177–96 in *Homosexuality, Science, and the 'Plain Sense' of Scripture*, ed. David Balch. Grand Rapids: Eerdmans, 2000.

Smith, Mark D., ' Ancient Bisexuality and the Interpretation of Romans 1.26, 27', *Journal of the American Academy of Religion*, 1996, 64: 223–54.

Thiselton , Anthony C., *The First Epistle to the Corinthians: A Commentary on the Greek Text*. Grand Rapids/Cambridge: Eerdmans/Paternoster Press, 2000.

Vasey, Michael, *Strangers and Friends: A New Exploration of Homosexuality and the Bible*. London: Hodder & Stoughton, 1995.

Theological Ethics and Homosexuality

Banner, Michael, *Christian Ethics and Contemporary Moral Problems*. Cambridge: CUP, 1999.

Bonhoeffer, Dietrich, *Cost of Discipleship*. London: SCM, 1959.

Bradshaw, Timothy, 'Baptism and Inclusivity in the Church', pp. 447–66 in *Baptism, the New Testament and the Church*, ed. Stanley E. Porter and Anthony R. Cross. Sheffield: Sheffield Academic Press, 1999.

Clapp, Rodney, *Families at the Crossroads: Beyond Traditional and Modern Options*. Downers Grove: IVP, 1993.

Grenz, Stanley J., *Welcoming but Not Affirming: An Evangelical Response to Homosexuality*. Louisville: Westminster John Knox Press, 1998.

Holmes, Stephen, *Listening to the Tradition*. Carlisle: Paternoster Press, 2003.

John, Jeffrey, *'Permanent, Faithful, Stable': Christian Same-Sex Partnerships*. London: Darton, Longman & Todd, 2000.

Jordan, Mark D., *The Ethics of Sex*. Oxford: Blackwell, 2002.

Leal, Dave, *Debating Homosexuality*. Cambridge: Grove Books, 2001.

Lloyd, Michael, '"God Made Me This Way": What Is Natural in a Fallen World?' *Latimer Comment* (63).

Macourt, Malcolm, *Towards a Theology of Gay Liberation*. London: SCM, 1976.

McCarthy Matzko, David, 'Homosexuality and the Practices of Marriage', *Modern Theology*, 1997, 13: 371–97.

Null, John Ashley, 'Grace: God's Power to Make Us Right', *The Living Church*, 1991 (23 June): 11–13.

Pannenberg, Wolfhart, 'When Everything Is Permitted', *First Things*, 80 (February 1998): 26–30.
http://www.firstthings.com/ftissues/ft9802/pannenberg.html

Ramsey, Paul, 'Self Love, Love of Happiness, Love to God and to Neighbor', pp. 25–40 in *The Essential Paul Ramsey: A Collection*, ed. Wiliam Werepehowski and Stephen D. Crocco. New Haven and London: Yale University Press, 1994.

Rogers, Eugene F., *Sexuality and the Christian Body: Their Way into the Triune God*. Oxford: Blackwell, 1999.

—— *Theology and Sexuality: Classic and Contemporary Readings*. Oxford: Blackwell, 2001.

Schmidt, Thomas E., *Straight & Narrow? Compassion & Clarity in the Homosexuality Debate*. Leicester: IVP, 1995.

Stuart, Elizabeth, *Just Good Friends: Towards a Lesbian and Gay Theology of Relationships*. London: Mowbray, 1995.

—— 'Is Lesbian or Gay Marriage an Oxymoron? A Critical Review of the Contemporary Debate', pp. 255–83 in *Celebrating Christian Marriage*, ed. Adrian Thatcher. Edinburgh: T. &T. Clark, 2001.

Thatcher, Adrian, *Liberating Sex: A Christian Sexual Theology*. London: SPCK, 1993.

Thielicke, Helmut, *The Ethics of Sex*. London: James Clarke, 1964.

Turner, Philip, 'Undertakings and Promises or Promises and Undertakings? The Anatomy of an Argument about Sexual Ethics', *Studies in Christian Ethics*, 1991, 4(2): 1–13.

Turner, Philip, 'Sex and the Single Life', *First Things*, May 1993: 15–21.

Wannenwetsch, Bernd, 'Old Docetism – New Moralism? Questioning a New Direction in the Homosexuality Debate', *Modern Theology*, 2000, 16: 353–64.

Williams, Rowan D., 'The Body's Grace', pp. 309–21 in *Theology and Sexuality: Classic and Contemporary Readings*, ed. Eugene F. Rogers. Oxford: Blackwell, 1989.

Science and the Study of Homosexuality

Burr, Chandler, *A Separate Creation: How Biology Makes Us Gay*. London: Bantam Press, 1996.

Corvino, John, *Same Sex: Debating the Ethics, Science and Culture of Homosexuality*. Lanham MD: Rowman and Littlefield, 1998.

Jones, Stanton L., and Yarhouse, Mark A., *Homosexuality: The Use of Scientific Research in the Church's Moral Debate*. Downers Grove: IVP, 2000.

—— 'The Use, Misuse, and Abuse of Science in the Ecclesiastical Homosexuality Debates', pp. 73–120 in *Homosexuality, Science and the 'Plain Sense' of Scripture*, ed. David Balch. Grand Rapids: Eerdmans, 2000.

McKnight, Jim, *Straight Science? Homosexuality, Evolution and Adaptation*. London: Routledge, 1998.

Murphy, Timothy F., *Gay Science: The Ethics of Sexual Orientation Research*. New York: Columbia University Press, 1998.

Ridley, Matt, *Nature via Nurture: Genes Experience and What Makes Us Human*. London: Fourth Estate, 2003.

Rosario, Vernon A. (ed.), *Science and Homosexualities*. London: Routledge, 1998.

Siker, Jeffrey S., 'Homosexual Christians, the Bible and Gentile Inclusion: Confessions of a Repenting Heterosexist', in *Homosexuality in the Church: Both Sides of the Debate*, ed. Jeffrey S. Siker. Louisville: Westminster John Knox Press, 1994.

Stein, Edward, *The Mismeasure of Desire: The Science, Theory, and Ethics of Sexual Orientation*. Oxford: Oxford University Press, 1999.

Van Leeuwen, Mary Stewart, 'To Ask a Better Question: The Heterosexuality–Homosexuality Debate Revisited', *Interpretation*, 1997, 51 (April): 143–58.

Whitehead, Neil and Briar, *My Genes Made Me Do It! A Scientific Look at Sexual Orientation*. Lafayette, Lousiana: Huntington House Publishers, 1999.

Socio-Cultural and Political Dimensions of Homosexuality

Brooten, Bernadette, *Love between Women: Early Christian Responses to Female Homoeroticism*. Chicago: University of Chicago Press, 1996.

Davies, Jon and Loughlin, Gerard (eds), *Sex These Days: Essays in Theology, Sexuality and Society*. Sheffield: Sheffield Academic Press, 1997.

Giddens, Anthony, *The Transformation of Intimacy: Sex, Love and Eroticism in Modern Societies*. Cambridge: Polity Press, 1992.

Gill, Sean, *The Lesbian and Gay Christian Movement: Campaigning for Justice, Truth and Love*. London: Cassell, 1998.

Greenberg, David F., *The Construction of Homosexuality*. Chicago: University of Chicago Press, 1988.

Irigaray, Luce, *An Ethics of Sexual Difference*, tr. Carolyn Burke and Gillian C Gill. London: Athlone Press, 1993.

Jordan, Mark D., *The Invention of Sodomy in Christian Theology*. Chicago: University of Chicago Press, 1997.

Ray, Peter, 'Determined to be Different: Social Constructionism and Homosexuality', pp. 135–58 in *Marxism, Mysticism and Modern Theory*. ed. Suke Wolton. New York/Basingstoke: St Martin's Press/Macmillan Press, 1996.

Scruton, Roger, *Sexual Desire*. London: Phoenix, 1994.

Stewart, Jacqui, 'The Family in a Technological Society', pp. 85–102 in *The Christian Family: A Concept in Crisis*, ed. Hugh Pyper. Norwich: Canterbury Press, 1996.

Storkey, Elaine, *Created or Constructed? The Great Gender Debate*. Carlisle: Paternoster Press, 2001.

Stuart, Elizabeth, *Gay and Lesbian Theologies: Repetitions with Critical Difference*. Aldershot: Ashgate, 2002.

Sullivan, Andrew, *Virtually Norma: An Argument about Homosexuality*. New York/Toronto/London: Alfred A.Knopf/Random House/Picador, 1995.

——*Love Undetectable: Notes on Friendship, Sex, and Survival*. New York: Alfred A. Knopf, 1998.

Webb, William J., *Slaves, Women & Homosexuals: Exploring the Hermeneutics of Cultural Analysis*. Downers Grove: IVP, 2001.

Yip, Andrew K. T., *Gay Male Christian Couples: Life Stories*. Westport: Praeger, 1997.

Historical Debate and Homosexuality

Brown, Peter, *The Body and Society: Men, Women, and Sexual Renunciation in Early Christianity*. New York: Columbia University Press, 1988.

Boswell, John, *Christianity, Social Tolerance and Homosexuality: Gay People in Western Europe from the Beginning of the Christian Era to the Beginning of the Fourteenth Century*. Chicago: University of Chicago Press, 1980.

——*Same-Sex Unions in Premodern Europe*. New York: Villard, 1994.

Cozzens, Donald B., *The Changing Face of the Priesthood*, Collegeville, MN: Liturgical Press, 2000.

Hinkle, Christopher, 'A Delicate Knowledge: Epistemology, Homosexuality and St. John of the Cross', *Modern Theology*, 2001, 17: 427–40.

Laqueur, T., *Making Sex: Body and Gender from the Greeks to Freud*. Cambridge, MA: Harvard University Press, 1990.

Reynolds, Philip Lyndon, *Marriage in the Western Church*. Leiden: Brill, 1994.

Sheehan, Michael M., 'Christianity and Homosexuality', *Journal of Ecclesiastical History*, 1982, 33(3): 438–46.

Smith, Mark D., 'Ancient Bisexuality and the Interpretation of Romans 1.26, 27', *Journal of the American Academy of Religion*, 1996, 64: 223–54.

Witte, John, *From Sacrament to Contract*. Louisville, KY: Westminster John Knox Press, 1997.

Wright, David F., 'Homosexuals or Prostitutes? The Meaning of *Arsenokoitai* (1 Cor. 6:9; 1 Tim. 1:10)', *Vigiliae Christianae*, 1984, 38: 125–53.

Church Policy and Pastoral Care

ACUTE, *Faith, Hope* & *Homosexuality: A Report*. London: Evangelical Alliance, 1998.

Anglican Communion, 'Report 1. Theme 3 Human Sexuality', pp. 93–95, and 'Human Sexuality Resolution 1.10', pp. 381–2, in *The Official Report of the Lambeth Conference 1998*. Harrisburg, PA: Morehouse Publishing, 1998.

Cantlon, Christopher L. and Thompson, Pauline A., *An Honourable Estate: Marriage, Same-Sex Unions, and the Church*. Toronto: Anglican Book Centre, 1998.

Catechism of the Catholic Church, paras 2331–90. London: Geoffrey Chapman, 1994.

Cozzens, Daniel. B., *Sacred Silence: Denial and Crisis in the Church*. Collegeville, MN: Liturgical Press, 2002.

Gomez, Drexel W. and Sinclair, Maurice W., *To Mend the Net: Anglican Faith* & *Order in Renewed Mission*. Carrollton: Ekklesia Society, 2001.

Gomez, Drexel W., Goddard, Andrew and Walker, Peter, *True Union in the Body? A Contribution to the Discussion within the Anglican Communion Concerning the Public Blessing of Same-Sex Unions*. Cambridge: Grove Books, 2003.

Hallett, Martin, *Out of the Blue: Homosexuality and the Family*. London: Hodder & Stoughton, 1996.

Harries, Richard, 'More Talk than Listening', *The Tablet*, 15 August 1998.

Harvey, John, *The Homosexual Person: New Thinking in Pastoral Care*. San Francisco: Ignatius, 1987.

Holben, L. R., *What Christians Think about Homosexuality: Six Representative Viewpoints*. North Richland Hills, TX: BIBAL Press, 1999.

House of Bishops, Church of England, *Issues in Human Sexuality: A Statement*. London: Church House Publishing, 1991.

Humphrey, Edith, 'Why This Issue? A Reflection on the Crisis in Anglicanism', 2003. http://www.prayerbook.ca/articles/c3w.htm

Meilander, Gilbert, 'The First of Institutions', *Pro Ecclesia*, 1997, VI(4): 444–55.

Moore, Gareth, *A Question of Truth*. New York and London: Continuum, 2002.

Siker, Jeffrey S., *Homosexuality in the Church. Both Sides of the Debate*. Louisville: Westminster John Knox Press, 1994.

Sipe, A.W. Richard, *Sex, Priests and Power: Anatomy of a Crisis*. London: Cassell, 1995.

Sugden, Chris, and Samuel, Vinay, *Anglican Life and Witness: A Reader for the Lambeth Conference of Anglican Bishops 1998*. London: SPCK, 1998.

Torrance, David W. (ed.), *God, Family and Sexuality*. Edinburgh: Handsell Press, 1997.

Turner, Philip, 'How the Church Might Teach', pp. 137–59 in *The Crisis in Moral Teaching in the Episcopal Church*, ed. Timothy Sedgewick and Philip Turner. Harrisburg, PA: Morehouse Publishing, 1992.

——' Abstinence: A Divine Test for the Churches?' in *The Power of Orthodoxy: The Future for Global Anglicanism*, ed. Peter Walker, 2002.

Index of Scriptural References

Index of Names and Subjects